DATE DUE

SUCCESS SECRETS
OF THE
ONLINE
MARKETING
SUPERSTARS

MITCH MEYERSON

Dearborn™
Trade Publishing
A **Kaplan Professional** Company

President, Dearborn Publishing: Roy Lipner
Vice President and Publisher: Cynthia A. Zigmund
Acquisitions Editor: Michael Cunningham
Senior Project Editor: Trey Thoelcke
Interior Design: Lucy Jenkins
Cover Design: DePinto Design
Typesetting: the dotted i

Published by Dearborn Trade Publishing
A Kaplan Professional Company

Printed in the United States of America

05   06   07   10 9 8 7 6 5 4 3 2

Library of Congress Cataloging-in-Publication Data

Meyerson, Mitch.
    Success secrets of the online marketing superstars / Mitch Meyerson.
      p.   cm.
    Includes index.
    ISBN 1-4195-0501-7
    1. Internet marketing.   2. Internet advertising.   I. Title.
    HF5415.1265.M47 2005
    658.8'72—dc22

                        2005003058

C o n t e n t s

Babe Ruth, Joe Montana, Michael Jordan, Tiger Woods, Clark Gable, Marilyn Monroe. These are superstars that are known to almost everybody in America.

Robert Allen, Marlon Sanders, David Garfinkel, Yanik Silver, Declan Dunn. These are also superstars, but because they shine in cyberspace rather than from the cover of *People* magazine, they are unknown to almost everyone in America.

The contributions of the online marketing superstars are no less thrilling and impressive than those of the nonmarketing superstars. They have blazed trails, set records, established new benchmarks, and most importantly, left a trail of wisdom that allows you to follow their steps to stardom.

Mitch Meyerson has captured lightning in a bottle by speaking extensively with these superstars and distilling the essence of their wisdom into the words that appear in the pages of this extraordinary book.

These are their words, their ideas, their experiences, their insights, their genius. These are their secrets, their advice, their observations. By learning them firsthand from the people who have talked the talk and walked the walk, you are able to act upon these ideas, and then breathe life into them for your own business.

Because this book has been conceptualized, then created by Mitch Meyerson, I'm confident that you'll be captivated by his clarity of communication. As Paul McCartney would say, "Nobody does it better." This book exists not to raise questions but to answer them for you.

One of the more astonishing aspects of this book is that although it contains actual interviews with actual superstars, all of them have achieved their stardom by taking different routes.

Some have built their empires on sales letters, others on e-zines, others on attracting traffic, and still others on converting leads into customers. This book does not focus on any one technique, but instead, delivers the goods on a plethora of techniques so that you'll be given a cornucopia of tactics to select from for your own business.

Many dot-coms that bit the dot-dust would be rolling in dot-clover if they had the benefit of the brilliance in this book before inaugurating their ventures.

Each page of *Success Secrets of the Online Marketing Superstars* is teeming with mind-boggling revelations—directly from the superstars themselves—and in their own words. In my opinion, Mitch Meyerson is presenting you with the tickets to the gold mine. There are enough nuggets in these pages to fill your bank account to overflowing.

By interviewing the brightest stars in the galaxy we call cyberspace, Mitch Meyerson has made a timeless and major contribution to the body of online marketing knowledge.

Jay Conrad Levinson
Author of the *Guerrilla Marketing* series of books

	A *c k n o w l e d g m e n t s*

Special thanks to Michael Cunning-
ham at Dearborn Trade Publishing for believing in this idea from the beginning; Alex Mandossian for introducing me to many of the Online
Marketing Superstars; Peggy Murrah for her brilliant virtual assistance
on this project from the beginning; Susan Schulman, our wonderful lit-
erary agent; Laurie Ashner for inspiration and for cowriting my first
three books; Bea Fields and Michael Port for the big thinkers and great
people they are; Trey Thoelcke for his insights on the manuscript; Tara
Kachaturoff for her contributions to this work: Jay Conrad Levinson for
supporting my creation of "Guerrilla Marketing Coach"; the Certified
Guerrilla Marketing Coaches I have trained; Jane Johnson, Kathy Rice,
Lisa Wilder, Mickey and Nona Siegel; and to all the musicians that help
keep passion alive.

'**ve** always been a proponent of studying the masters. As a psychologist, I studied the likes of Jung, Adler, Berne, and Perls. I wanted to understand why people behaved in the ways they did. After consolidating years of study and inquiry into models of my own, I wrote and published my first three books, *When Is Enough Enough?*, *When Parents Love Too Much*, and *The Six Keys to Creating the Life You Desire.*

As an Internet marketer, I adopted the same philosophy. In writing this book, I spent two years studying and interviewing over 24 of the world's top online marketers. I analyzed their tactics and strategies to determine why they were more successful than countless others. I wanted to know exactly how a typical small- to mid-sized business owner might develop an online business presence that would similarly thrive and prosper. This adventure has been no short of amazing in light of the wealth of information I've learned. I've used their techniques on my own Web site and in my business, and they work.

Knowledge is power. With annual e-commerce expenditures in the billions of dollars and with predictions for growth to continue at unprecedented rates, it's critical that you have the knowledge to successfully attain, sustain, and compete in the highly competitive world of online marketing. *Success Secrets of the Online Marketing Superstars* provides you with the answers you need.

Just as I explored the greats in the field of psychology, we're going to delve into the minds of some of today's greatest online marketing gurus. Once inside, the secrets of their success will be revealed, along with steps you can take, today, to create the success you desire.

You'll meet Rob Bell, the president of a company specializing in shopping cart systems used by today's top Internet marketers. With over 20 years of sales and marketing experience, Rob shows you how to grow your profits, saving time and money, by automating your sales through the latest in shopping cart technology.

We'll also check in with Jim Black. He's revolutionizing how business is done by bringing people together through innovations in audio and web conferencing technologies. He'll introduce you to the ins and outs of bringing the full sensory experience to your customers.

You'll learn:

- *How to build a solid foundation for success online.* Learn the rules of permission marketing that can pull thousands to your Web site, how to create multiple streams of income on the Internet, the secrets of online branding, the eight simple Guerrilla Marketing techniques to maximize your Web site's effectiveness, and more.
- *How to write compelling Web copy to convert visitors to buyers.* Learn Web copywriting secrets that position your prospects to say "yes," three proven formulas for writing attention-grabbing headlines, a 12-step system to create powerful sales letters that attract buyers, how best to position client testimonials for maximum impact, and more.
- *How to attract traffic to your Web site.* Learn how to create an influx of traffic to your Web site, to develop profitable joint ventures through affiliate programs, the five elements that affect your search engine placement, how to select a winning domain name, and more.
- *How to create e-products, targeted e-mail campaigns and other powerful online strategies.* Learn how to create low-cost, profit-producing products like e-books, how to build large opt-in mailing lists following 12 simple steps, the 8 types of sales-generating announcements to send to interested subscribers, how to use shopping cart technology to make you money, and more.
- *How to maximize your profits from seminars, coaching, and selling.* Learn how other top marketers have used online marketing to successfully promote their virtual businesses.

From Robert Allen's presentation on multiple streams of Internet income to Yanik Silver's tips on Web copy that sells, from Declan Dunn's models for affiliate marketing to Jimmy Brown's masterful e-mail marketing techniques, you'll be provided with the information you need to stand out from the mass of congestion and clutter on the Internet.

I'm a firm believer that you don't need to reinvent the wheel. In today's fast changing marketplace, there just isn't enough time. Opportunitics move by swiftly. You must be ready to take advantage of them. You can save time, money, and energy by going directly to the source— our Online Marketing Superstars. They've blazed the trail, cleared the path, and are sharing their secrets of success. You can create a successful online presence, today, by following tips, techniques, and processes proven to work. There is no time like the present to take the first step forward. Let's go!

Mitch Meyerson
Scottsdale, Arizona
http://www.mitchmeyerson.com

We're conducting a research study of Internet Marketing Skills. To assess your Online Marketing IQ and receive your free multimedia marketing e-course, take our complimentary assessment found at http://www.onlinemarketingsuperstars.com.

1

MARK VICTOR HANSEN
THE MILLION DOLLAR MINDSET

Legendary author and marketing expert **MARK VICTOR HANSEN** has sold more than 80,000,000 books and products in the past ten years alone. When it comes to thinking big and implementing big plans, he is a master. Mark's latest book series, coauthored with Robert Allen, is *The One Minute Millionaire,* and their goal is to inspire one million new millionaires this decade.

FOR MORE INFORMATION: http://www.markvictorhansen.com

In This Chapter You Will Learn:

- What the Million Dollar Mindset Is
- How to Master the Art of Marketing
- Goal Setting Guidelines
- How to Think Big, Act Big, and Realize Your Dreams

THE MILLION DOLLAR MINDSET

It's time to stop tiptoeing around the pool and jump into the deep end, head first. It's time to think *bigger,* want *more,* and achieve *all* your goals at any age. Merely stumbling through eight hours at the office is no longer enough. So-so commitments and standoffish relationships with our family members will no longer get the job done.

- We want more for ourselves.
- We want to live our dreams.
- We want the abundance we were born to live.

The majority of people meet with failure because they lack the persistence to create new plans to take the place of failed plans. But you were meant to experience abundance in every facet of your life. It's your job to choose what that abundance is.

One question I'm often asked is, "How does one go about creating a million dollar business?" The truth is, when you take control of your life by asking for what you want and need, you can accomplish *anything* your heart desires. No doubt, you know of people who seem to walk into any situation and any relationship expecting success. They achieve success again and again because they've learned, and acted on, one simple truth: You will reach your goals only with the help of others.

There are some common characteristics shared between people who have mastered the art of asking.

- They know what they want. They are clear about their vision, purpose, and goals.
- They believe that what they're asking for is very possible.
- They are passionate about what they are requesting.
- They act even when they're afraid or feel fear.
- They learn from experience so that they become better "askers" every time they ask.
- They are persistent. If at first they don't receive, they ask, ask, ask until they do.

MASTER THE ART OF MARKETING

A huge vision. That's what we're trying to instill in our audiences—how to think and act big. But to create this type of big vision and to generate money on demand, you must master the art of marketing.

Marketing is the ability to effectively reach out to a customer and offer them your product, your service, your personality, your information. This is called Information Entrepreneurship, which is the best of all possible businesses.

For example, I'm working on several new information products. If I have a content rich report that you desperately want to have, for example, on book publishing strategies, you'd be willing to pay $7 for that . . . maybe even $39, $49, or $99. Especially if it contained new information or insights that could potentially save—or make you—thousands of dollars.

What I'm trying to do is show people how to turn their ideas into best-selling books and other profitable information products. I want to sell you on it, motivate you on it, empower you on it, offer telephone conference calls on it, seminars on it, trainings on it; even coaching programs.

What I'm doing is creating a market. That's what we've done with *Chicken Soup*. Now I'm going to do it with information publishing advice. I've got the next ten products I'm ready to finish writing on and get done, because once you catch on to how to be a marketing maven and a marketing master, you become a no-limit, fully-functioning person.

And then, if you put your team in, and TEAM means "Together Everyone Accomplishes Miracles," you start accomplishing financially what everyone else considers a miracle. It's normal and natural to be able to multiply yourself and replenish yourself and then share all that. So you earn all you can, save all you can, invest all you can so that you can give all you can.

THE BIG PAYDAY

Everyone can have a normal payday. You go to work and you get paid. But look what happened with the *Chicken Soup* series. At our zenith, we were selling 15,000,000 books a year, and we had 15 of the top 50 bestsellers on *USA Today*.

That was all done by design and strategy. Jack Canfield and I sat down and mentally muscled through it again and again and again, because *planning* is everything. The plan is nothing because the plan changes once you're into execution. You've got to be flexible and keep moving around. But when you start to plan, your 18 billion brain cells go to work, and they say, "Look at the infinite opportunity. We've got stuff here that no one else sees." We still are going to pull off selling a million books in one day.

I think I've finally found an executive that can really pull this off by going inside the companies and making the companies happy to pull off what we want to pull off. So everybody wins and nobody loses when you get to do a bigger job. And one of my biggest clichés is, "Whoever has the biggest idea rules."

GOAL SETTING GUIDELINES

To achieve these big ideas, you've got to set goals. You've got to set goals as simple as, "What would your ideal home look like if you had the home of your heart's desire?" You know, what it would look like if you acquired it and it worked for you. And that's down to what does the front door look like, what does the entryway look like?

When you're looking out the windows, are you looking at whatever winds your clock? Not where you are, but where you want to be, your heartfelt desire. I just got back from our Hawaii beachfront home, and as far as I'm concerned, we have the best piece of beach in Kona, Hawaii. But everyone needs whatever they're seeing, whether it is a mountain scene or a desert scene or a forest scene. I'm not biased. I think maybe if you're really doing well, you want all four of those available to you.

And then what you do is start acting on that and bring yourself forward at levels that no one else has ever thought to bring themselves forward. Everybody that becomes a millionaire directly and indirectly employs ten other people. So it becomes really exciting because this is, with good marketing and great thinking, a way to get full employment in America.

I've told people thousands of times that they've just got to ask for what they want. The problem with that is they don't know what they want!

TURNING DREAMS INTO REALITY

I'm going to start you on a wonderful path of painting your dreams into reality. I'm going to teach you the secrets behind setting—and achieving—your greatest ambitions.

Before we set off on this path together, let me make one thing very clear: The word "goals" can be intimidating; it can feel so overbearing that it keeps people from even beginning the process. So, let's instead think of goals as a "To Do List with Deadlines."

Do the deadlines have to be tomorrow? Next week? Of course not. This is *your* To Do List for the rest of your life. Goals can be added to, subtracted from, and, most importantly, scratched off the list as you move through your life.

Here's a checklist to ensure you're using a successful framework to set your To Do List:

- *Your most important goals must be yours.* Not your spouse's. Not your child's. Not your employer's. Yours. When you let other people determine your definition of success, you're sabotaging your own future.
- *Your goals must mean something to you.* When you write your goals, you must ask yourself, "What's really important to me?" "What am I prepared to give up to make this happen?" Your reasons for charting a new course of action give you the drive and energy to get up every morning.
- *Your goals must be specific and measurable.* Vague generalizations and wishy-washy statements aren't good enough. Be very specific!
- *Your goals must be flexible.* A flexible plan keeps you from feeling suffocated and allows you to take advantage of genuine opportunities that walk in your future door.
- *Your goals must be challenging, exciting.* Force yourself to jump out of your comfort zone to acquire that energy and edge.
- *Your goals must be in alignment with your values.* Pay attention to your intuition, your gut. When you set a goal that contradicts your values, something inside will twinge. Pay attention.
- *Your goals must be well balanced.* Make sure you include areas that allow time to relax, have fun, and enjoy people in your closest circle.

- *Your goals must be realistic.* Be expansive but don't be ridiculous. If you're four feet tall, you will probably never play in the NBA. Also, be sure to allow yourself time to get there.
- *Your goals must include contribution.* Unfortunately, many people get so wrapped up in pursuing their goals that they don't have time in their lives to give something back to society. Build this into your goals program.
- *Your goals need to be supported.* Share a few of your dreams with a number of people, or share all of your dreams with a select few people. In either case, you're creating a web of support and accountability for yourself.

Open your mind to all the possibilities. Start each goal with "I am" or "I will." Don't even think about restricting yourself!

THE AMBASSADOR OF BIG THINKING

What I suggest is that marketing is really effective storytelling. I also suggest that your life is a series of stories. You're in the "before picture" of your life. There's a picture we show in my Mega Marketing Seminar of a little baby kitten looking in the mirror. In the "after picture," the kitten sees a roaring lion.

All of us are a "before picture," and storytelling is about where you are with your picture and where you want to be. If it's not where you wanted it to be, what would you like it to be if it could be anything you want? Because there's a bigger, better, brighter you and once you know how to do that, then you get to multiple streams of marketing.

I've only touched on marketing, but you also want to do media, publicity, high-profile endorsements, word of mouth, joint ventures, and cross-promotions. *Chicken Soup* did a cross-promotion with Campbell's Soup and were on 4,000,000 Campbell's Soup cans. A foldout label described the promotion. All the consumer had to do was collect three labels and send them in to Campbell's for a free special edition *Chicken Soup for the Soul* book, coauthored with Campbell's. Campbell's won. *Chicken Soup* won. The consumer won! Campbell's was willing to pull off our dream with this. So then you get the big word of mouth. It was bypass marketing because we sold a lot of books off the Campbell's labels that no one believed we could do, and our book still went to number one, because you get 4,000,000 exposures to those who are reading labels. That's pretty good.

Everyone should have marketing affiliates. Annually, I hold a Mega Book Marketing Seminar where we discuss book marketing and promotion strategies. Licensing is something that has been enormously big for us. I have 39 number-one licenses. We sold 5,000,000 greeting cards last year, and 897,000 albums with Rhino Records. We, right now, are selling $2,000,000 worth of dog food a month under the *Chicken Soup* label.

Obviously you've got to sell all your existing customers. You've got to keep doing direct mail, which we call "snail mail." We've got all kinds of cool stuff, like we've got a guy talking about "lumpy" mail at our seminar, where if I sent you a bank bag in the mail and your wife got it, and it had your name on it marked personal and confidential, and it was security locked, believe me, you'll open it.

We get almost 100 percent openership and it goes to the person you want to open it. Then we've got newspapers and magazines. You've got to have multiple streams. We teach you how to have multiple streams of income, multiple streams of residual and flat, multiple streams of marketing to make your life go great.

GETTING THE VISION

Back in 1990, Jack and I did breakfast talk together in the Los Angeles area. He mentioned that he was going to do a book containing all the inspiring and motivating stories that got him standing ovations in his presentations. I said let's do it together. He asked me to send him some stories and we agreed to do it.

We started working and it took us three years, 24/7, 365, and our wives said we ought to live together because we spent so much time together. We knew we were going to hit not a home run, but a grand-slam home run.

Did we know what we'd sell? Now we're at 100,000,000 books, if you count everything worldwide, and it's still growing. Our goal is a billion books by 2020 AD. Did we know that we could get this far then? No.

Not a chance, because a big shot is a little shot that keeps shooting. If you have big targets, and this is why I'm the Ambassador of Big Thinking. I want everyone to have 5-, 10-, 50-, and 100-year goals. Most of us are underperforming ourselves.

In spiritual language, sin is an Aramaic term and it means to miss the target; miss the mark. Well, you miss the target if you don't have a target. If you don't have a dream, you can't accomplish the dream. It doesn't just fall from heaven, it falls on those of us who have great and inspired dreams and hopes and desires.

I publish a "Rich Results" newsletter. We e-mail it out free every week and it takes you through, step-by-step, how to get 101 goals. You've got goals in all areas of your life. You've got your health and your finances, both earning power and net worth. You've got your social goals, your spiritual goals, your mental goals, and you really start writing down who you want to meet, when you want to meet them, and where you want to meet; what you'd like to do; and who you'd like to partner with.

I can tell you that when I started writing my goals 30 years ago, I never believed that I could be where I am now. I really caught on to this for the first time when I was bankrupt and upside down financially and in an absolutely have-not-ness and chaos. And you know, most people ask if I want to go any further.

The reason I want to go further is there's nothing more exciting than creatively using your mind and applying it at a high level and knowing that other people are going to get better results than you do. I have all these people saying, "Well, I'm making more than you did in less time." I say, "Good, good, good. That's that goal, get reflected glory. I want to see what you can do and what's possible." That's so exciting.

I've got a student right now that's definitely going to make a billion dollars in the next year and he said he'd like to give me part of it. I said, "Well, I'm into accepting this week, so it's very good we're both on the same page." It was nice because he said, "I never would have done this because before you came along I was thinking little." He's a money guy and he said, "I did loans of $100,000 and then you told me, 'Don't do loans of less than a million.'" I found out there were more people that need over a million and we've got one client that he's going to lend $5,000,000 to in a couple of days.

THINK BIG, ACT BIG, AND REALIZE YOUR DREAMS

If you're just starting out, don't be intimidated by the people who have already made a big impact. Start where you're at. I've got an audio program called, "How to Think Bigger Than You Ever Thought You Could Think," and I think everybody ought to listen to it.

Second, if you can, come to any of our Mega Seminars. My belief is it's the blitz courses done by top guys in their fields where you have 5 or 10 or 20 teachers, over a 3- or 4-day immersive weekend where you get inundated for 12–18 hours a day. By the end of that time, your mind is expanded.

As Oliver Wendell Holmes said, "A man's mind, stretched by a new idea, can never go back to its original dimension." Well, you're now in a new shape and if you do all the stuff we tell you, like buddying up, teaming up, and partnering up with at least three or four people in the room that are going to hold you accountable on what it is you're supposed to do, you're going out with a new set of marching orders.

I'm touched. I'm thankful. I'm blessed. And you know, a lot of it is getting done because I get to dream it and other people get to figure out how to make it happen. It's amazing how this all works.

2

ROBERT ALLEN
CREATING MULTIPLE
STREAMS OF INCOME ON
THE INTERNET

ROBERT ALLEN is the author of some of the largest selling financial books in history. His colossal New York Times bestsellers, *Nothing Down* and *Creating Wealth*, have sold over a million copies each. His recent bestsellers include *Multiple Streams of Income, Multiple Streams of Internet Income: How Ordinary People Make Extraordinary Money Online,* and *The One Minute Millionaire: The Enlightened Way to Wealth.*

FOR MORE INFORMATION: http://www.robertallen.com

In This Chapter You Will Learn:

- The Importance of Multiple Streams of Income

- How to Test Your Market

- What a USP Is

- The Power of Reverse Engineering

- How to Create a "Feeding Frenzy"

CREATING MULTIPLE STREAMS OF INCOME ON THE INTERNET

You need to have your Web site generating revenue streams from all kinds of different avenues. It can't be just one; it has to be multiple streams of income because it makes your Web site much more versatile. It also forces you to think like a businessperson. You start to think, "How can I squeeze out the most amount of profit out of every single activity that I am doing on the Internet?"

The other reason is you never can tell when one of the streams of income that you are focusing on might be the big one, the big kahuna. It may be the one that is going to make you enormous amounts of money.

STARTING AN ONLINE BUSINESS

Online is the most profitable way for launching your business. It may take you a little while to figure it out because it's a little bit of a different animal than traditional business. But once you figure out how you make your online presence successful, then you have the best of all worlds because:

- You can do market testing without a lot of expense.
- You can do advertising that is dramatically less expensive than in the real world.
- You have the ability to communicate instantly with just a few pushes of the buttons.

Compare this to direct mail in the real world. Normally, you have to go down to a print shop to get your letters stuffed and take your mail and send it out into the real world. You cross your fingers and you hope that it all gets delivered because about a third of the mail in bulk mail doesn't get delivered anyway. When you go online, you can do all of that in a matter of minutes instead of a matter of days or weeks or months, and you can get your response back immediately.

We did a test here recently. We tried to determine which of four different approaches would be best. We did four tests of 10,000 e-mails a piece.

Each one of these was a separate and different test with a different headline, a different offer, and a different price point. We were able to determine within one day after sending out 40,000 e-mails that one of the approaches was, hands down, the best approach. One offer generated 400 responses, which is about a 4 percent response rate. None of the other offers on the same idea generated even near that. One offer generated only one response out of 10,000 e-mails instead of 400 responses, so one offer was 400 times better than the other offer.

If we had done this in the real world, sending out direct mail letters and testing and seeing which one offer might work, first of all, it would have cost us $40,000. And $30,000 of it would have been a total loss. It would have taken a week to two weeks to get the full response back. We were able to do the exact same test in 24 hours and find out which of our offers was the best. Now not only do we have more money in our pocket, because it didn't cost us any money to test these other ideas, but we also have speed on our side. Now we know in 24 hours which offer works. And so we can start to roll out the offer that does work.

If you can crack the code of the Internet, and figure out how to find the customers and how to deliver your product to them in a way that is profitable to you, then you have all the advantages of the Internet. With all of the cost efficiencies of the Internet and all of the speed of the Internet, there is just no better place to be.

FAIL FAST FOR FREE

I've often said that on the Internet you can *fail fast for free*. And if you can fail fast for free, that means you get to fail, fail, and fail at no cost. You can't do that in the real world. And the cost is so inexpensive. Your cost on the Internet is not technically zero but it's close to zero. You can keep failing and failing and failing until you figure out how to succeed. There's just no better place to do it. It's the best.

You have to be much, much more careful in the real world. I call it the real world and the online world. In the real world if you aren't really, really careful, you end up losing all your money on your marketing.

build one in. This way, people can really tell the difference between you and your competitor.

Next you have to make an offer that is outrageous; you have to "Ginsu knife" your offer. You have to add much more to it. Most people don't do this. They just say, "We have this widget, we're selling it, here's the price, and that's the way it works." But the way I encourage you to do it is to reverse engineer everything. Create your product and the price points. Then factor in costs to build in the ability for you to add other items to your offer to make it even more sensational or more advantageous. Make it look better to your customer.

In my case, we offer training programs. Each training program has a $5,995 price point. There are four training programs, so if you were to buy them all, it would cost you almost $25,000. Of course, each one of these training programs we offer is extremely valuable and extremely focused, and each one is absolutely worth $6,000.

So, in our offer we say you can choose the one you want, with the additional offer that, if you choose today, I will give you a scholarship to the other three programs at no charge to you. I want your spouse to attend at no charge as well. You just select the one program that you want the most and if you will do that today I will give you a $2,000 discount. And you will get a three-day training program that goes with that and you will also receive 90 hours of audiocassettes.

Then reverse engineer it to be able to make your offer extremely irresistible to the customers you are dealing with.

Then finally you have to make a powerful promise. In our promise we want you to make a million dollars this year. There are very few people who make that kind of promise. This is the year we are going to become millionaires.

You need to reverse engineer your business and deliver those three advantages for your unique selling proposition. If you do, you will be 99 percent ahead of every one of your competitors. Very few of them ever think through their ultimate advantage; very few of them ever create a sensational offer. You're going to be ahead of them!

CREATING A FEEDING FRENZY

The first step in creating a feeding frenzy is to find the fish that are already hungry. I learned from Jeff Paul, and I have heard it in other places since, that you've got to find addicts. *An addict is a person who has got to have your product.* If it's not going to be from you, it's going to be from somebody else. And there are all kinds of classifications of customers. For example, golfers are some of the biggest addicts on the planet. If they come up with a new way to shave a stroke off their score, golfers are going to buy some silly product to help them do that. A videotape, a new kind of driver, a new kind of putter, it doesn't matter. These people are addicted. That's what you're looking for, someone who has a positive addiction.

Whether it is exercise, chocolate, or belonging to certain kinds of groups, there are all kinds of addictions. Just make sure you are dropping your hook in front of a group of people that are already addicted—those who are disposed to say yes.

Most people do it just the opposite. They create a product then say, I wonder what those fish want. For the bait, they kind of think, "Well if I was a fish, this is what I would want." They create a product that really has nothing to do with what their fish want. Therefore, they go out and look for a market to drop their hook into. Just the opposite is the way you need to approach it.

THE 12 PRINCIPLES OF PERSUASION

Find a market that is already addicted and go talk to them. Find out exactly what they want. Organize and design it exactly the way they tell you to do it. Then you drop your hook into that group of fish, and you've got yourself a feeding frenzy. The way you feed a feeding frenzy is through what I call the "12 Principles of Persuasion."

Principle #1 is to give gifts. If you give gifts to people, they are predisposed to buy. It increases the probability that they will buy.

Principle #2 is to take baby steps. Cause them to make little tiny commitments instead of big commitments. As Seth Godin says in his book, *Permission Marketing,* when you go to a bar you don't turn to the gal next to you and say, "Hi, I'd like to get married." Instead, you ask, "Would you like a drink?" You take little baby steps, letting people know they don't have to make big commitments.

Principle #3 is popularity. You show that your product is popular and that other people have bought it. For instance in my case, you introduced me as a bestselling author. That creates the belief in the mind of the listener that this guy has been popular, he is popular. Other people like him, therefore I should as well.

Principle #4 is credibility. If you've got degrees behind your name or if you've got credentials, you flaunt them. You let people know about it.

Principle #5 is create scarcity. Probably one of the fastest ways for you to create a feeding frenzy is to create scarcity. You engineer it so that your product is scarce. And you stick to that. It's not an artificial thing; you literally design scarcity into your product so people will act. They need to act because of a time deadline.

Principle #6 is honesty. This is always important. When people hear that you have flaws, they actually like that. If you just tell the truth about yourself, people will believe you more and you will get a greater response than if you tried to act like you're the greatest thing on the planet.

Principle #7 is create rapport. Build a relationship with people, establish a connection. People buy from those with whom they have a relationship.

Principle #8 is create urgency. There's a difference between scarcity and urgency. Scarcity is a limited number. Urgency is limited time. It's critical to your marketing. It causes your customers to act rather than wait around and think about it. If they wait around and think about it, you've lost them. Someone else will put the bait in front of them and they will bite that bait. Whoever can get the fish to bite first, the fastest is going to be the one who wins this game.

Principle #9 is greed for pleasure. Make your offer so incredible that they can't say no.

Principle #10 is fear of loss or pain. Sometimes in your marketing you need to just point out that if they don't take advantage of the offer you're providing here they don't get the ultimate benefit that they want, which is a better life. Just think about it: You live ten years trying to search for the right ideas and not acting on what you find, then you wait another ten years, and eventually you run out of life. Your marketing has got to reach both segments of your marketplace.

There are those who are what we call "moving toward," and other people who are "moving away from." Some people are drawn toward your product or services because they have a bright future. They want to improve their lives and they are moving toward their goals. Other people are motivated because they are moving away from pain or fear or loss. It's generally about 80 percent of your audience steadily moving toward something, and that's how you reach them. You say, here's the bright future, let's go get it. But 20 percent of your audience is going to be motivated by fear, lack, and loss; by moving away from pain instead of moving toward pleasure. So your marketing has to have both of them in there because you need to reach both of your types of thinking audience.

Principle #11 is belonging. Get people to belong to a club, or group, or somewhere they can feel a part of what you're doing. Some people are motivated by this, and it creates action.

Principle #12 is curiosity. Some people just have to check it out. The thought that they are going to lose out somehow without checking this out drives them nuts. One of the phrases that I say at the end of my program or a marketing call is, "If you miss this, you will kick yourself." Sometimes I will have people come back five months later and say, "You know, the reason I did this is because I found that I was kicking myself thinking that I was going to miss it."

If you use all 12 of these principles in your marketing, you *will* create a feeding frenzy. You will create people who will act, and this action will be a result of the way you created your marketing approaches.

LEARN FROM SUCCESSFUL PEOPLE

The most important point of Internet marketing is to figure it out as quickly as you can. The Internet is amazing. One of the stories I talk about in *Multiple Streams of Internet Income* is about a gentleman in Mississippi who markets a $1,600 set of tapes. He had just bought some products from one of the Internet gurus, and decided to follow his advice. He started his own Web site and an e-zine. Six months later he was sending out wonderful information every single month, but with no response. He was getting discouraged and ready to quit. He makes one quick phone call to his guru and asks, "What's the matter? I spent all this time and all this effort, sending out all this free information, but nobody's responding."

The guru asks first of all, "Did you make an offer in your e-zine? Did you actually have an ad in your e-zine that said, 'Oh, by the way, I have this for sale?'"

He says, "No, I didn't. I just assumed people would call me back and say they wanted to get hooked up with my stuff." The guru replies, "Well you need to have an ad at the very beginning of the e-zine and an ad in the middle and an ad at the end. You need to offer something specifically."

So, the very next week he sends out his e-zine and gets $3,500 worth of orders. Boom, the lights went on. It just took a little tiny bit of tweaking to shift from a monthly e-zine to a weekly e-zine. This way, he could make that money every single week. Now he makes tens of thousands of dollars every single month. It was just a tiny little adjustment in his approach. So I would highly recommend that you don't try to figure this stuff out by yourself. There are a lot of resources online to learn how to make your Internet marketing work. Find somebody that you really like. Learn from them. Learn from their mistakes. It's going to be the fastest way for you to get there. Frankly, it may cost you thousands of dollars to have someone point you in the right direction, but if you don't, you will have to learn it by yourself and it will take years longer. You will waste all kinds of time and money on the wrong approach. Find somebody you can trust, follow their advice, and go for it.

The first step you can take right now is to do what I have been encouraging you to do here, go to http://www.robertallen.com to sign up for our free e-zine and join my Maybe Lake. Watch the way I do it, and if you're really smart, you will do this with all of the people you want to test. Join their e-zine and watch how they market it to you.

C h a p t e r

3

JAY CONRAD LEVINSON
GUERRILLA MARKETING
ONLINE AND OFFLINE

JAY CONRAD LEVINSON, author of the bestselling marketing series in history, *Guerrilla Marketing,* plus 24 other business books, has so influenced marketing that today his books appear in 37 languages and are required reading in many MBA programs worldwide. He has written monthly columns for *Entrepreneur Magazine,* articles for *Inc. Magazine,* a syndicated column for newspapers and magazines, and online columns published monthly on the Microsoft and GTE Web sites. Jay has served on the Microsoft Small Business Council and the 3Com Small Business Advisory Board.

FOR MORE INFORMATION: http://www.gmarketing.com

In This Chapter You Will Learn:

- The Importance of Marketing Online and Offline

- How to Be Proud of Your Site

- The Eight Elements of a Successful Web Site

- What Fusion Marketing Is

- How to Get the Most Out of Your Favorite Search Engine

- How to Spot Major Trends

Because I live in the San Francisco Bay Area, I'm not too far from Silicon Valley. In the early 1990s I kept hearing about the Internet from those people and I realized it was going to be a fantastic marketing venue. I thought it would be a good idea for me to have a *Guerrilla Marketing* book on it, however, I knew it would take me a year or two to learn about the Internet.

I contacted a good friend who was living in Sedona, Arizona, Charles Ruben, and I said, "Let's do a book together about marketing on the Internet." He agreed and so we cowrote the first edition of *Guerrilla Marketing Online.*

My publisher, Houghton Mifflin (who published Mark Twain and Henry David Thoreau) initially said "Oh, no" when I told them I wanted to write a book about guerrilla marketing on the Internet. When I asked why, they said, "We don't want to publish books with new words and no one knows what the Internet means."

"The people *will* know what Internet means; it's going to be a big, big thing," I told them. They insisted they had learned not to use new words in a title, so the book came out as *Guerrilla Marketing Online* in 1993. We were way ahead of the game, but not in using the word Internet.

The Internet has been around since the 1970s and it took a while for people to start wrapping their minds around it. As you can see, my Boston publisher wasn't ready for it in the early 1990s, but now everybody knows what the Internet is.

I was interested in it because anybody in marketing is trying to learn every possible way that they can be marketing, and online was one of the ways that entered my mind. I also knew it would be of poor service to the *Guerrilla* readers to make them wait a year. That's why I got in touch with Charlie Ruben. Luckily, we were able to put out one of the first books about marketing on the Internet.

That's the story of how *Guerrilla Marketing Online* got started and why it got started so early. As you can see, because the Internet actually started in the 1970s, we weren't really that early because the book came out in the early 1990s.

TWO WORLDS OF MARKETING

Once you've gotten even a spark of a notion to go online, you've got to let that spark ignite thoughts of how to promote your Web site. You've got to have the insight to know what this means; you've got to start thinking imaginatively about two worlds.

People who are in the online world think that's the only world. That's where you think in terms of multiple links to other sites and banners leading to your site, search engines directing browsers to your site, making postings on forums alerting onliners to your site, chat conferences that are heralding your site, recommendations of your site by other Internet powers, and, of course, e-mailing to parties who are demonstrably interested in learning about the topics covered at your site.

You can write articles for other sites in return for links back to your site. This is a very unused way to marketing on the Internet—writing articles for other sites, mentioning your site in your e-mail signature and advertising online to entice people to visit your site.

It means preparing an online version of your press kit to publicize your site online. That world also means connecting with as many other online entities as possible. All of them are on a quest for you to make your site part of the online community, actually to make it an Internet landmark to your prospects, a not-to-be missed feature of the Web.

Now, a lot of people do that, but that's only one world and most people don't live there. There's the second world in which your imagination should run rampant.

THE OFFLINE WORLD

In a mission to achieve top-of-mind awareness of your site is the offline world, because most of the real world still resides there. That's where people continue to get most of their information, at least for now, although the number one reason people go online is to get information. So offline is the way you've really got to let them know of your online site, and it's got to be teaming with information that can shower them with benefits for their businesses, their lives, or both. This means you've got to live in that online world touting your site on your ads, on stationery and your business cards, on signs and brochures and flyers, in Yellow Pages ads, on ad specialties, on packages or business forms or gift certificates, and on reprints of PR.

You can market your site in catalogs, newsletters, and classified ads, and on radio spots or TV. More than one company now has a jingle that's just heralding their Web site. You should never neglect directing folks in the outside world to your site in the online world; in direct mail letters and postcards and in all your faxes, almost anyplace where your name appears. The world begins to think that your last name is dot-com, which means you're going about your offline promotional activities in the right way.

Some companies think that by mentioning their site in tiny letters at the bottom of their ad or by flashing it at the end of their TV commercials that they're taking care of offline promotion. Not true. They're only going through the motions. People have got to talk about their Web site the same way they would talk about their child: with pride, enthusiasm, and drive. Mostly, you've got to make people excited about your site. Let them see your pride.

Will industry or local newspapers write about your site? The answer is of course they will, if you make it fascinating enough for their readers. That's your job. Promotion will lure them to your site, but it's killer content that will encourage return trips. Killer content means information that gets people to respond emotionally. The best way to do this is to write articles on their greatest problems and struggles and then offer laser-focused solutions to these problems. Another powerful way to engage readers is to offer specific and current statistics on issues that resonate with them. When they can see themselves in your words, they will keep reading and come back for more. A good way to improve your skill in this area is to visit other Web sites that offer relevant and compelling copy for their visitors.

The most important thing that I just said in that message is that people live in two worlds; it's not just the online world. People live mainly in the offline world. No matter what you are doing online, you've got to be excited about it offline as well. That's where most people still reside and they always will, no matter how big the Internet gets. Most people will spend their time not being online, but being in the other world where there are no keyboards or mouses or search engines.

And it seems to me, like using the basic principles of *Guerrilla Marketing*, that there are multitudes, there are dozens, a hundred, marketing weapons and strategies. We can take these and use so many of them online and offline, and there are more combinations than ever when you mix the two mediums.

EIGHT RULES FOR CREATING AN EFFECTIVE WEB SITE

There are certainly rules for Web sites that produce the desired result, the first one being that nothing is for sure on the Internet. Everything I'm saying is correct today, but the rules are constantly changing.

Right now, today, you've got to *equally emphasize eight elements* if you're going to succeed online. Notice all four of those words begin with *E: Equally Emphasize Eight Elements.*

I. Planning

The first element, which comes as a shock to most people, is *planning.* You should ask yourself why you want to build a Web site in the first place. A lot of people don't have Web sites and run thriving businesses. A lot of people put up a Web site because they think they're supposed to because they're in business, just like you're supposed to have a telephone. You don't necessarily need a Web site. It's the most powerful tool in the history of marketing, but it's definitely not mandatory. You've got to know ahead of time what you wish to accomplish with your Web site.

The best example I know of this is a man who has a company called European Sleep Works. It's a store that sells beds and mattresses in Berkeley. This man was kind of technophobic and did not really want to have a Web site, but the young people working for him in Berkeley wanted to have a Web site. Eventually, it dawned on him that one of the keys to his success was attracting great people. One of the ways he attracts them is by giving them a piece of the business once they've been working for him for a year.

Now he was hearing that if he didn't get an online presence, he might lose some of those people. So he told them, "Okay, give me a Web site, but know this ahead of time: I don't want to sell *anything* from my Web site. It's too hard to ship mattresses to people."

So the people who worked for him agreed and they put up his site, EuropeanSleepWorks.com, and what he does now is use the offline world, radio and newspapers, to talk about his Web site. All of his radio commercials and all of his newspaper ads direct people to the Web site.

The Web site tells a whole lot more than he could ever say in the context of mass media. He told me just a short time ago that in the 30 years he's been in business, by far the most effective marketing tool he's ever used is having an online presence and having a Web site. Yet he's never sold *anything* from the Web site and has never wanted to. All he tries to do is direct people to his showroom, and it works like crazy.

People have to remember the *fourth* most important reason people go onto a Web site is to buy things. The first most important reason is to get information, so he intrigues them enough that they want more information.

Everybody and their cousin seems to be wired these days, and as a result, they hear the commercial, they go to the Web site, and they learn way more than they ever could before. My friend has a radio commercial, and it's broken the bank for him. He got past his fear of technology by finally coming up with the right answer to "What do I want to accomplish with my Web site?" And his answer was to direct traffic to his store, which is different than what most people think of.

2. Great Content

The second element is *great content*. That's really what's going to attract people to your site. It's going to make visitors happy when they're there; it's going to keep them coming back for more visits on a regular basis. Make sure to keep your content specific, relevant, and focused on their current concerns.

3. Design

The third of the eight elements is *design*. Right now, there is what's called a stay-or-bail moment when people go to a Web site. That means that within the first three seconds, they take a look and decide if they're going to stay there and look for more, or if they're going to think it's too confusing or it's shouting so loud that it may give them a migraine headache, and they leave immediately. So there's this big hang or click moment; it happens in the first three seconds when people see your site. Should they hang around and read more, or should they click away? And it's the design of the site that influences their decision. A good rule of thumb is to keep it simple. Research has shown that when people are presented with too many choices, they get confused and often leave. Make sure your navigation is clear and allows the reader to easily reach the most essential content.

4. Involvement

The fourth element, and a lot of people overlook this, is *involvement*. The Internet, and having a Web site that's an interactive medium, is very different than radio, television, magazines, or newspapers; it's really a back and forth dialogue, so guerrillas take advantage of the Internet's interactivity by involving visitors rather than just requiring that they read.

Involving visitors means you give them a quiz or you let them sign up for a prize or for a free e-book or a PDF file, or maybe they enter your contest—whatever it is, you involve them. Make it a give-and-take; transform it from a visit into a dialogue. Radio and television do not involve people nearly to the extent that the Internet does, and you've got to realize that a Web site is not a place to run your commercial or put your ad or put up your brochure. It's an involving thing, and the more you involve people, the more they'll be involved with you.

5. Production

The first four are pretty easy. The fifth element is the easiest of all, the *production* of your site. This means just putting your first four elements online. If you don't know how to do it yourself, there are lots of companies out there who will produce your Web site and even post it online for you.

6. Follow-Up

The sixth element is where people start falling on their faces. They're pretty good at planning, and they're not too bad at content. These days, they get some good help and they have a fine design and get a realization of the interactivity that lets them wrap their minds around this idea of involvement, and they think they've done their job. But they haven't done their job because there are three more tasks that they've got to emphasize.

So the sixth element is *follow-up*. People visit your site and then they e-mail you; they ask you a question, and what guerrillas do is they follow up. They immediately follow up. The old rule used to be to get back to people in 48 hours, and then it became 24 hours. The reality is, guerrilla marketers know you should get back to them in 2 hours. I have one client who tries to get back to people in 30 minutes! The name of that game is follow-up. You've got to acknowledge that people visited your site and involved themselves. You must acknowledge it with follow-up, even an autoresponder will do, but you've got to let them know you know of their existence.

7. Promotion

The seventh element is *promotion*. You must promote your site online buy registering it with search engines and by linking with other sites. You've also got to be promoting it offline in the mass media and mailings, wherever your name appears. As I said before, the moment you think of marketing online, you've got to think of promoting your site offline.

8. Maintenance

The eighth element is *maintenance*. Unlike marketing, a Web site is just like a little baby. It requires constant changing, updating, and refreshing and renewing. You've got to pay close attention to it, and you've got to realize you don't just put up a Web site and walk away. You put up a Web site and then maintain it and keep it ever fresh, and keep it changing and keep offering new things. Again, people fall on their face when it comes to those last three—a follow-up promotion is maintenance.

This way, huge guerrilla companies can have the warmth and close connection of small guerrilla start-ups. I think if people equally emphasize those eight elements, they're going to find that a Web site is a pretty easy way to make money, as long as you start out with quality in the first place.

GUERRILLA RELATIONSHIPS

Fusion marketing is based on the idea of "I'll scratch your back if you scratch mine," and other words for this are tie-ins, comarketing, or collaborative marketing. Let's say you see a commercial, and you think it's for McDonald's. Midway though, you think it's for Coca-Cola. But by the time it's over, you realize that all along it was for *Finding Nemo!* That's because of fusion marketing between Disney, McDonald's, and Coca-Cola.

There's lots of fusion marketing going on in other areas, and the most lush area and opportunity for guerrillas in fusion marketing is in the area of trading links with people, doing favors for other Web sites and trading links with them. The world is teaming with potential allies for you. Many of them want to help you, they want to team up with you, and they want you to help them. This can happen when you trade links with them.

Your site calls attention to them, their site calls attention to you. This kind of marketing partnership can attract a lot of visitors to your site and each one is visiting not because of money that you've invested online, but because of the friends that you've made. Guerrillas know that not linking is not thinking and to find appropriate online marketing partners with whom you might trade links, think in terms of connecting with companies who have the same kind of prospects and the same kind of standards as you.

Guerrillas engage in what we call a "weekly surf" to locate potential partners. When they can find them, they don't think in terms of entering into a long-term arrangement, they think of the short-term relationship to see if everything works out for both of you. So don't think marriage; instead think fling. If it's fun, you'll both do it again.

If you've got a banner on your site, put it on another site in exchange for you returning the favor for the other site owner. You can discover there are loads of exchange opportunities; there's lots of back scratching going on in cyberspace. The old phrases that we used to call this were tie-ins, collaborative marketing, and comarketing.

Guerrillas call this fusion marketing and today all those phrases refer to trading links. What you ought to really do is go to your favorite search engine and mine it for the names of potential online marketing partners, because it is a goldmine.

BUILDING YOUR ONLINE BRAND

Making money online depends on the level of the company, corporation, or endeavor that you're talking about. The Internet has proven to be a challenge for the large dot-com companies that really need to be able to sustain and justify a large amount of capitalization.

There is an absolutely phenomenal, enormous opportunity, and it's almost even easy, for the small guy to net $100,000 to $150,000 a year on the Internet. I have friends that are 19 and 20 years old in other countries, for example, one friend is in Poland, making $50,000 (US) a month. I have a friend in the United Kingdom who's 19, and he's making a six-figure income.

The Internet is custom-tailored and custom-made for the smaller marketer. It's a challenge if you want to have a successful billion-dollar dot-com business, and the reason is how you reach everyone on the Internet. The Internet is well, well suited for niche marketing, but if you want to reach everyone with your message, it's not like direct mail, where you can go and buy a list and roll it out to a million people. It's a different entity.

ONLINE BRANDING

First, let's talk about why online branding is important or essential. There are good and difficult things about the Internet.

The Internet brings an awful lot more players in. Because there are a lot more players, I think you see that it's much more difficult to maintain customer loyalty. Customer loyalty is really built on branding and on building a relationship, and those two go together.

You have to build this bond with your customers and prospects. You have to build a relationship with them, but at the same time, part of building that relationship is maintaining a consistent theme, identity, and message. That's really what branding is about.

Branding is about communicating a message. I come from the old direct mail, direct response background in marketing, and in the old days, I think that if you talked about branding to a direct response marketer, they would have laughed at you. But you know it's not the old days. It's the new days, it's the days of the Internet, and I think that even direct response marketers are seeing you have to leverage every asset, every opportunity that you have online.

You have to develop that loyalty, and try to keep it. The only way that you maintain price value is by having a brand in this relationship, and that's how you keep out of cutthroat, price-oriented competition. That's the need for branding.

CREATING A BRAND

There are several things that are important when it comes to building a brand. Number one, you look at the models for good branding.

One of the good models, for example, is the whole series of books "for Dummies." You have *Computers for Dummies,* this for dummies, that for dummies, and they all have the same character logo used on the covers and on their Web site. It maintains a consistent color theme, which is black and yellow. Everything has the same graphic design, and so what that means is whether you're looking at the Web site or whether you're looking at the book, you know the company, you know the look.

If you think of Starbucks, what colors do you think of? Starbucks is associated with that green color they have, and so this is subconscious association. Psychologists call it contiguous association, and that's really what you're trying to build in branding. Here's what we do to bring this down to something concrete.

FOUR STEPS TO CREATING YOUR BRAND

1. Look at the Model

I mentioned the *Dummies* series. Another good model is the RichDad .com and the *Rich Dad, Poor Dad* series of books that have the purple/gold, which is their consistent theme of colors. They use a consistent graphic design. When you see a new *Rich Dad* book come out, you instantly recognize it at the bookstore. When you go to their Web site, you instantly recognize it.

2. Look at Your Internet Properties

Chances are, you have multiple Web sites, and you want to maintain a consistent look and theme among your Web sites. If you go to our Web sites, whether you go to PushButtonLetters.com, AmazingFormula.com, or PRCash.com, they all have something in common that lets you know where you are. Our theme is "marketing that roars," and we have a lion that appears on every Web site. We maintain the same colors, the same theme.

A really great place to learn some of the basics of branding is the book *E-myth* by Michael Gerber. It's kind of odd that he would be talking about branding in a book that really talks about the entrepreneurial urge. But I think that Michael talks about branding in a more practical application than some of the books that are written about branding.

Part of branding is the logo that you incorporate, and they have this little four-quadrant logo that they have incorporated. When Michael speaks, it's really interesting. He has this whole stage set, and part of that stage set is that quadrant made up into a big image, a graphical representation that actually sits there on the stage when he speaks. And so, the books, the Web site, the seminar speaking, the colors, the theme, the graphic design, it all blends together.

So, look at models, then look at your own properties and look at them with a dispassionate eye and say, "Do I get the same feeling? Do I see the same colors? Do I see the same graphics? Do I instantly know and recognize this company?" And, if you don't, then you know you're not doing a consistent job of getting your message across.

3. Go to Your Customers

Ask them who your company is and what your company is about, and see if your customers all say you're about the same thing, or if they have conflicting messages. If your customers all have conflicting messages of who you are and what you're about, then you have a problem, because you haven't portrayed or gotten your branding and your message, and your theme, across to your target market.

4. Go to Your Own Staff

Ask, "Who are we? What do we stand for? What do we represent? What are we about?" Does your staff know who you are, what you are, your identity, your theme, and your branding? Is your own staff clear about it? These are, I think, the core issues. It's about your identity. Who are you? What do you stand for? What are you about? That theme and that message and that persona have to permeate every part of your company; this is done through a consistent theme, consistent message, consistent slogan, consistent logo, and so forth.

BRANDING *THE AMAZING FORMULA*

This was interesting because our lead product is *The Amazing Formula,* and it was an inadvertent branding, in that I didn't start out to do it that way, but we became known for that. When you're branding, you're faced with some interesting dilemmas. For example, did I want to make every product in my group of products "The Amazing" this, "The Amazing" that? Or, did I want to make everything "The Formula" this or "The Formula" that?

We sat down, we analyzed it, and we thought about it, and we decided not to do that because we were concerned that it would detract from *The Amazing Formula* product itself. So we decided to go with a completely different branding, which is "Marlon Sanders, Marketing That Roars." The logo is a lion, and the unique angle is that the Web site actually roars. When you receive an e-mail from us, the e-mail actually roars, bringing in the auditory element so it's both visual and auditory.

In short, customers can immediately associate my products, myself, and my identity. Consistency is so important. Chet Holmes, who's worked a lot with Jay Abraham, says that based on the research he did, the average consumer gets 3,000 commercial messages per day—from TV, billboards, telephone, Internet, and other sources. That's an enormous amount of noise and clutter. How do you cut through that enormous amount of noise and clutter? You must have a consistent message. You must have something that you focus in on and hone in on so people identify it with you. If you don't have a laser-focused message, then there's no chance of cutting through the noise in the marketplace.

THE FIRST E-BOOK ON
INTERNET MARKETING

The Amazing Formula would be my most famous e-book because, to my knowledge it was the first e-book on Internet marketing, and was 100 percent digitally downloaded. There were some e-books that were being given away free, but to my knowledge, no one else was selling them. It is the one I'm best known for, but I don't necessarily think it's the best. At least, it's not my favorite product.

My favorite product is actually called *Gimme My Money Now*. The only reason that it's my favorite is because it's really an action plan. It's "Step 1, do this. Step 2, do this. Step 3, do this," and so on. However, it is simply for information marketers, so if you're in a noninformation product business, it's not as relevant. *The Amazing Formula* is broadly applicable to all types of businesses.

"Gimme My Money Now" is really simple. Basically, what it tells you is Step 1, target a market. Step 2, do a 12-product survey to find out what that market wants to buy. Step 3, put together a sales letter and put it up on a Web page for that product. Step 4, trade an initial supply of inventory prototype, an initial product that you can deliver, then test it. What we shoot for is a 1 percent conversion of unique visitors to buyers, and you either meet that or you don't. If you don't make it, then you tweak yourself over and retest. If you do make it, then what you want to do is roll out more.

What we recommend is rolling out with an associate program because it's the single fastest, simplest, and easiest way to get a large volume of traffic online. Even with all the affiliate competition, it's a proven model and I believe that without spending a lot of money, it's the best way to get traffic to your Web site, and the great thing is you pay after the fact. You don't pay your affiliates until there's a sale. And so, that's really "Gimme My Money Now" in a nutshell. In fact, one of my friends, Paul Myers, tells me that he attributed buying his new house to the money that he earned from just using this simple formula. You can find it at http://www.gimmesecrets.com.

WHATEVER THEY'RE BUYING, YOU'RE SELLING

I want to throw out a little philosophy, because I like to have some specifics, but I also like to have philosophy. A long time ago, I had this little retail store. I was really struggling and I wasn't making any money. One day, this guy came in who was in sales and obviously doing well. I said, "Oh man, I'm not any good at sales." He used what is called the Feel Fell Fall method, "I know how you feel, I used to feel the same way. Tell you what I found . . ."

He said, "I found sales is easy once you do this: *Whatever they're buying, you're selling.*" For all the bells and whistles of Internet marketing, technology marketing, and direct response marketing, I really think it comes down to something really simple: Whatever they're buying, you're selling. In other words, your job is to not take a product and ram it down peoples' throats. Your job, and sometimes the challenge, is to find out what people want to buy, and not only allow them to buy it from you, but give them a unique, sustainable advantage for doing so.

In the marketplace today, with all the competition on the Internet, now more than ever, you have to have what's called a sustainable advantage. Michael Porter talked about this at length in his books on competition. You can't just have an edge over your competitors, because society now moves at Internet speed. They're going to knock off that competitive advantage overnight unless it's what's called *a sustainable competitive* advantage. A sustainable uniqueness means that you're able to sustain it over a period of time because there's a barrier to entry. In other words, there's some reason that your competitors cannot easily match the unique value, the unique benefit, the unique proposition you're offering to your customers.

CREATE A SUSTAINABLE ADVANTAGE

Jay Abraham, the marketing consultant, is famous for popularizing the term, "unique selling proposition," though he didn't invent it. Rosser Reed did that. But, Jay Abraham is famous for really popularizing it in today's marketing world. The problem with the unique selling proposition (USP) is, that if you have a USP that's easily knocked off by your competitors, you're not on Internet time. You're going to have that USP for about a month before one, two, three, or four competitors knock it off. You have to be thinking about how you can create a competitive advantage with a unique benefit and value to your customers that is not easily knocked off; something that you can sustain over time.

This is what I think a lot of marketing is today. By finding out what people want to buy, allowing them to buy it from you, and being able to deliver a benefit to them, you are able to sustain over a period of time.

TARGET A HUNGRY MARKET

I want to give you a brief overview of what *The Amazing Formula* is really about. *The Amazing Formula* teaches you to target a market. It's kind of the same thing. It's the same things I've talked about, echoed in a different manner. You target a hungry market. These are people with money to buy products and services that really help, and people that are really hungry for a certain class of products or services. You find out what they want to buy, and then you create the sales process for buying it from you. Make no mistake, marketing is about the who, the what, and the why. Who's going to buy from you? What product is it they're going to buy? And, why are they going to buy it from you?

If marketing is about who, what, and why, sales are about the how. How are you going to sell it to them? So, *The Amazing Formula* really combines the who, the what, and the why, and the how. The how, when you sell online, is with sales letters. I'm a big advocate; in fact, I created a software program that writes your sales letters for you. You can find it at PushButtonLetters.com, and it's one of our bestselling products. Two competitors have now knocked off that product, but it maintained its competitive advantage for about two years. I should have patented it, but I didn't and that was a mistake. In today's world, you have to have trademarks, patents, and copyrights, and you have to try to maintain your competitive advantage.

USING SALES LETTERS

In any event, the sales tool that I teach is dominantly using a sales letter, however, the same psychology that I teach in using a sales letter applies to telemarketing and in-person calls. A lot of it is understanding how to create perceived value for the customer. As Zig Ziegler once said, "When a customer looks at you and your products and services, they're visualizing their stack of money, and they're comparing it to your stack of value. Your stack of value has to be a lot higher in their mind, or they're not buying from you." I teach what I call the "ten times perceived value factor." I teach that your perceived value needs to be a minimum of ten times the money they are spending in order to make a sale because if your stack of value is equal to their stack of money, they're probably going to just keep their money.

PERCEIVED VALUE TIMES TEN

Let's take something simple like your dry cleaner. If you can dry clean your clothes just as easily yourself, and for less money, you're not going to use their services. The only reason you go to the dry cleaner is because you perceive that they're going to save you five to ten times the amount of time, energy, effort, money, and so forth. For the dry cleaners, it's dominant. They're charging you, so it's not the money they're saving. What they're really saving is time, frustration, aggravation, and they're giving you convenience. Now, they're doing that in a much larger proportion than the money you're spending, or you would just choose to do your clothes at home. They're also saving you money, in that if you're washing your clothes at home, those clothes are going to fade really quickly, and you're going to have to go spend money to buy new ones. So while they're charging you to do the clothes, in the long run, they're actually saving you the money you have to spend on new clothes because the clothes you washed and dried are now faded.

That's a really basic simplistic example, but I think it gets the message across. When people buy my information product, they better see that they're going to make 10 or 20 times the cost of that product from what they learned about marketing. They'd better get some immediate techniques they can apply and make money because if they don't, they're just going to keep their money. Why should they buy the product? So, in other words, if a product costs $67, I want them to see that they're going to easily, without a lot of effort, make $670 to $1,000. For them to be willing to spend the $67, they need to see themselves make a lot more than just $120, or they're probably going to keep their money.

I would like to say a few things to people just getting started on the Internet:

1. Find a group of people with a common interest, problem, passion, desire, or need that you can solve or provide a solution for.
2. Find out what it is they want and need.
3. Supply it to them.
4. Do this with a sustainable competitive advantage.
5. Brand yourself with a consistent message, theme, logo, appearance, colors, and design so that you build equity with your customers. Then, over the long term, build your loyalty base.

The final step is to concentrate on building your relationship with your customers by e-mail, teleconference calls, in-person contact, and so forth. This way, you're really building a long-term relationship with your customers. You're branding, you're creating equity, and you're creating a sustainable competitive advantage that's going to keep you in business a year from now.

5

YANIK SILVER
WRITING WEB COPY
THAT SELLS

Just 31 years old, **YANIK SILVER** is recognized as the leading expert on creating automatic, moneymaking Web sites and he's only been online full-time since February 2000. Yanik is a highly sought after speaker and attendees regularly pay up to $4,995 per person to hear his secrets. He is the author, coauthor, or publisher of several bestselling online marketing books and tools including: InstantSalesLetters, InstantInternetProfits, 33DaysToOnlineProfits, Mind-Motivators, and InstantMarketingToolbox.

FOR MORE INFORMATION: http://www.ultimatecopywritingcourse.com

In **T**his **C**hapter **Y**ou **W**ill **L**earn:

- How to Write Great Web Copy

- How to Use Testimonials

- How to Write "The Catch"

HOW TO WRITE GREAT WEB COPY

Writing great Web copy is a lot like writing great sales letters. And this is going to sound a bit unusual, but one of the best ways to learn how to write a great sales letter is to *read a lot of sales letters* by others who promote via direct mail and on the Web. Whenever you see one that really resonates with you, one that you really love and makes you want to buy, even if you know you can't afford it, but it makes you want to buy the product, it's a winner! If it's on the Web, print it out.

Then, actually copy it. I mean, get a pad and pen and write it out by hand. As you handwrite several of these winners, you will start to learn the process for what makes a good sales letter. It is a skill, and you can learn it by doing it.

For me, writing sales letters is not like writing the next great novel. A great sales letter is personal salesmanship in print. We want to grab attention so we do unconventional things, ones you wouldn't necessarily find in great literature.

Like a one-word paragraph, for instance. We will also write sentences that are written for the eye and sentences that are written for the ear.

The best thing I can do for you is to give you my 12-part formula. This is exactly how I write a sales letter, and you can do the same thing. I will also highlight some of the key points.

STEP I: PUT UP A WEB SITE

The first step is to begin planning a Web site. One thing I do want people to realize is that I use a simple approach to our Web marketing: Our entire Web site is a sales letter. That's it! And that's why we spend a lot of time on our headline and sales letter.

People look at any of our sites and its just one long scrolling letter. Almost like the same kind of letter you get in the mail. That's why I say that the Web is much more like direct mail than it is like TV.

If you can simply do what we do, it will cost you a lot less money, rather than trying to fill your site with hundreds of pages of content, and then hope someone will buy something.

We're just being very direct. There are three things that people can do when they come to our site: they can give me their e-mail, they can buy our product, or they can leave. There is not much else that they can do. That's the key: You want to limit what visitors can do so you can maximize your revenue from each visitor.

Long scrolling copy will turn off some readers. But let me explain. There are two types of readers: one will read everything and the other will skim and scroll looking for key points.

For this reason, I have an editing process. I edit our sales letter at least a half-dozen times. In each of the edits, I am editing for a different purpose.

One of the edits is an edit for all the subheads. One of our best sites makes a quarter million a year and that is InstantSalesLetter.com. If you scroll through that site, you will see the subheads and you'll notice that you get a complete sales message, even if you're just a skimmer. So that's one of the key secrets for writing for the Web, you appeal to both types of readers.

Layout also is very important. You want to write and design your site in such a way that it helps the eye of the reader. Reading Web pages on a computer monitor is harder than reading a letter you hold in your hands.

We bring in our margin. There is a bit of blue space around the sales letter so you won't have to read all the way across the screen. We also use a light background with dark type on it. We use color very sparingly. I don't use ten different colors, such as purple, blue, red, and green, all over the place. I stick to a main color scheme. For points I want to highlight, testimonials, for example, we put these in a yellow shaded box, black on yellow. That's the highest contrast colors. This increases readability, 1,000 percent.

STEP 2: WRITE A POWERFUL HEADLINE

If you've been around marketing long enough, you've heard over and over the importance of a great headline. It doesn't matter if it's in print or on the Web.

On the Web it's especially important because people are literally whizzing by at the speed of light; clicking everywhere, going from one Web site to the next. So, your headline has to reach out and grab them.

Create a Swipe File

Even if you're not a great writer, you can create a great headline. What you need to do is use models from great headline writers.

All great copywriters have what they call a "swipe file." That's probably a bad name for it, because we don't literally swipe things or copy things, but we use the headlines of others as models. We use them to brainstorm and to get "the big idea" out of it.

I created my own "best headlines" file that I use all the time. People can get that at UltimateCopywritingCourse.com. You can get headlines that have worked over and over again. (Plus, the course has over 1,529 pages of swipe file material.)

For instance, let's take one of the classic headlines and I'll show you how to model it for whatever product you're selling.

A Classic Headline

A classic headline is, "Do You Make These Mistakes in English?" It's an ad for a home-study course for English language that ran for 40 years. It was created by Maxwell Sackheim

You can use this formula to sell anything that puts in the reader's mind that you make mistakes and want to avoid them. I've used this headline before: "Do You Make These Mistakes with Your Online Marketing?" It fits perfectly. "Do You Make These Mistakes in Real Estate Investing?"

One of the keys to that headline is the word "these." It forces the readers to ask themselves, what are the mistakes I make? It doesn't say, "Do You Make Mistakes in English?" They might just say "yes" or "no" and move on, but they may be making *these* mistakes. They ask, "What are the mistakes I do make?"

Because headlines are so important, one more point is to use power words. You can use simple words like *amazing,* for example, or *great.* Words like *discovery, discover, new,* and words like *announcing* and *introducing,* work as well. Words that you see literally, in the National Enquirer—these are power words that get your attention. These are old words that have been used forever and ever. And sometimes the simplest words are the best!

FIGURE 5.1 Using Simple Words

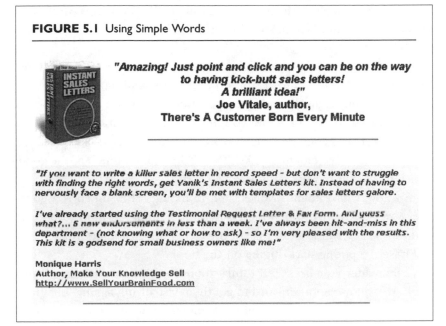

"Amazing! Just point and click and you can be on the way to having kick-butt sales letters! A brilliant idea!"
Joe Vitale, author,
There's A Customer Born Every Minute

"If you want to write a killer sales letter in record speed - but don't want to struggle with finding the right words, get Yanik's Instant Sales Letters kit. Instead of having to nervously face a blank screen, you'll be met with templates for sales letters galore.

I've already started using the Testimonial Request Letter & Fax Form. And guess what?... 5 new endorsements in less than a week. I've always been hit-and-miss in this department - (not knowing what or how to ask) - so I'm very pleased with the results. This kit is a godsend for small business owners like me!"

Monique Harris
Author, Make Your Knowledge Sell
http://www.SellYourBrainFood.com

STEP 3: BUILD INTEREST

The next step of the formula is to build interest by discussing a problem, expanding on your headline, or incorporating a story.

FIGURE 5.2 Building Interest

```
Dear Friend,

How much is one good sales letter worth to your business?

Suppose you could sit down, write a simple letter to your prospects and
customers, mail it and then have your phone start ringing off the hook.

Imagine...one letter could bring you tons of hot leads and new customers,
get them to keep buying over and over again, reactivate 'lost'
customers, and even provide you with a constant stream of referrals. So
anytime you need more business - you simply turn the tap on... it's like
having the goose that lays the golden egg.

Sounds too good to be true?

Well, it isn't if you have the right tools. You see, dollar-for-dollar,
nothing provides a better return on investment than direct mail and it
doesn't matter what product or service you sell.
```

There's an old advertising formula called AIDA, which is Attention, Interest, Desire, and Action. You will see how this works as we walk through each element.

The first part of the formula is *attention*. This refers to the headline. Next we want to build *interest*. You do that by expanding on your headline or by stating a problem or incorporating a story.

For instance, I will show you how the first paragraph of our InstantSalesLetter.com Web page works. The sales letter asks a question, and gets great involvement. It asks, "Dear Friend, How much is one good sales letter worth to your business?"

So now, I have them involved and thinking, "How much is a good sales letter worth?" And then, it has them imagining: "Suppose you can sit down, write a single letter to your prospects and customers, mail it out, and have the phone start ringing off the hook?"

The reader visualizes, and thinks about their phone ringing off the hook. We will use another word to get them visualizing again. "Imagine, one letter could bring you tons of hot leads and new customers, get them to keep buying over and over again, reactivate 'lost' customers, and even provide you with a constant stream of referrals. So anytime you need more business, you simply turn the tap on. It's like having the goose that lays the golden egg."

So it goes on from there. It really gets them involved and visualizing. It answers the questions in the minds of the readers. Questions like, "What are the benefits of a sales letter and how can it help my business?"

A little further into the copy, I use a story and that really helps to keep readership up.

STEP 4: SHOW HOT BENEFITS

Now on to step 4 in the formula, which is the Web reader's desire for hot benefits.

The best people to model are people from *Bottom Line Reports*. They publish many newsletters. I got a direct mail piece from them. They have a big black book of insider medical and health knowledge. The sales letter is almost entirely bullets.

Literally one bullet is so powerful that it can cause a reader to make a buy decision. It makes them think, "Oh, I really need to have that!"

FIGURE 5.3 Showing the Benefits

And that's why I want to let you in on a little-known secret to creating powerful sales letters, by sharing this story with you...

* * * *

In 1904 a man named Albert Lasker, the head of the Lord and Thomas advertising agency, received a peculiar note. The note read:

"I am in the saloon downstairs, and I can tell you what advertising is. I know that you don't know. It will mean much to me to have you know what it is and it will mean much to you. If you wish to know what advertising is, send the word 'Yes' down by messenger." Signed - John E. Kennedy.

Unknown to Kennedy, Lasker had been searching for the answer to this question for over 7 years. He immediately summoned Kennedy, a relatively unknown copywriter, to his office. During this fateful meeting Kennedy uttered 3 words that changed advertising forever. Those words were "Salesmanship in Print".

* * * *

A simple concept, yet nobody has been able to improve on it.

And the results?

So, in our sales letter the subhead says, "Which of these fill-in-the-blank, sales letter templates could you use to grow your business?"

And then it has a number of check marks for the bullet lines. It says, "Turn 'lost' customers into active paying customers or patients."

And next, "Compel current customers or patients to immediately send referrals to you," "Introduce new products or services and sell them right away," "Create a surge of hot, qualified leads, sales appointments and new customers," "Gather testimonials that are worth their weight in gold," and goes on from there.

Benefits are the results your prospects are looking for. If you sell a book, people don't want to read the book, they want the "secrets" and information inside.

You can incorporate benefits into your bullets (which are really "mini headlines"), so use the same powerful words to build desire and stress benefits on how they can avoid pain. InstantSalesLetters.com shows a variety of them. There is definitely an art to writing bullets, but it's a learnable art. You use almost the same formula for writing a headline.

With bullets you want to create more curiosity. You're hitting them over the head with bullets, bullets, and bullets. Each bullet talks about a benefit, not a feature.

FIGURE 5.8 Creating Greed Desire

---

3 FREE Bonuses For Ordering By Midnight
Wednesday, October 11

Bonus#1: As a special free bonus for acting immediately I'll also give
you a copy of a special e-book "Surefire Sales Letter Secrets: How
To Create a Fortune in Your Business With Powerful Direct Mail."
This is a $39.95 value.

> *"I recently bought your Instant Sales Letter Kit. As a bonus, Surefire Sales Letter Secrets came with it.
> This book really exceeded my expectations. I read it all in one sitting and couldn't put it down. It is so
> concise, yet says so much. I found it very clearly written, to the point, well organized and packed with
> tremendously useful information, but not too long. You have an amazing ability to get the most content
> with the least amount of words. I'm finding myself referring to it constantly as I write."*
> **Ruth James**
> **Virginia Beach, VA.**

Bonus#2: My Surefire Direct Mail Profit Worksheet.This pre-done
spreadsheet gives you a powerful analysis tool for all your direct mail
projects. You simply enter in basic information like number of pieces
mailed, mailing costs and number of responses -- then this worksheet
automatically performs the important analysis calculations for you --
instantly! This essential tool is another $39.95 value.

Bonus#3: Ultimate Sales Letter Tool Box: All The Openings,
Bullets, Copy-Connectors, Selling Words, Phrases, Guarantees,
Closes, and P.S.s You'll Ever Need To Create Killer Sales Letters
(A $39.95 value).

I like to pile on the bonuses and really get people excited. Sometimes they buy the main product just because of the bonuses. Do I care? No! Your bonuses should be so good you could sell them on their own.

The more irresistible you can make your bonuses, the better. Some people will buy your main product just to get the bonuses.

One way you can entice your readers even more is to throw in bonuses later on in your letter, like "bribes."

STEP 9: GIVE AN
UNCONDITIONAL GUARANTEE

Step 9 is giving them an unconditional guarantee. You want to take away any fears that you're going to rip them off or they are going to lose in some way. I like to use a better-than-risk-free guarantee, which means that even if they return the product they can keep all the bonuses. The more risk-free you can make it for people to take action, the better.

FIGURE 5.9 The Guarantee

100% Risk-Free Guarantee:

Your success in using these powerful, pre-done sales letter templates is completely guaranteed. In fact, here's my 100% Better-Than-Risk-Free-Take-it-To-The-Bank Guarantee:

> I personally guarantee that if you make an honest effort to try just a few of these proven sales letters in your business, you'll produce at least 100 times your investment in profits within the next year. That's right, 100 times extra profits you wouldn't have made if you didn't send out these sales letters. You've got a full 12 months to prove to yourself these templates really do work. But if you aren't 100% satisfied, let me know and I'll issue you an immediate, no-hassle refund right on the spot. Plus, the free bonus gifts are yours to keep regardless, just for your trouble.

Is that fair or what?

That means you can try out all the sales letters at my risk, while you see if they work for you or not. And if they don't produce, I honestly want you to ask for your money back. And I'll let you keep the free bonus gifts as my way of thanking you for giving the sales letters a try.

There is absolutely no risk, whatsoever on your part. The burden to deliver is entirely on me. If you don't produce immediate profits using these instant sales letters then I'm the loser, not you.

You want to make it totally lopsided in their favor. Obviously it's easier for me, because I am selling mostly digitally delivered products for people to access online. They get to keep them no matter what. They say they want to return them; I am not going to go into their house and take it off their hard drive. So you might as well give it to them anyway.

There are many options you can offer in your guarantee. For example, mine says, "Simply try out these letters and if they don't give you at least a hundred times return on your investment, then we'll refund your money, no hassle, no questions." You will get a lot more sales by giving a great guarantee than you will by not having a guarantee.

STEP 10: DEMAND IMMEDIATE ACTION

We're up to step 10 and that's where you need to demand immediate action using scarcity or a time deadline. Stress what they are going to lose if they delay. Nobody likes to make a decision. That's why you have

---

FIGURE 5.10 Prompting Action

```
Look at it this way -- $39.97 is really a painless drop in the
bucket compared to the money you're going to waste on ineffective
mailers and marketing this year. That's why...

              You Really Can't Afford Not To Invest In
                These Instant Sales Letter Templates!
```

---

to help them along by incorporating a time deadline and reminding them of what they'll miss out on if they don't take action.

There are only two reasons people do anything and that's for gain or fear of loss. They'll either move toward something or move away from something.

Basically, you want to hit them over the head with both of those. You need to tell them exactly what to do. So you're going to demand immediate action using some scarcity, which will move readers toward an action.

And you're also going to insert a time deadline, for example, "Special offer is only good until 'X' date." Then, you have the right to go back to regular price, for example (that instills fear of loss), or you can say, "You only get bonuses if you order by 'X' date."

Stress the "pain"—what they will lose—if they don't do something. Here is a little paragraph, it says, "Look at it this way—$39.97 is really a painless drop in the bucket compared to the money you're going to waste on ineffective mailers and marketing this year. That's why you really can't afford not to invest in these sales letter templates." It can be something just as simple as that.

STEP 11: TELL THE READER
WHAT TO DO NEXT

Step 11 is to make it absolutely clear what they need to do next.

Here's where a lot of sales letters wimp out. Don't make people guess what you want them to do. Tell them to "click here" to get started right away.

FIGURE 5.11 What to Do Next

It's easy to get started right away. Just <u>click here</u> and you can have immediate (and unlimited) access to all of the *Instant Sales Letter Templates* right on the spot. You just fill-in-the-blanks, right on your own computer. No retyping and no recopying. It couldn't be easier or faster.

Get ready to create a flood of new customers, get them to buy over and over, and refer others - just by using these powerful sales letters. Why not take 2 ½ minutes now to create a powerful sales letter for your business? <u>Order Now!</u>

You need to tell them exactly what to do. Remember, your copy is for online, so it's going to say, "Click here, and get immediate access to the product." Or, "Click here to get started and get your order processed right away." You lead them by the hand and tell them exactly what to do. It also helps if you have multiple links on your order page where people can take some action at several points.

STEP 12: THE POWER P.S.

The last step is what I call the "The Power P.S." A lot of people just scroll all the way down to the end of the screen, but I give people another chance to get additional information. "P.S. Click here if you've decided not to order," takes them to a page where it answers even more questions.

It may say something like, "I know that this is a terrific deal but I know that a certain percentage of people won't take me up on this offer,

---

FIGURE 5.12 The Post Script

<u>P.S. Click here if you've decided not to order.</u>

P.P.S. Just think! You'll never again suffer through the pain and hassle of trying to write a powerful sales letter yourself. Or pay big bucks hiring a top copywriter. Now, you can get everything all done for you, practically handed to you on a silver platter. You simply fill-in-the-blanks...and you're done in about 2 ½ minutes -- flat!

so here is a list of frequent questions we get asked." Then there are questions and testimonials after those questions.

"The Power P.S." is not like the same kind of P.S. you see in sales letters that you get in your mail. "The Power P.S." either stresses the benefits again or the guarantee, or restates the offer or anything like that. It's another chance to get them to think about the offer and maybe take action.

This formula works. We're getting about 1 in 32 visitors to buy our product; simple formula, great results.

There you have it. Apply these 12 steps to your next sales letter—you'll see sales soar! Of course, if you really want to master copywriting for the Web, then the UltimateCopywritingCourse.com is an ideal resource.

Chapter

6

MARIA VELOSO
THE SEDUCTION OF
THE ONLINE SURFER

MARIA VELOSO is widely acknowledged as a leading expert in Web copywriting, and the premier advocate of frame-of-mind marketing™. Her reputation for writing compelling Web copy is well known in Internet marketing circles. Through her unique model of Web copywriting, she has sold several million dollars' worth of products and services for her online clients, sometimes selling a few thousand copies of a book in a single day, and sometimes $18,000 worth of e-classes in two days.

FOR MORE INFORMATION: http://www.webcopywritinguniversity.com

---

In This Chapter You Will Learn:

- How to Make the Sales Process a Seduction
- How to Get Your Prospect Tuned In to Your Sales Message
- How Virtual Salesmanship Will Increase Sales

THE SEDUCTION OF THE ONLINE SURFER

Various metaphors have been used to describe the *sales process*. Some call it a *game*, wherein the player with the best moves wins. Some call it a *battle*, wherein the one who is craftier, stronger, or has the most powerful weapons emerges the victor.

I prefer to call the sales process a *seduction*.

Particularly when it comes to selling on the Web, there is a need to *seduce* your reader with words and devices, rather than rushing through the sale in such an abbreviated way that the reader doesn't have time to get emotionally involved. Remember the marketing adage: *People buy on emotion and justify with logic.*

Rushing the sale and shortchanging the sales "foreplay" in order to grab the reader's wallet is one of the most consistent weaknesses I've observed in the majority of commercial Web sites. Most copywriters "cut to the chase" by making their selling motives immediately known, and as a result, they remove all doubt that all they really want is to sell you their wares.

SHORTCUTS DON'T WORK!

In the academy award–winning movie *A Beautiful Mind,* Russell Crowe plays the role of John Nash, a socially inept, genius mathematician. In one scene of the movie, Nash tells a woman:

> "I find you very attractive. Your assertiveness tells me that you feel the same way about me. But ritual remains that we must do a series of platonic actions before we can have intercourse. But all I really want to do is have sex with you as soon as possible."

This is not the way we normally expect a man to seduce a woman because it's not only *offensive*—but, quite frankly, it's *uncivilized.*

Believe it or not, that's exactly how most Web sites come across to their visitors. They start with *blatant sales pitches* that virtually say, "Marketing etiquette says I must first entice you with valuable content that's of interest to you. But all I really want to do is sell you my product as soon as possible.

This way of selling is equally offensive. It tells the reader that you're not even willing to go through the motions to win their business. When it comes to selling on the Web, shortcuts don't work!

"NEVER SELL A WINE BEFORE ITS TIME"

The art of seduction in copywriting is more pronounced on the Web because *people online do not want to get sold to.* This is a proven fact documented by a study conducted by Web usability experts, John Morkes and Jakob Nielsen. If Web visitors ever do get "sold" on something, they first want to be finessed, cajoled, informed, served, "seduced"—not bombarded by blatant advertising.

The problem with most online marketers is that they start selling from the *get go,* the moment their Web visitors arrive at their site—long before their visitors have been *primed* to buy. When you start selling prematurely, your sales message falls on deaf ears. Remember that old advertising slogan: Never sell a wine before its time.

You have exactly five seconds to make your intentions known in the first screenful of your Web site—because that's all most online surfers will give you.

That's why your Web site's first screenful (or the first eyeful) is the prime real estate of your Web site that you must use to set the stage for the seduction. What you put in it makes or breaks the sales success of your Web site.

HOW TO SEDUCE YOUR WEB VISITORS

Seducing your Web visitors is like a dance, wherein you lead and they follow. You make a move, they respond accordingly, you take another step and they follow your lead in a *seamless relay* that ultimately leads to the sale.

The only objective of your headline is to get your prospect to read the opening sentence. The only objective of your opening sentence is to get your prospect to read the second sentence. The only objective of your second sentence is to get your prospect to read the third sentence—and so on and so forth until the prospect pulls out their credit card and buys what you're selling. When the sale is consummated, the seduction is complete. But if you let go at any step, the sales process comes to a screeching halt.

Using the dating example once again, which of the following opening lines would get a positive response from a woman?

- A: "I'm a movie producer, I own a mansion in the Hollywood Hills, and that's my Porsche parked across the street. So what'll it be, your place or mine?"
- B: "Excuse me, Miss. My friend and I can't seem to agree on something. Was it Russell Crowe or Mel Gibson who starred in *Gladiator*?"

Most people would agree that opening line A would strike out—and maybe even warrant a slap in the face. And yet that's exactly how most marketers sell on the Web. They virtually say to their Web visitors, "I have the world's greatest widget at the cheapest price. Buy it now!"

Now, let's take a look at opening line B. It certainly wouldn't offend a woman, and it's likely to get a polite response. But where does the seduction come in, you ask?

That's the whole point. The seduction starts by getting someone's attention and putting that someone in the proper frame of mind to know you better. No matter how good your offer might be, the online population is still a skeptical bunch, and they're not likely to buy unless they know you and trust you.

On a Web site, you don't start selling the moment your Web visitor arrives. All you want initially is for your prospect to *respond* to you in some way. Then, you get a virtual dialogue going and build rapport that paves the way to the sale. Isn't that the objective of all direct-response marketing?

How exactly do you get your prospect to respond on a Web site? Some of the most powerfully seductive mechanisms I use are *involvement devices*.

Involvement devices are devices used to get people "involved" with your sales copy. They magnetize people to read every word of your copy. Getting your Web site visitors to read your copy is Job 1 if your objective is to sell them something.

When you use involvement devices, you effectively "own your audience." That is, you hold your audience captive.

I've always been aware of the power of involvement devices, but I never saw firsthand the amazing results they can produce until early 2001 when I started experimenting with various Web copy–related devices that could boost the response of a sales offer.

Back then, I was the Director of Creative Web Writing at Aesop Marketing Corporation. I wrote a promotional piece for a product we were selling for a famous TV personality, Matthew Lesko. More particularly, we were promoting Matthew's e-book entitled, *Free Money for Entrepreneurs on the Internet,* which was an e-book about how to get government grants to start or grow an Internet business. The promotional endorsement that I wrote on behalf of Mark Joyner is shown in Figure 6.1.

The promotional piece, which segued into the "Free Money for Entrepreneurs on the Internet" Web site was wildly successful, and accounted for more sales than its initial product launch two or three months earlier.

So what's the success secret of this little promotional piece? It's the involvement device that allowed them to articulate their problems in their own words, and type them into that little box. It got a lot of people "involved" in the sales copy, and made them admit they had problems that needed solving.

You see, when people read on the Web, they generally do so with a lot of skepticism, and they take everything you say or write with a grain of salt. They keep you at arm's length, so to speak, and don't allow you to get too close. Involvement devices (like the one I used in the above example) get people "caught in the Web" of your sales process.

Here's what happened when I got people to type their problems into that little box: I got them to raise their hands and virtually say "Yes, I've got problems, and boy, I'd really love it if you could solve them!"

Do you see how seductive the device was? It made them not only respond in the proper frame of mind, but also got their hearts beating a little faster in anticipation of what I had to offer.

So, in other words, they prequalified themselves as my target audience. And at that point, all I had to do was demonstrate how my product (free money from the government) could solve their problems. The sale was, thereafter, a done deal.

You see, I'm not a mind reader. I couldn't possibly know what my readers' top three business problems were. So I made them identify

---

FIGURE 6.1 The Magic Quiz

The Magic Quiz That Solves Your Money Problems Instantly
By Mark Joyner

Here's a magic quiz that's sure to **amaze** you: I want you to name the **top 3 problems** you are facing right now in your Internet business.

(Type your 3 problems in the box below.)

Of the 3 things you listed above, how many of them would be **solved** if I handed you **$150,000** right now?

Chances are, <u>all</u> of them, right?

Well, maybe there are problems that are best solved by having marketing <u>expertise</u>, <u>time</u>, or other <u>resources</u>—but which of those can't you acquire if you had $150,000?

My guess is none.

There's magic in making **business problems disappear** with the wave of a **money** wand. That's probably why American author, Washington Irving, coined the term **"almighty dollar"** back in 1836. The almighty dollar cures most, if not <u>all</u>, business ills *when utilized effectively.*

While most magicians would never tell you the secret behind their magic tricks, I'm going to tell you how to do the **trick** of the "disappearing business problems."

Did you know, for instance, that . . .

. . . you can fill out a simple, one-page form and get a $150,000 low-interest loan from the government?

. . . the U.S. Government will give you a $15,000 loan without collateral?

. . . you can get a grant of any size for your Internet business, and you don't have to pay it back?

<u>**Click here to find out how.**</u>

---

their own problems right there in black and white in that little box because I knew I had a product that could solve any money problem.

Ultimately, all marketing (both online or offline) is simply about solving people's problems and meeting people's needs, isn't it? But no matter how intimately you know your target audience, you never *really* know exactly what moves them, what grieves them, what turns them on, what turns them off, what their hot buttons are—you can only make educated guesses. And sometimes, educated guesses can be wrong!

In this particular involvement device that I invented, I made them name their own problems instead of attempting to identify them myself, and running the risk of missing the mark.

Due to the success of that involvement device, I decided to test a variation of it on the Web site of a client who sells affirmation software. This client already had existing Web copy that had a decent conversion rate. I rewrote his copy and added an involvement device similar to the one I used for the Matthew Lesko's e-book. See Figure 6.2.

FIGURE 6.2 Revised Copy with an Involvement Device

"Name the Top 3 Things You Want in Life"

... then use your computer for 10 minutes a day to magically manifest the things you want in your life now.

I want you to name the **top 3 things** you desire to have, or wish to improve, in your life right now. Examples: money (name the *specific* amount you want), a loving relationship, an ideal job, perfect health, your dream house, a brand new car, etc.

(Type the 3 things you desire in the box below.)

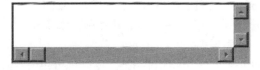

Okay, are you done typing the 3 things you want?

What if I told you that there's a way you can achieve those 3 things—*and anything else you desire*—by using the power of your computer for just **10 minutes** a day for 12 days?

In the next few minutes, I will show you an **advanced technology** that enables you to manifest everything you want through the results-amplifying use of *computerization*. This information is not available anywhere else on the Web, or the world, for that matter. So I urge you to **read every word** of this article because the secret that can single-handedly turn your desires into reality is **hidden** in this webpage—and I don't want you to miss it.

The results: By installing this seductive involvement device in the first screenful of my client's Web site, the sales tripled the very next day. During subsequent weeks, it maintained sales that were 200–300 percent more than the previous daily sales, and even had days when six times as much product was sold.

My client's former headline was as follows: "Learn how to be prosperous, successful, and happy in just ten minutes a day." So you see, the client had taken a stab at what he "thought" were the hot buttons of his target audience. But in the process, the headline ended up sounding vague and definitely *not* riveting. It didn't call out to the real desires of the target audience.

On the other hand, the involvement device asked readers to identify their wants, needs, and dreams. What could be more riveting than the specific dreams of your target audience, the dreams they wouldn't dare tell another living soul? That's what the involvement device asked them to do, and it gave them a "safe" place to type in specific dollar amounts, or even describe in detail the man or woman of their dreams, because the information they typed in wasn't being captured or compiled in any way. Typing in their desires brings their desires into focus so that the product (affirmation software) can be presented as a solution for achieving those desires.

Do you see how powerful and seductive that is?

GET THEM TUNED IN TO ONLY ONE SIGNAL—YOUR SALES MESSAGE

Involvement devices break people's preoccupation.

Consider this: At any given moment, a person's attention is preoccupied with dozens of things at the same time—everything from how they are going to pay for their child's college education, to how to earn more money, to what they are going to have for dinner tonight. Think of your prospect's mind as an antenna that receives signals from everywhere. It receives radio waves from all over the world.

An involvement device is just like a radio tuner in that it gets people tuned in to only one signal—one station or one channel—that is, your sales message or your Web copy. Getting someone's attention on the Internet is probably the biggest challenge you face because attention is in short supply—what with over 3 billion Web pages on the Net clamoring for attention.

In Figure 6.3 is an involvement device I used to sell the electronic prepublication edition of my book, *Web Copy That Sells*.

FIGURE 6.3 Marketing Quiz

Here's a quick marketing quiz that could make a *dramatic impact* on the amount of money you earn on the Web.

Answer these 5 questions:
(Simply check YES or No)

1. Do you want to learn **psychological devices** you can use on your website that can make people pull out their credit cards and buy what you're selling?

   YES ❑   NO ❑

2. Do you want a **website that sells phenomenally well** even during the worst economic times, even in highly competitive markets, and even when the price of your product or service is well above your competitors' prices?

   YES ❑   NO ❑

3. Do you want to **boost your website sales and profits** significantly *without spending a single penny?*

   YES ❑   NO ❑

4. Do you want to discover little-known *involvement devices* that can easily **double or triple your website sales** overnight?

   YES ❑   NO ❑

5. Do you want to instantly conquer the top 3 mistakes that keep 9 out of 10 commercial websites from making as much money as they'd like to make?

   YES ❑   NO ❑

If you answered YES to any (or all) of the above, the good news is this: You can easily achieve all these things you want with the **specialized knowledge** I'm about to reveal in this article.

This quiz or questionnaire type of device is designed to get prospects to get involved by clicking on the YES boxes. This "trains" them to respond with a YES so that the final YES (which is YES to buying your product) would be hardwired in their subconscious. The order page I designed also started with a YES box that needed to be checked, and therefore, there was continuity and consistency of action, which is something that people subconsciously gravitate toward.

Figure 6.4 is another example of a multiple-choice involvement device I crafted for one of my clients. The key is to give multiple choices—enough to cover the entire spectrum of needs of your target audience. That way, whoever among your target audience reads it, they'd be able to relate to at least one of the choices you featured there. Then, they are effectively magnetized to your sales process because that's just like getting them to raise their hands and say, "Yes, I'm your qualified prospect. I'm interested in what you're selling."

FIGURE 6.4 Another Involvement Device

Which of the following describes you? (Check all that apply.)

❑ "I've got a **website** and I've started building a **mailing list,** but I don't know how to make money using them."

❑ "I'm fairly new online. I know a **few things** about Internet marketing, but nothing I do seems to generate enough leads, customers, sales, or profits for me."

❑ "There are so many *bewildering* offers that promise to make me a fortune on the Internet, which ones should I choose? Who is **genuine** and who's **bogus,** and who should I believe?

❑ "I hear about Internet marketers making so much money on the Internet, when will I get my share of the billions of dollars that are changing hands on the Web?

If you checked one or more of the above, then *you're in for an eye-opening revelation.*

I recently wrote the Web copy for an e-book titled, *Megabolic Weight Loss: How to Melt Away Body Fat, Lose Weight, and Create Your Ideal Body Eas-*<u>*ily*</u> *and* <u>*Permanently*</u>*, Even While You Sit in Front of Your Computer or Desk All Day.*

In the body copy, when it came time to close the sale, I wrote what's in Figure 6.5, which is an example of an involvement device that uses the power of commitment.

WHY IS THIS SEDUCTIVE?

According to master of persuasion, Robert Cialdini, "Writing is believing." When you ask your readers to write down (or in this case, type out) the things they desire, they admit the need for your product or scr-

---

FIGURE 6.5 The Power of Commitment

A well-known success coach once said that in order to be successful, one has to do only 2 things:

1. Learn how to succeed, and
2. Do what it takes to succeed.

Now that you know *Megabolic Weight Loss* is the surefire way of losing all your unwanted weight, all that's left is for you to do what it takes to succeed. In order to do that, you need to **get leverage on yourself.**

Quite frankly, *Megabolic Weight Loss* simply cannot fail when it is implemented <u>exactly as prescribed</u>. But no weight loss program, no matter how powerful, will work if there isn't the **power of commitment** behind it.

So **type your name, the number of pounds you want to lose, and the reasons you want to lose the weight** in the blanks below, and read the completed statement out loud to reinforce the commitment that will lead to your ultimate success.

I, _____, have decided I want to lose ____ pounds, because _____ and I'm committed to following the Megabolic Weight Loss Program until I reach my desired weight.

vice, and a written commitment is more lasting than a mental commitment. One who writes out a commitment has a higher likelihood of following through on what they have written.

In this case, too, I make the reader close themselves on the sale by making *Megabolic Weight Loss* part of their commitment statement.

THE NEXT WAVE OF VIRTUAL SALESMANSHIP

There is an exciting new involvement device that I'm positive will *revolutionize* the way we sell online. I've heard of the dramatic sales results it has brought to Web sites that employed the device—and I'm therefore in the process of beta testing it as we speak before I give it my final "thumbs up."

By now, you've heard that adding audio to your Web site brings a sales-pulling dimension to Web sales. Now, the "next big thing" is *creating a video presentation for your Web site* that becomes your virtual salesperson. See Figure 6.6.

A video presentation on your Web site compels action much better than a static Web page, and it takes the drudgery out of reading blocks of text. Because it puts the entire sales seduction in a polished, informative video, it's a remarkable and seductive way to engage potential customers. The combination of sound, graphics, text, and special effects grips an audience like nothing else can. It's marketing seduction taken to the highest level.

The beauty of this technology is that you cannot only place your video presentation on a Web site for download, but you can stream it over

FIGURE 6.6 A Virtual Salesperson

the Internet, send your compressed videos in an e-mail, burn them on a CD-ROM, or share them on your corporate network. All your audience needs to view your shows is the RealOne Player or the standard Windows Media Player that is already installed on all Windows PCs and most Macs.

Best of all, it literally takes *less than an hour* to produce a video presentation with the professional look of a TV newscast, made right there in the comfort of your home or office without requiring the services of a videographer. Furthermore, it doesn't require the traditional "post-production" approach of editing, which involves shooting video, digitizing the footage, marking each clip, creating custom graphics, sequencing the clips with graphics and effects in a time line, and finally rendering the output video.

In the past, average Web site owners could not really consider paying someone to produce videos for them because the price was so prohibitive that they couldn't justify the cost. However, this new technology now costs less than $150, and allows you to create an *unlimited number of video presentations in a do-it-yourself manner.*

I predict that when combined with the principles of Web copywriting, video presentations will be the wave of the future in Web site selling. For more information on this revolutionary technology, as well as the results of my beta testing, e-mail me at videoinfo@webcopythatsells.com.

RECOVERY DEVICE THAT COULD POTENTIALLY INCREASE YOUR WEB SITE SALES BY 50 PERCENT TO 100 PERCENT

There is an involvement device I *invented* a few years ago that not only gets people involved in the sales copy—makes them raise their hands and prequalify themselves as your target audience—but it also captures their contact information. This device has the *recovery principle* of marketing as its foundation. The recovery principle is not new. It's something used often in direct response marketing.

Here's how this "recovery" involvement device works in a nutshell: If you fail to sell your Web visitors on your primary product at the full price, but succeed in selling them the same product (or maybe even a different product) at a lower unit of sale, you recover the effort and cost of getting them to your Web site, and plug them into your income stream. That's why it's called a recovery device.

Through a series of seductively crafted follow-up e-mails, you can convert a considerable percentage of prospects into customers. Even if you don't make as much profit on each of these sales, you recover costs and make a considerable amount of extra profit in the process. More importantly, you turn someone into a customer who might have otherwise never done business with you at all. And of course, that customer has a lifetime value because he or she will be buying future products from you.

The recovery involvement device that I used in the Web copy I wrote for Jay Conrad Levinson's "Guerrilla Marketing Boot Camp" is shown in Figure 6.7.

This little recovery device managed to amass over 2,000 prequalified prospects' names, and accounted for almost 50 percent of the seminar attendees. Conversely, had we not installed this recovery device, we would've had only half of the attendees. Once you understand that you don't have to just offer your product at one price, but that you can adjust your offer on the fly, you can make much more profit than if you

---

FIGURE 6.7 Recovery Involvement Device

Before you do anything else...

...you <u>must</u> lock in your position. Even if you're not yet **100% certain** that **you're going to attend**, you can secure your position with just **your e-mail address** so that you won't lose out. <u>Don't worry that you haven't read everything yet</u>—because you'll **pay no money** now, and you will <u>not</u> be obligated to attend the Boot Camp should you change your mind later.

When you enter your e-mail address below, you will be given a **priority reservation code** that will guarantee you **preferential** treatment over others when the limited number of seats is allocated.

If <u>you don't</u> lock in your position, there's a **93% chance** that you won't secure a seat, even when you decide you want to attend. Lock in your position by entering your **e-mail address** here:

[   ]

When you press GO, your entry will be **time-stamped** for preferential handling, and don't worry, you won't be taken to another site. You'll remain right on this Web page.

had not employed a recovery device. Knowing this can dramatically improve your Web site's profitability.

EPILOGUE

Seducing the online surfer is both an art and a science that requires the knowledge of consumer psychology as well as an intimacy with the mindset of the Internet population. Involvement devices are simply the catalyst that gets your prospects to respond so that you can start a dialogue and create rapport with them.

It bears repeating that you must create a *seamless relay* from the first screenful of your Web site all the way to your call to action that engages and holds the attention of your prospect. I have a proprietary system that I call the "Million-Dollar Blueprint for Writing Web Copy That Sells" that enables you to create seductive, sales-pulling Web site copy from start to finish, even if you've never written a word of copy in your life. That blueprint is featured in both my Web Copywriting Mastery Course (http://www.webcopywritinguniversity.com) and my e-book, *Web Copy That Sells: The Secret to Creating a Profitable Web Site* (http://www.webcopythatsells.com).

Chapter

7

DAVID GARFINKEL
THE MAGICAL POWER
OF HEADLINES

DAVID GARFINKEL is known by many as the world's greatest copywriting coach. David is the author of *Killer Copy Tactics, Advertising Headlines* and he's also author of the e-book *Secrets Exposed*. David has made millions of dollars for his clients with his promotions. A travel agency made $5 million in annual recurring sales from a three-page sales letter David wrote for them.

FOR MORE INFORMATION: http://www.killercopytactics.com

In This Chapter You Will Learn:

- What a Headline Is

- The Types of Headlines That Work on the Web

- What Type of Headline to Write

- What Winning Headlines Look Like

- The Do's and Don'ts of Headline Writing

THE MAGICAL POWER OF HEADLINES

I know you're reading this book to learn about Internet marketing, but before we make our way over to the fields of endless riches you can plow and later harvest on the Internet . . . well, first, I'd like you to take a quick trip to the streets of Chicago.

In fact, I'd like to invite you to go backwards in time with me. A couple of decades ago, I lived in the Windy City. At the time, my home was seven blocks away from "Big John," the 100-story John Hancock building.

Now let's say you and I had a meeting scheduled for 10 AM Tuesday morning at an office on the 27th floor.

A taxi drops you off in front of 875 North Michigan Avenue (the address of the John Hancock building). After you get through security, you enter the lobby and head toward the elevators. You get in; push "27"; take a high-speed ride up into the sky; get out; turn right; and you find your way to the office where we're having our meeting.

Simple enough, right?

Well, doing business on the Internet is very much like the imaginary voyage and meeting you just envisioned:

The taxi ride is like the form of traffic that got you to my Web site.

The John Hancock building is like my Web site itself.

The elevator ride is like reading my Web site, and, *coming into the office on the 27th floor* is like taking the action I wanted you to take—making a purchase, signing up for a newsletter, requesting more information, etc.

But wait a minute! Did you notice I left out a very important part of the process?

Darn right I did. I left out:

The front door of the John Hancock building!

Why is that so important? Because if I can't get you in the front door, then what chance do I have of getting you to the elevator; in the elevator; up 27 floors; and into the office?

Answer: I have no chance at all . . . until I get you in the front door!

Now, why the convoluted analogy?

Here's why. I've given you this elaborate example to emphasize how *crucial* your headline is to your Web site, or any other piece of sales copy you write (on the Web or off). And yes, you guessed it:

The front door of the John Hancock building is your headline!

And an important front door it is. Advertising experts estimate that between 75 percent and 90 percent of any advertising's effectiveness comes from the headline.

Here, then, is why what you learn from this chapter is so vitally important to your success as an Internet marketer:

With a good headline, you stand a fighting chance of having anything from minimal to overwhelming success.

But without a good headline, your chances of success are next to zero.

So, let's start at the beginning. By the time we're done with this chapter, you'll have a whole mini seminar on Web headlines under your belt, from the very basic to the moderately advanced. For now, though, we start with the basics.

WHAT IS A HEADLINE?

A headline is the first set of words that your prospect sees on any piece of copy you write. It's just like the headlines you see in a newspaper:

- Economy Improves as Unemployment Drops, Consumer Spending Swells
- Ninth-Inning Grand Slam Saves the Day
- Flu Vaccine Shortage Worries Health Officials
- Spring Rains Flood Farmlands
- New Computer Chip Promises Better Video on Handheld Computers

While all these headlines would work well to sell newspapers and get readers interested in reading the news stories that follow, only the last one would work in marketing, 99 percent of the time. Why? Because most newspaper-style headlines merely sell the reader on reading the story, but they aren't designed to create interest in, and desire for, a product or service that you'd be telling the prospect about.

However, the last headline in the list—New Computer Chip Promises Better Video on Handheld Computers—has a characteristic that could make it work just as well for an ad as for a news story. It's this: The headline conveys a *benefit* ("Better Video on Handheld Computers") of a *product* ("New Computer Chip"), and this not only creates *interest* in the product, it also creates a *desire* for that product, if, that is, you're the kind of person who likes video on your computers.

In short, a headline not only needs to capture attention and keep your prospects reading, it also needs to *set the tone* for what the prospects are about to read and to *create a mood* in the prospect that will begin to make them receptive to taking the *action* you will eventually invite them to take in your sales copy.

That action might be *to buy what you are selling*. It could be just *to request more information*. Or, it might be *to request an application form,* which would lead to the next step of the sales process.

Whatever action it is you desire your prospect to take, your headline has an important job to do: *Prepare the prospect emotionally for the invitation you are soon about to make.*

TYPES OF ADVERTISING HEADLINES THAT WORK ON THE WEB

You'll almost always use a *single headline* with the following types of marketing copy:

- *Sales e-mails.* When you are sending out an e-mail that requests some sort of action, the subject line of the e-mail serves as your headline.
- *Short text ads for e-zines.* These are short ads, four to ten lines or so, that publishers run in their e-mail newsletters (e-zines). These ads look a lot like classified ads in a newspaper, although sometimes they are considerably longer than the two to three lines you see in the paper.
- *Google AdWords ads.* You've seen these when you use Google, but you might not know what they're called. AdWords ads are the "sponsored listings" in the right-hand column of each page of search engine results. You can buy these (as opposed to search engine listings on the left-hand side, which you have to compete for), and you can even pay for position. If you want yours to be the first ad everyone sees at the top of the heap, it's entirely possible, although in some categories the very top spot might cost more than you want to spend.

But you may use *more than one headline* on . . .

- *Web pages.* On a Web site, you may have *multiple headlines* at the top of your page. You might want to use a *prehead,* which is a short phrase in small type before the headline; a *main headline,* which states the main promise of what you're offering your prospect throughout the copy; and even a *subhead* right after the main headline, to flesh out and highlight the benefit that you introduce in your main headline.

We'll cover examples of all types of headlines as we proceed.

WHERE MOST PEOPLE GO WRONG WITH HEADLINES

Headlines can make a tremendous difference in the dollars-and-cents effectiveness of any piece of copy. Changes in a headline can easily double and triple closing rates. I know one marketer who claims *he increased his sales on the same ad 18 times* just by changing the headline!

Most people, unfortunately, write really bad headlines. It's not necessarily that they use bad grammar or spelling. The problem is that their headlines don't "reach people where they live." These headlines don't create interest, desire, or receptivity to taking action. They don't do their job, so they're not good headlines.

Here are the three main underlying causes of headline problems:

1. *The headline doesn't pass the "So what? Who cares?" test.* A merely factual headline doesn't cut the mustard, because facts by themselves rarely stir people's emotions. Also, when there's a promise spelled out that the prospect doesn't instantly see as valuable, then the headline doesn't have relevant emotional power—and it, too, fails the test.
2. *The headline is cute, clever, or obscure.* You see lots of headlines like this. They include plays on words, sexual innuendo, attempts at humor, or displays of what the headline writer thought was exquisite sophistication. While this approach may raise a chuckle and even get the prospect reading the rest of your Web page, unless

what's being sold in the copy is *directly* related to the cuteness up top, a headline of this type *never* sets the tone and puts the prospect in the mood most conducive for taking action afterwards.

3. *The headline means everything to the business but nothing to the prospect.* If your company has just celebrated its 25th anniversary, that's terrific! Very few businesses last that long. But a self-congratulatory headline trumpeting that fact has no power to motivate prospects to take action . . . unless the prospect has a gnawing, burning need to do business with a 25-year-old company, and is *already* aware of that need *before* he or she reads the headline.

Most headline problems can be traced to the failure of the person who wrote the headline to stand in the prospect's shoes (mentally), and see things (in his or her mind's eye) from the prospect's point of view. It's a very valuable skill to learn. And it's key to writing good, powerful headlines.

HOW DO YOU KNOW WHAT KIND OF HEADLINE TO WRITE?

Here are five rules of thumb to help you get in the right frame of mind to write a winning headline:

1. Start where your reader is. Most people writing copy start where *they* are. This is a big mistake, unless you are selling to peers—people who are as knowledgeable about what you are selling as you are (which is rarely the case). Typically, s*tarting where your reader is* means focusing on the biggest *benefit* your product or service provides.

On the other hand, starting where *you* are—which, again, you *don't* want to do—means focusing on a *fact, accomplishment,* or *feature* that you consider important, but that will have little or no meaning to your reader.

Example: You sell office supplies over the Internet. Because of skillfully negotiated contracts with manufacturers, you have wider access to more varieties of products, at lower prices, with faster delivery, than anyone else in your industry.

Here's a typical example of starting where *you* are:

Our Supply Chain Relationships Are Second to None!

Anyone who wants a stapler or some new inkjet cartridges will have no idea what you're talking about, and couldn't care less about learning more.

Compare that with a headline that starts where *the reader* is:

Office Supplies: Lowest Prices, Best Selection, and Fastest Delivery. We Can Prove It and We Guarantee It!

The second headline is about the *benefits* of all those skillfully negotiated supply chain relationships. And anyone looking for office supplies will be motivated to read further.

2. Look at the end result your reader wants. As a marketer, whether you're writing copy for your own business or for someone else's, you have to learn every little detail about the products, services, and whatever else is for sale. It's easy to get wrapped up in the details and forget that people aren't buying what you're selling—they're really buying *what it can do for them.*

The O.M. Scott and Sons Company was founded in 1907 as a mail-order seller of grass seed. Mr. Scott once told his employees that their customers weren't buying grass seed from the company, "They're buying greener lawns."

Your headline is strong and attractive when it talks about the beneficial end result of using what you sell. What's *your* "greener lawn"?

3. Spell out how what you're selling provides the solution to a problem, or the attainment of a desire. Once you know where your readers are and what end result they're looking for, figure out what's on their mind that would lead them to wanting what you have. Chances are very good it's either something that's bothering them, or something they have a strong, persistent desire for, but they haven't been able to get yet.

A golf pro may teach concentration, posture, better swing, and better attitude. But what's bothering the golfer is this: too many strokes to get to each hole. What the golfer wants is to get to each hole with fewer strokes. A headline that promises fewer strokes and a better score will far outperform a headline that talks about concentration, posture, better swing, or better attitude.

- Each headline points to an *end result,* and that is what people are looking for most of the time. Some of the end results in the original headlines: "People Like You"; "*(implied benefit:* not being) Tongue-Tied at a Party"; "Win Friends and Influence People."
- The headlines are made from *short words.* Most are one-syllable words, and in all six original headlines, there's only one three-syllable word: influence.
- These headlines both arouse curiosity and stoke desire. The copywriters probably thought long and hard about what people *really* want before they settled on the final version of the headline, and, they artfully arranged the words to make people reading them wonder "what's this about?" as they felt an inner emotional tug moving them toward getting the end result.

Note: For more information about how to modify proven, classic headlines to use with your own copy, visit http://www.advertisinghead linesthatmakeyourich.com.

REAL-WORLD EXAMPLES: HEADLINES FROM INTERNET MARKETING

Now that you understand the psychology and function of headlines, and you've seen some examples of winning headlines from the real world of paid advertising, you're in a much better position to take advantage of what you're about to learn.

So let's get into the nitty-gritty. It was important to lay the groundwork first, because effective headlines are almost like a foreign language to most people, even though the words are all in English!

E-MAIL SUBJECT LINES

An important principle to burn into your brain is: *It's very, very risky (and difficult) to* start *an Internet relationship with a prospect using e-mail.* That's because of the spam problem. E-mail is inherently a very personal medium, so you're better off getting prospects through search engines, ads in e-zines, pay-per-click ads (like Google AdWords), referrals from other Web sites, and e-mail lists where people already have a relationship with another person or business.

E-mail is most effective, then, when you *already* have a relationship of some sort with a prospect or customer.

Bear that in mind as you look at the following examples.

Dr. Dave Woynarowski is a physician who has come up with pharmaceutical-grade supplements that also use alternative-healing ingredients. He has a daily e-mail newsletter that talks about his supplements in relation to various health issues. Here are some excellent subject lines he has used:

- How to Energize Your Life!
- Fish Oil and Lung Cancer
- Sacred Cow, or a Pile of Cow Dung?

Just as with any kind of headline, the key to writing successful subject lines is knowing what's of interest to your reader, and starting where your reader is. Dr. Dave has the advantage of a full patient load at his medical clinic, so he knows firsthand what's on the minds of his customers. You don't need to be a doctor, though, to engage in some kind of dialogue with your customers and prospects—and it's important that you do.

Now, to someone who's never heard of Dr. Dave and isn't familiar with his supplements and his philosophy, these subject lines could come across somewhere between meaningless and annoying. But to his loyal and informed readership, these are excellent phrases . . . they cause interest and prompt the reader to open the e-mail and read it.

I know that for a fact. How come? Because I'm one of his customers, and I'm interested in what he has to say.

Incidentally, if you're curious, you can find out more about what Dr. Dave's up to at http://www.drdavesbest.com.

HEADLINES FOR SMALL ADS ON THE INTERNET

Small classified ads are different from e-mails in that they will not be seen as intrusive if you don't already have a relationship with the person reading them. You typically pay to place these ads in e-zines or on Web sites.

Headlines are like the headlines on Google AdWords ads, and single headlines for Web pages, both covered below, so we won't spend a lot of time with small ads.

There are a couple to look at in Figure 7.1.

Notice the headlines (in boldface type) follow the same rules that we've been talking about all along: they feature a beneficial end result, they are designed to stoke desire, they use short words, and they put the reader in the frame of mind to read more and possibly to take action.

GOOGLE ADWORDS ADS

Google AdWords ads are in a special category all by themselves. They're small ads that appear on the right-hand side of the results page when you do a search on Google.

I wrote the one in Figure 7.2.

FIGURE 7.1 Google Ads

Become a Best-Selling Author Online!
E-books are a low-cost, high-profit way
to make money on the Internet, and you
can become an author even if you don't
write the e-book yourself! Learn how.
http://www.ebooksecretsexposed.com.

How to Meet a '10' on the Internet
It all starts with your picture. No matter
what you look like, the odds are high
that your online photo isn't doing
you justice. Get a top pro trained to
take pictures that look GREAT for
Internet dating, at a reasonable price!
http://www.DateBetter.com.

FIGURE 7.2 An AdWords Ad

Hot New MLM

This one puts money in your pocket

two ways. Get your share! Aff.

www.davidgarfinkel.com/travel

What's the headline? "Hot New MLM." My 12th-grade English teacher at Richard Montgomery High School in Rockville, Maryland, would have flunked me for writing a sentence like that. But the marketplace, that is, the people who typed "MLM" into Google, gave me an "A." I got 3.5 percent of the people who saw a page where this ad appeared to click on it. (Google requires a minimum of 0.5 percent click-throughs to keep an ad running. My ad performed at *seven times the minimum*. Not a world record—not even a personal best for me—but very successful, nonetheless.)

A couple points about this headline:

- *Relevancy*. People who saw this ad had "MLM" on the brain—because those are the letters they had typed into Google in the first place. So I'm already a step ahead because I'm talking about what they're already looking for.
- *Emotion*. The other two words in the headline, "Hot" and "New," spark excitement. For a contrasting example to put this in perspective, imagine if I had used "Old, Cold MLM" as my headline! (Yes, it would have worked *great* as a *joke*, but in the serious, grown-up world of actually getting results and making money, it would have flopped like a gasping fish on a dry dock.)

Another very successful AdWords ad is shown in Figure 7.3. This is an ad that pops up when people type "Google AdWords" into Google. It's the work of Perry Marshall, who, for my money, is the preeminent authority on using this advertising medium to get results.

FIGURE 7.3 A Successful AdWords Ad

Beat the AdWords System

Access 100 Million People in 10 Min

The Definitive Fast Start Guide

http://copy.adwordsadvertising.com

Perry's headline is clever, in a productive way. "Beat the AdWords System" implies there is a system, which, of course, most people don't know about; that it's possible to beat the system (which is inherently appealing, all by itself); and that he can show you how.

And, once again, there's a word in the headline ("AdWords") that was already on the prospect's mind (because that's what he or she typed into the search form in order for the ad to come up). That's very important.

Copywriting legend Robert Collier, who sold millions of books in the 1930s through direct mail and advertising, admonishes copywriters to "enter the conversation already going on in the prospect's mind." By using the same words they typed into the search engine in your ad, you're pretty much guaranteed to do that.

Now, check out the AdWords ad in Figure 7.4.

It's for a very specialized market: people who publish e-books on the Internet, and want to make audio recordings of their e-books so their customers will have another way to purchase, and take in, the information.

FIGURE 7.4 A Specialized AdWords Ad

Free Ebook on Recording

The tools and support to make audio

information products on your PC.

http://www.recordyourself.com

Mike Stewart, who goes by the moniker "The Internet Audio Guy," wrote this ad. It shows up when people type things like "record yourself" and "recorded e-book" into Google.

The headline is great, because it makes a *free offer.* Anytime you can give something away for free that your market will perceive as valuable (and related to what they're looking for that you can provide them), do it.

Notice again that neither the headline nor the rest of the ad adheres to the rules of English composition. No matter. Mike says he gets plenty of business from this little ad, and as you study it, you can see why.

HEADLINES FOR WEB SITES

The same rules apply for Web site headlines, but with a twist . . . you can have more than one headline. This is especially the case when your Web site is selling something that has a lot of desirable dimensions to it and you want to get your prospect mentally prepared to learn about a lot of different benefits.

Figure 7.5 shows what I call a "headline package" for a very successful site selling a self-improvement course.

The first headline is actually a banner graphic that runs across the top of the Web site. "How to Get Lots of Money for Anything—Fast!" is the title of the book, but it's also a very compelling headline.

"Wanted: People Who Need Money FAST!" is the second headline. To the *rational* mind, this is obviously redundant. But to the *emotional* mind, this is very telling. It says, "Oh! They're looking for people like me."—if, that is, the prospect is someone who needs money fast.

FIGURE 7.5 A Headline Package

Wanted: People Who Need Money FAST!
How YOU can **cash in** on the $25,000-a-day secret that's **made millions**

The third headline, "How YOU can cash in on the $25,000-a-day se-cret that's made millions," again, seems to be repeating what the first two headlines are saying. But take a closer look. The third headline takes a big, conceptual promise and makes it a little more specific. Now the reader's curiosity and desire are building to a fever pitch.

And that's exactly what a headline—or, in this case, a headline pack-age—is supposed to do.

For more information about this course, visit http://www.getanythingfast.com.

Next, a headline for an audio CD/searchable e-book package about dream interpretation is shown if Figure 7.6.

There are three parts to this Web page headline:

1. "WARNING"—the prehead.
2. "Your Dreams Are '911 Emergency Calls' from Your Subcon-scious Mind!"—the main headline.
3. "Don't Ignore Them, They're Trying to Tell You Something"—the subhead.

People who come to this Web site have clicked on links in ads or ar-ticles that talk about the interpretation of dreams. It's a preselected group of prospects, the perfect target market for this product.

This headline package is what I refer to as a "wake-up call" (pun in-tended). Though some people wake up in a cold sweat, and trembling, from a particularly horrible nightmare, most people are at most con-fused by their dreams, or else ignore them altogether, and in any event, don't give them a second thought.

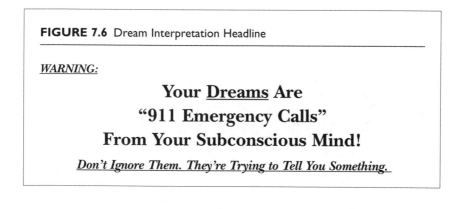

FIGURE 7.6 Dream Interpretation Headline

WARNING:

**Your <u>Dreams</u> Are
"911 Emergency Calls"
From Your Subconscious Mind!**

<u>Don't Ignore Them. They're Trying to Tell You Something.</u>

The owner of this Web site, Dr. Michael Wolf, is a clinical psychologist who knows better. He realizes that dreams have great importance, although most people will do anything not to get the message. That is why he chose to inject so much shock value into the headline package.

As you can see, besides sounding an alarm, this headline package arouses great curiosity in the reader and makes them highly receptive to the solution that will be offered later on the Web page.

You can see the whole Web page at: http://www.dream-analyst.com.

Another example:

Adriana Dodge is a real estate expert who has put together a manual, which includes legal documents, for people who want to buy a home but wouldn't qualify financially under normal conditions. The headline package for her Web site is shown in Figure 7.7.

The header graphic contains the first headline: "Adriana Dodge's No Cash No Credit Home Buying System." Her name starts the headline because the way she drives traffic to the site is by radio interviews. People already know her name, and may even feel like they know her a little bit.

The last seven words of this top headline tell the whole story about her product while extolling its benefits. The benefits more or less describe the target market—people who have little cash and possibly bad credit, who want to buy a house.

The second headline, "Get our FREE newsletter about how you can buy a home with No Cash and even No Credit. Sign up now!" makes a very appealing offer that, once accepted, begins a nonthreatening relationship between Adriana and the prospect.

FIGURE 7.7 A Headline for Adriana Dodge

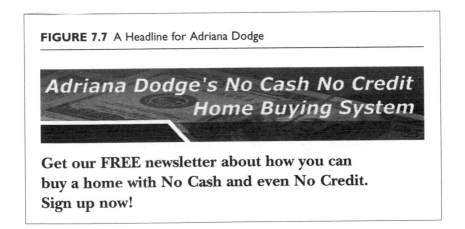

Adriana's free newsletter gives her a way to begin communication with wary prospects; build trust; and eventually make more sales than if she depended solely on the one visit to the site to get her all her business.

You can find more information at http://www.askadriana.com.

And, finally, the headline package I wrote for the first issue of my own "World Copywriting Newsletter" is shown in Figure 7.8.

The main headline, "The Tip of the Iceberg," could mean just about anything, but it has a dual emotional appeal: first, it could mean "danger ahead"; second, it could refer to a visible clue of a much larger and more substantial something-or-other beneath the surface.

The second headline, "Or, How An Advertising Secret That Created A Six-Year Backlog In Orders for Pianos Can Get You More Business Than You Ever Imagined Was Possible!" creates closure for the ambiguity caused by the first headline, but opens up even more ambiguity to keep the reader reading!

It creates closure by making more tangible what "The Tip of the Iceberg" means. Clearly, it means something about an advertising secret.

But when you learn that this secret created a six-year backlog in orders—and that this secret can work for your business as well—this creates a wracking curiosity that can only be relieved by continuing to pay attention and read the newsletter.

By the way, if you'd like to see my newsletter yourself, it's free to subscribe. Go to http://www.world-copywriting-institute.com.

FIGURE 7.8 World Copywriting Newsletter Headline

The Tip of the Iceberg
Or, How An Advertising Secret That Created A Six-Year Backlog In Orders For <u>Pianos</u> Can Get You More Business Than You Ever Imagined Was Possible!

TEN GOLDEN RULES FOR WRITING POWERFUL HEADLINES

We've covered a lot so far, and if your mind is awhirl from all the information and examples, I don't blame you one bit.

It took me about 30 years of working on newspapers, magazines, and my own books (on the content-producing, editorial side) along with 15 years of writing copy and teaching others to do the same (many of those were the same years . . . I'm not *that* old!) to learn what I've just shared with you.

I've found that simple rules of thumb are very helpful in assimilating new knowledge and translating it into productive action. With that in mind, here are five "do's" and five "don'ts" to guide your headline writing, both on the Internet and in non-Internet (print, radio, and TV) formats.

Do

1. *Make it conversational.* Learn how people talk, and even how you talk when you're not being self-conscious or trying to sound "professional." Strive to put that in your copywriting, *especially* your headlines. The more it sounds like real conversation, the more engaging it will be for your reader.

2. *Enter the conversation already going on in the customer's mind.* This famous piece of advice from 1930s copywriting legend Robert Collier may be the single most important thing to remember when you start writing copy. It's a more specific version of my rule: Start where the *reader* is, not where *you* are.

3. *Remember VERVE—Visceral, Emotional, Resounding, Visual, Empathic.* It's a memory-jogger to help you build the kind of headlines that get results. Point-by-point:
   - *Visceral* literally means having to do with your intestines, your guts. A visceral headline is very physical and immediate.
   - *Emotional* means the headline appeals to your reader's *feelings*.
   - *Resounding* means it sounds like someone talking. Your reader can "hear" you saying the headline, because it comes across as conversational language.
   - *Visual* means the reader can *picture* what your headline is about.

- *Empathic* means the reader feels you understand how he or she feels.

4. *Walk the fine line between fact and hype.* A timid headline won't do you any good, but neither will one that is so over-the-top that no one will believe it. Make the biggest claim you can make, and still prove in your copy.

5. *Understand the ultimate purpose of your headline is to get your reader to read the next line of copy.* Don't sum up everything you're about to say later in your headline. Create intrigue, curiosity, and desire. Leave 'em hungry for more!

Don't

1. *Be clever.* Most of the time, the urge to be clever is a short cut to avoid doing the work of creating an enticing promise that will prepare the reader to take the action you are looking for. Resist the temptation; a straightforward headline almost always works better than a clever one.

2. *Be boring.* Remember that, ultimately, what you are looking for is *action.* Action involves *motion.* Motion is prompted by *emotion.* And emotion is generated by *excitement.* Don't settle for a headline that is more likely to produce a yawn than anything else.

3. *Don't assume your prospect knows what you know.* It's easy to fall into the trap of forgetting all the time and effort you put into building the knowledge and expertise you have on the product, service, or information you are marketing. Make the effort to turn back the clock, in your mind, to when you knew far less. Don't write your headline for sophisticated people; write for the person who needs to learn more.

4. *Don't focus on your process.* Remember Mr. Scott and the grass seed? People aren't interested, initially, in how the seeds are selected, or developed, or, for that matter, stored or shipped. People are interested in greener lawns, their end result. Don't focus on your process; focus on what the prospect *gets.*

5. *Don't merely try to arouse curiosity.* You have to do better than that if you want your prospect to get up enough of an emotional head of steam to be ready to buy, or take some other crucial action, after they finish reading your copy. Curiosity at the outset won't do it. Curiosity's good, but what's more important is desire. And intrigue.

ALEX MANDOSSIAN
TRAFFIC CONVERSION
SECRETS

ALEX MANDOSSIAN has helped his clients generate over $203 million in sales from TV spots, infomercials, coaching clients, QVC and Home Shopping Network, national retail catalogs, space ads in Parade Magazine and USA Weekend, and direct mail and postcard marketing. He has also helped to develop and distribute spot TV and infomercial mega-hits such as the Thigh Master (Suzanne Somers) and RONCO Food Dehydrator (Ron Popeil). Alex is also one of the top Web site Traffic Conversion strategists in the world.

FOR MORE INFORMATION: http://www.accesstoleaders.com

In **T**his **C**hapter **Y**ou **W**ill **L**earn:

- What Traffic Conversion Is

- How to Understand and Improve Your VPV

- The Difference between Principles versus Tactics

- The Five Web Traffic Drivers

WHAT IS TRAFFIC CONVERSION?

The first thing people need to realize is that traffic conversion is different than traffic creation. Traffic creation is all those search engine optimizers, directory optimizers, and pay-per-click search engine optimizers that bring traffic to you.

My job begins where their job ends: at the point of digital sale or, in this case, the Web site.

When a visitor visits a Web site, my job is to create some drivers and some psychological tactics to get people to either give a shy "yes" in the form of an opt-in request for more information, or to go ahead and just order from the first-time visit.

One thing I want to make very, very clear: It's not about conversion. When we talk about conversion, it's not about how well we convert, it's about visitor value. Specifically, VPV means Value per Visitor.

If we can increase the VPV, which is my expertise, then we can have all kinds of relationships with co-op partners and affiliate partners. Then we can afford higher pay-per-click traffic coming from pay-per-click search engines like Overture.

For example, let's say we had a 5 percent conversion, which is enormous. That means 5 out of 100 people are buying something from you. And let's say the product and the service that we offered was $10. So that's $50 for every 100 visitors or a $.50 VPV, value per visitor. Now that's not very good. Because if you have affiliate traffic coming in and you're giving away a 50 percent commission, which is not that extraordinary, you're making $.25, they're making $.25, and it's very likely you will not have a lot of affiliate relationships because they can make a lot more money elsewhere.

However, say you had a 1 percent conversion, that is 1/5 of the 5 percent you were getting and your product was $100. Now if you make $100 per 100 visitors, then the match isn't so difficult, your VPV, or value per visitor, is $1, or twice as much as before.

Even though you had only 20 percent of the previous conversion rate, many affiliate partners would love to do business with you if they knew they could make $.50, or 50 percent, out of every dollar that comes in, because that's a pretty decent VPV to be reckoned with. So it's not just about conversion rates, it's all about value per visitor and increasing that value per visitor is the key to the game.

METRICS AND MEASURING

Tom Peters said, "You can only improve what you measure." So if you're not measuring the dollars that are coming in divided by the number of visitors that are coming in, then you are really playing pin the tail on the donkey with your marketing dollars.

There are far fewer principles than there are tactics. They cause predictable, sustainable, and capital-efficient growth or sudden changes in losses in business if you're using the wrong principles.

Principles answer why your marketing works or doesn't work and specifically in this case your e-marketing, or online marketing. I like to also call a principle a driver or a strategy.

A tactic is a technique, some people call it a trick, or tricks, of the trade, and they help execute the e-marketing or marketing that you do in the form of the tools that you use.

Let's say a tactic is an e-mail or an autoresponder or an opt-in box on your Web site. The tactic answers how your e-marketing works. So whereas the *principle is **why** it works, the tactic or technique is **how** it specifically works,* and unfortunately, the single biggest difference between a principle and tactic is endurance.

Principles often work forever. For example, if something is scarce, like gold, it's very valuable. Diamonds, platinum—those are the principles of scarcity that are in effect there. But tactics are often obsolete overnight. Selling gold by mail may not be the way to go anymore because people just don't believe what you have to say.

So the point is, where the tactic can be obsolete overnight, principles last forever. Focus on principles. Stephen Covey said it better than anybody else when he said, "The power behind principles is that they are universal, timeless truths." If we understand and live our lives based on principles, we can quickly adapt and apply them anywhere. And in my case, I apply principle-centered tactics to increase visitor values, in many cases to make them soar.

WEB CONVERSION DRIVERS

There are five Web conversion drivers and all of them end in "ING." This is something I've learned from Jay Conrad Levinson. He's big on memory rich words so that you can remember them, not only easily but so they have some meaning. In his *62 Free Ways to Grow Your Business Profits,* you are familiar with all the different types of words that end in the same, such as amaze*ment,* commit*ment,* etc.

In this case, all these words and drivers are principles and they end in "ING." They specifically end in "ING" because I like to think of them as always in action. They are ongoing. They didn't happen. They are not about to happen, they are always happening. I call them "drivers," which are interchangeable with strategies and principles. So there is no particular order for using them.

Baiting

The first driver is *baiting.* Baiting lures and hooks more first-time visitors to opt in. An opt-in is a shy yes. It's not an immediate order but an exchange for an e-mail address and a name, often times your zip code, and even more information. With the opt-in, a person is getting an ethical bribe of some kind, and we call it "bait." We're baiting them to get their e-mail address and their name in exchange for something valuable.

It could be a white paper; it could three free chapters like I give away on MarketingWithPostcards.com. If you have software, it's ideal to be baiting with a 21-day free trial or 30-day free trial like many software companies do. If you are a radio show host like Mike Litman, at MikeLitman .com, the appropriate strategy is to give away real audio samples of your audio, of your interviews with Mark Victor Hanson or Jay Conrad Levinson. You have to look at the appropriate bait because baiting is kind of like trying out a new lure in a lake.

You know right before the strike that it's really exciting but you don't know if that particular lure is going to work. You've got to make sure that it's the right bait for the right fish.

I use baiting for my marketing with postcards site to create five figures, that's five-figure cash profits, not just gross, month after month, with less than a hundred visitors a day. So that is a very, very high value per visitor; in fact, upwards of $4 value per visitor. This had generated over a quarter of a million dollars of annual revenue between August 2001 and August 2002.

Of course, I do sell coaching off this site in addition to my postcard manual, which is only about one-fifth of the total sales. But these were all strangers that were baited with the three free chapters. I demonstrated my knowledge and I monetized that traffic, which is the name of the game.

When baiting comes into play, just make sure you're baiting with the appropriate type of bait.

Baiting a white paper or baiting a special report would be ideal if you are selling information. Bait an excerpt from a teleclass. If you teach teleclasses, it would be awesome in the form of an audio as a Real Audio file.

Just make sure that the bait is luring in and hooking first-time visitors in an appropriate way. It's absolutely inappropriate to bait, let's say if you're selling software, three free chapters of the user manual on how to use the software. That makes no sense. So just make sure it makes sense and it's appropriate—in other words, use common sense.

Make sure the first bait you're throwing out there is not only very innocuous but that you're not asking too much information from them. At the same time, make sure it's compelling for them to strike at it. That's driver number one.

Bundling

Driver number two also starts with a B and is called *bundling*. Bundling has been used for years and years by huge corporations like McDonald's. You may remember that McDonald's only sold hamburgers at one time. Then some genius at McDonald's University suggested they have all their people across the checkout counter ask, "Would you like fries with that?" And those few words generated $35 million in net profit the following year.

Then someone came up with a new bundling strategy. Instead of allowing the person at the register to ask if the customer would like fries (because often times they would forget or they may be in a bad mood) they decided to create Happy Meal Deals. So now instead of spending $.99 on a burger, your typical ticket at McDonald's is somewhere around $3.50 to $4, because there is a Happy Meal Deal that is a bundled product.

Now bundling has been used with reckless abandon in the computer industry. You don't just buy a monitor, you don't just buy a CPU unit, and you don't just buy a keyboard. If you call Dell Computers, they ask, "What can I build for you today?" So you're building and bundling your computer.

Here is a great example of bundling, which has a very, very high conversion rate, 42 percent. It increased my value per visitor by about 10 percent and there are zero customer acquisition costs. I have done nothing. I've done this while I sleep. It's a very simple bundling strategy that anyone can eavesdrop and take a peek at CopywritingCoach.com.

I sell the course Copywriting Classics for $77 and there's a bundling up-sell. In this case a cross-sell, because I'm selling something else at the digital point of sale, which is the order form.

So if you go to http://www.copywritingcoach.com, click on "order now" and take a peek at the up-sell, which is a $19 sell at a $20 savings for a digital product called "Public Speaking as Listeners Like It." It's a lost classic written by Richard Borden who was the chairman of the public speaking division at NYU, New York University, back in the early 1930s. That was in the time of Dale Carnagie and all the greats like Napoleon Hill. But this man was lost in obscurity. Now it's public domain and I made it into a digital e-book. It's sold as a bundle with Copywriting Classics and four out of ten people are taking it.

In the copy of the order page, it says, "Today's Special Value, Public Speaking as Listeners Like It, Write Like Richard Borden. Order this and take advantage of the special value and save, in this case, $20." All you do is replace the number one where the zero is next to the book title; the shopping cart automatically increases it to $19 more. I make $19 more pure profit because there is no cost of product—it's a digital product—and it's a great little bundling strategy.

Another great bundling strategy that I have seen out there is by Zone Alarm. It's one of the best virus detection and best firewalls you can get, and it's dirt cheap. You go to ZoneAlarm.com and purchase the $39 program, it's just for one Zone Alarm, and it's called Zone Alarm Pro. Automatically you see this thing that says "get pest control": Use pest control to kill bugs your anti-virus product doesn't even look for. What a great up sell! $19.95 and you just add it to your shopping cart. What's great about the Zone Alarm bundling strategy is that they offer two or three different bundles so they can nab you for close to $100, and many people take advantage of this offer.

It's not rude, it's just actually convenient. They think you need this anyway, which I know I did, so why not get you at the point of sale instead of spamming you with an e-mail later. So bundling eliminates spam, and it increases average orders at the digital point of sale, and it is a very, very fast and easy way to increase your average order size at zero cost.

Recycling

The third Web conversion strategy is *recycling*. This is my absolute favorite because it's something that has been overlooked by virtually every Internet marketing expert who I personally know. I can't believe it's been overlooked because it's so important.

Now, if you have a supersuccessful site, I mean really successful, you're converting 3 percent. It may astound some people but if 3 out of 100 people purchase something from you, you are supersuccessful. Five out of 100 is just stratosphere proportions.

Well imagine if you have 5 percent conversion. That means 95 out of 100 people are leaving. What do you do with those people? I mean 95 out of 100 people are leaving you and they are never coming back.

So what recycling does is try to get back to those people and say, "Hey (taps them on them shoulder)! Perhaps you overlooked something or how would you like to come back. Let me call to your attention . . ."

The best example is something I did for 1ShoppingCart.com. If you go to http://www.1shoppingcart.com and you let the Web site load and just click off the browser as if you are not interested, all of a sudden you see an exit pop-up that reads, "We need your advice before you leave us. What is the biggest reason you decided not to give 1ShoppingCart.com a try?" Of course, 1ShoppingCart.com has a merchant account, built-in autoresponders, affiliate manager programs, and e-book delivery systems.

It's very powerful and it does all the metrics for you. If you go to 1ShoppingCart.com and you exit, I try to recycle you and here's what the recycling exit pop-up looks like: It says, "What's the biggest reason you decided not to give us a try?" There are four check boxes. Number one says, "I need a merchant account." Number two says, "I need to build an autoresponder system." Three says, "I need an affiliate manager program." Four says, "I need a digital e-book program." Well guess what? 1ShoppingCart.com offers every single one of those things.

So if I check one of those and I click the submit button, this little thank-you page comes up. In the pop-up itself, that thank-you pop-up says, "Did you know that 1ShoppingCart.com puts the power of affiliate tracking systems at your fingertips, plus many more advanced features?" And there are two buttons that say "No thanks, I'll pass" or "Please tell me more."

Five percent of all the exit traffic that leaves 1ShoppingCart.com comes back to those specific pages and we close a portion of those to give the $3.95 trial. If not for our recycling efforts, we would have lost those people for life.

That is recycling in action—it happens every single day while you sleep. It boosts your value per visitor quickly, reliably, and economically. Don't just go after the people landing on your Web page who are interested. Go after the people who are disinterested, that 98 percent that left you. Go after those people; see if you can get them with exit strategies.

You can do it with pop-unders too. You can see an example of this at EBookGenerator.com, which is Armand Morin's site. He's a genius. He has an e-cover generator at eBookGenerator.com that creates e-book covers for you in less than five minutes. However, if you exit that site, he feels it is possible that you might need an e-book cover right?

He has that site pop right under, so instead of an exit pop-up, it's an exit Web site and he just pulls a bunch of business that way, by recycling them into his other generator Web sites. He has a whole string of generators: eLetter generator, eCover generator, e-book generator, etc. So, recycling really works.

Gifting

Gifting is the fourth strategy. Here's the way I use gifting. I am just going to go over one example because it's very relevant to Guerrilla Marketing. There is actually a recorded Guerilla Marketing phone consultation during my Guerilla Marketing Coaching certification.

Now that one-on-one consultation is available at GMarketingCoach .com. Anyone can listen to that for free; it's 26 minutes.

What this does for me is it has gotten the fence sitters on the opt-in list, so people have now opted in for more information on marketing with postcards than on any other Web site property I own.

Around day five or day seven they get an autoresponder message that I've pre-written. It says, "Listen, how would you like a Guerrilla Marketing plan by phone, done by me, one-on-one, worth $125?" Ok, here's what you have to do, you have to write in and say 'yes' I want it. Secondly, you have to call in at the preassigned day. And thirdly, you can't be more than three minutes late otherwise the standby caller on that same day will take your place."

There are all these principles involved here, scarcity and gifting, which is the law of reciprocity. By me gifting a one-on-one consultation— and I do one per day—I have made $2,105 per hour. Doing this one strategy, investing only one-half hour per day, and I've done 82 consults, I've produced $82,300 in nine months—that's $2,105 per hour. The reason gifting works, the principle behind it, is it humanizes our virtual enterprise. It makes it a one-on-one consultation experience.

Impulses and Psychology of Persuasion by Robert Cialdini, PhD is a treatise of marketing. He says one of the most potent influence weapons is the *rule of reciprocation*. He says the rule states that we try to repay in kind what other people have provided us.

So one out of three, or one out of four, people I give these Guerilla Marketing plans to become clients. That's been the single most powerful tool I have used and it's a gift and I ask nothing in return. I don't bait and switch them into some selling process, I just tell them I hope our paths cross often, and because I have demonstrated my know-how, they come back for more.

Some people say, "Well, I can't do one-on-one consultations—that would be too many customers." Great, why don't you do a teleconference? Just give it away. There can be a lot of meat packed into a teleconference.

Gifting is a very powerful strategy and it's selfish because it applies the law of reciprocity to capture sales. So it is mutually beneficial. It's the definition of what I consider a good deal to be; where both sides feel they are getting the better end of the deal.

Sometimes it espouses guilt and that is not my intention, but gifting is very powerful. Think about it, you get a Hanukkah gift or a Christmas gift during the holidays; don't you feel like you need to give something back?

There is no such thing as an unconditional gift. It's always conditional in one way, shape, or form. So *gifting* is driver number four.

Engaging

Driver number 5 is *engaging*. That's the principle of engaging people. Engaging is very, very powerful. The key to engaging is getting people to use their mouse. There are many ways to do this.

Online you want people to use their mouse because the more often they get to use their mouse, the more engaged they are in their Internet marketing experience on your Web site. The way I do it, in many instances, is to use three words: Print this page.

If you go to my Web site, MarketingWithPostcards.com, that's 4,000 words. It's a long page and it's very, very engaging; however, I'm not so sure you're going to read every single word so the way I engage you is I get you to print it. By having you print it, I now have real estate in your home, which is the printed page that you can curl up with on your couch and read and highlight.

There is a lot of content in media information just on my sales page because I teach you how to use postcards for grand openings, for brick-and-mortar shops or stores. I have four or five pay studies on how people launch businesses whether you're a search engine optimizer or if you're launching a newsletter. Just with postcards. You've got to have good content first and foremost. But the way you engage people is number one, get them to use their mouse by having them print this page. It's very, very simple.

Another way to engage people you can see at DreamsAlive.com. There's a client whose name is Paul Bauer, who has a fabulous, fabulous piece of software. The cost is $77 to purchase the software plus $6.95 shipping and handling. Here's the problem, not everyone knows Paul Bauer. And not everyone knows how powerful the software is. So when they go there, they don't want to fork over $77. So we did a free CD-ROM using the Video Professor model that you see on TV. Instead of just selling 1 or 2 of these $77 CD-ROMs, we gave a 15-day free trial and we sold 42 CD-ROMs. We offered the CD free for 15 free days with a bunch of free bonuses. This increased the pulling power of that Web site by 940 percent. You can see it, you can read the copy—basically it's the same CD-ROM only they get a trial before they buy it for 15 free days, which is a combination of dating and engaging.

I'll give you one more great example of engaging. You can see it at CenterPointe.com. And the way that man uses the engaging strategy is he makes you click at the bottom of the page, one page after another, so to go to the next page you have to click page two, then page three, then page four. It is not good for printing but it is really good to get people to use their mouse.

Other examples include SmartCover.com, SpeakingWithJohn.com, and AccessToLeaders.com, just to name a few.

Those are the five principles of drivers: baiting, bundling, recycling, gifting, and engaging, and I have proven that using these five alone will make visitor value soar and increase conversion almost overnight.

These drivers work for all kinds of businesses: coaches, gardeners, brokers, insurance brokers, mortgage brokers, real estate brokers, information publishers, trash collectors. I have a trash collection company in California that has used these, along with hair dressers, cosmetic dentists, yoga instructors, seminar leaders, public speakers, and horse trainers.

Obscure companies and just everyday companies, whether brick and mortar or online, it doesn't matter. They use these types of principles because they've been used and have been working since the times of Caesar. Only the tactics have changed.

The most important point is to focus on principles, not tactics. Principles are enduring. Tactics can become obsolete overnight. Anytime someone teaches you a tactic, ask yourself, What is the principle behind this tactic? What is fueling this tactic to work?

Know when the tactic works and no longer works. Then keep using the principle in some other form. One day, pop-ups will not work. But the tactics of recycling will always work. So just find a good tactic and make it appropriate to the principle.

9

ROB BELL
HOW TO AUTOMATE YOUR ONLINE MARKETING

ROBERT W. BELL, President and CEO, creates and executes the overall strategic direction and vision for 1ShoppingCart.com Corp. Rob has more than 20 years of senior management, sales, and marketing experience in the high-tech industry. His work culminated over $35 million in sales to Nortel Networks. His first online business in the mid 80s was running a commercial online bulletin board system (BBS).

FOR MORE INFORMATION: http://www.easywebautomation.com

In ***T****his* **C***hapter* **Y***ou* **W***ill* **L***earn:*

• The Six Benefits of Automation

• How to Grow Your Customer Base

• How to Increase Customer Confidence

HOW TO AUTOMATE YOUR ONLINE MARKETING

Imagine a "hands-free" automatic sales and marketing machine that leaves you free to do what you want, when you want! Automation exists for thousands of merchants who have already taken in over half a billion dollars in sales in the past few years using a simple, yet powerful Internet strategy. Many merely check in remotely to find out how much money has been deposited in their accounts that day, while they pursue new ventures and personal projects.

What would you do with more free time and less hassles? You could focus on other areas to grow your business, travel, do charitable work, take more family time, or finally get to your favorite recreation or hobby. With the right online system, you can automate many of the processes needed to sell your products and services and support your customers.

If you're an online marketer or using e-commerce to complement your existing brick-and-mortar business, then you're most likely familiar with the importance of Internet marketing and shopping cart solutions. To automate these processes requires a combination of flexible, dynamic marketing systems, as well as secure credit card and order taking processes, to be efficient and profitable.

The *strategic use of automation* defines who wins when applying e-commerce solutions. With the power of automation, you'll see your online sales and profits excel beyond what you ever thought possible. To discover how automation works and what it can do for you, read the following strategies with references to one automated online sales and marketing tool called EasyWebAutomation.com.

BENEFITS OF AUTOMATION

The benefits of automation are so numerous you can't afford to ignore them. Automate your online efforts correctly and you'll reap the rewards. The primary benefit of "hands-free" marketing is selling to your customers 24 hours a day, seven days a week. Other benefits include:

- *Cost reduction*. Automation reduces your costs across the board. Everything from long distance phone bills to direct mail postage, and to reducing the need for hiring additional customer service and support staff.

- *Easy to run.* The number one complaint of most business owners is their inability to be away from the business. Your business becomes *much* easier to run and your presence becomes optional with online automation. With most systems you can quickly and easily check your sales and orders from any Web browser.

- *More time.* You gain more time to focus on priorities for the strategic growth of your company and to address those smaller problems that accumulate otherwise. This newfound discretionary time comes without your money-making activities coming to a halt, or hiring and training staff, while you finally take that vacation.

- *Happy customers.* Automation lets you serve your customers faster and more efficiently and raises your customer satisfaction levels. If you have employees, they can focus on other higher-value functions that demand human intervention. Automation also reduces the demand for the high cost of customer service representatives.

- *Targeted marketing.* While building your customer base, your prospects can be segmented. Once they respond to a specific offer, put them on a segmented list that identifies them, topics that interest them, products they want, and other personal preferences. Now you're able to market to your prospects more efficiently and personally with custom offers to produce larger profits.

- *Competitive advantage.* Automation gives you an edge over your competition. You can devote more time to identifying additional opportunities, enhancing customer service, and selling more to your best clients.

STRATEGY #1: GROW YOUR CUSTOMER BASE

The value of your business comes down to the size and quality of your customer base. If there's no market demand or buyers, then your business has little value or life expectancy! Capture the names and e-mails of prospects when they visit your Web sites. The fact that they clicked to your site shows they're interested. Rarely does a customer buy on their first visit to your site and they're just as unlikely to ever return without an invitation and further persuasion.

Permission-based opt-in. Seek the permission from your visitors to put them on your e-mail list. Send them additional information or preferred access. Use an unblockable, strategic pop-over window to have an offer appear automatically. A small script, like the Easy Opt-in script provided by EasyWebAutomation, works with a time delay on entry or exit to your sites. This tactic alone instantly increases opt-in conversions by as much as 30 to 40 percent. Once they've opted in to your list, they've "raised their hand" and identified themselves as part of your target market. Now feed them value-based, timely, rich content that encourages them to return to your site where you're more likely to convert them into customers.

Capturing e-mail addresses. Automate the most important role of your Web site: capturing the e-mail addresses of all your prospects. Your mailing list is critical to all your marketing and literally your most valuable asset. Offer special reports, e-zines, newsletters, insider information, mini-educational courses, advice, or free trials to entice visitors to share their name and e-mail. When the data is entered, it is automatically placed in your database and added to the appropriate list. Then, e-mail promotions and other benefits over time to build your relationship and gradually earn a prospect's trust, leading to more sales and frequent purchases.

Automatic response and communication. Once you have their e-mail address, put autoresponders to work. These automatically distributed e-mail messages are to motivate prospects to revisit your site for the latest offers. Create customized, brief, friendly, and conversational messages as content for your autoresponders. Do you read long e-mail?

E-mail should be used only to direct traffic to your sites *not* to deliver a ton of content.

STRATEGY #2: BUILD RELATIONSHIPS

The total number of purchases being made online is increasing gradually every year. However, shoppers remain as critical and demanding in their judgment of vendors. They only buy from people or businesses that they know, like, and trust.

Communicate automatically and frequently. Once you have an individual's e-mail you need to communicate with them frequently. This converts more original traffic and leads into buyers. Use autoresponders that give you the option of sending e-mail once, or in a series. The series are more effective because this creates multiple "touches."

Frequency builds trust and relationship. Controlling the frequency and intervals of messages moves your prospects forward in the sales process. Use merge codes within your autoresponders to customize and communicate in a personal manner. Merge codes automatically and use specific data like the recipient's first name, title, or company. Make sure to include personalization in subject lines, headers, and the salutation. Use multiple broadcasts for monthly newsletters, daily quotes, or stock tips. One-time e-mail, called "solo broadcasts," do have their uses, for example, as one-time special offers, seasonal announcements, and specific or urgent customer service bulletins.

Be SMART. Use a smart autoresponder system. It's more intelligent than the basic autoresponder first mentioned here. The smart autoresponder directs a new lead, or potential customer e-mail, into what is called the "hot lead" part of the responder. Picture sending out five or six autoresponder messages to a prospect and they subsequently come back to your Web site and make a purchase. You do *not* want to continue sending them a *prospect* message, now that they have become a paying *customer*. The smart autoresponder takes them off your *prospect* list and puts them on your *customer* list. Continuing communication with your customer this way makes sense.

The autoresponder is smart in other ways as well, adding to your marketing strength. Many systems have the power to serve a variety of products in the autoresponder database. For every product you're selling there is matching product information to compile appropriate autoresponder messages. Here's an example of just how this works:

1. You're offering vitamins at cost to win new business knowing it's a consumable product and the average customer buys a 30- to 60-day supply.
2. When your customer makes their first, promotionally-priced vitamin purchase, the autoresponder sends out product-specific information, along with offers for other products that you sell.

3. After that, the autoresponder sends out reminders to the customer a few days before the 30- to 60-day supply of vitamins is finished, asking them if they'd like to stock up and buy more.

4. In the reminder message for another vitamin purchase there's a direct link to that product in the shopping cart on the checkout page. How much more convenient can it be for your customers to make repeat purchases and give you recurring income?

Remember that the customers that you're already selling to are your *best* sales target and hold the maximum potential for profit. Repeat sales come from *staying in touch* with satisfied clients and that's the power of automating your online business.

Work with an automated service that has unlimited list creation and unlimited e-mail broadcasting (with no cost per e-mail) in their autoresponder system. Make sure you have the ability to cross-pollinate your lists and move prospects and customers from one list to another easily and automatically.

Use online automation to manage other communications that support your business like with your personal network, sales channels, the media, and suppliers.

Delivering your e-mail. Do *not* spam. If you're new to this, spam is unwanted and uninvited e-mail solicitation. Use an opt-in for all your e-mail marketing. Many Internet service providers (ISPs) have programs that filter spam. Be sure to avoid words identified and linked with common spam messages that prevent your lists from receiving your e-mail. Determine what words are flagged through a spam filter database tool. EasyWebAutomation includes free use of the Spam Assassin™ database checker. Before you send an e-mail you can "test" it to see if it will pass through the ISPs' spam filters. In addition, work with recognized, professional organizations that are on the "white lists" of all the major ISPs, such as AOL, MSN, and RoadRunner.

STRATEGY #3: INCREASE CUSTOMER CONFIDENCE

To build your online business it's vital that you have an e-commerce plan. Letting your customers place orders on your Web site is the major component. The key to the most profitable e-commerce today is the ability to influence prospects to confidently share their personal and financial data while making purchases.

"Pushing" your shopping cart. You'll notice a little shopping cart icon on many retail Web sites. Or perhaps when you click on a product, you're invited to add it to your shopping cart. A shopping cart is at the heart of your selling process online. No cart—no orders! What better way to assist consumers than with a shopping cart that operates in exactly the same way it would in a grocery store?

How a shopping cart works. Picture this: You're cruising down the aisles while pushing your shopping cart along, grabbing items and adding them to your cart. At the checkout you make the final decision about the items and discard any you don't want. An online shopping cart works in exactly the same way. Carts are used by millions of Web sites worldwide.

Instant delivery. Demand a shopping cart system that handles automatic digital product delivery. Net shoppers want to download your product instantly if it's software, music, or digital information, like an e-book. This is important because when it comes to the Internet today, *timing is everything!* Failing to take advantage of a shopping cart system severely limits your online capabilities.

Is it safe? This remains the most frequently asked question about online shopping. A few years ago most people were concerned about using their credit cards online. With ever-evolving security features on Internet browsers these days, using your credit card online is actually safer than using it at the local gas station. Implementing an online shopping cart makes it much safer to use credit cards online. A shopping cart employs something called a *digital converter.* You're given a secure certificate ensuring that your credit card and personal information is encrypted through the Internet browser. This makes it impossible for anyone to grab your data and steal it. The presentation of your order form and shopping cart application increases the trust your customer has in your online order system and makes them more likely to purchase. Point out any and all the security features on your site with written explanations and related logos and symbols.

STRATEGY #4: TAKE ORDERS ONLINE

When you're taking orders online for your business, there are a several factors you must address.

Order forms. Once you've convinced your prospect traffic to buy your goods, they'll click to your order form. Free shopping cart services online give you basic, bare-bones forms that don't look related to your company. However, with a superior and more adaptable system you can customize the HTML code to present your own custom, branded order form. At a minimum put your logo at the top of the page to maintain your site's look and feel. Additional suggestions include repeating benefits, clearly showing shipping and handling, restating your guarantee, and including and indicating what security features are in place. Together these contribute to decreasing shopping cart abandonment and increasing your sales.

Multimedia trust. You might consider appearing in or using audio or video clips on your order forms to provide helpful directions and confirm the sale. When prospects see and hear you, it helps to further establish trust with you, especially if you're personally and emphatically stating a guarantee.

PayPal. You can be selling online within 15 minutes, if you choose to accept payments through PayPal.com. As a third-party processor, they take customers' credit cards on your behalf and forward payment to your PayPal account minus their fee.

Merchant accounts. Today, it's a lot easier than in the past to open your own merchant account to accept credit card payments. Services called "gateways" compare your customer's credit card number against the personal information they enter, and confirm and approve it. Then they notify the appropriate creditor, such as VISA, MasterCard, or AmEx, to deposit the money in your bank account.

The shopping cart is the area in the online sales process where your customers are going to change their mind and leave your Web site without completing their purchases. Shopping cart abandonment can be as high as 75 to 85 percent. You must make sure your online ordering process is as efficient as possible and apply as many relationship and trust-building tactics as possible.

STRATEGY #5: USE A FREE SALES FORCE! YOU DON'T PAY UNTIL *AFTER* THEY SELL

Automating your sales process goes beyond your Web site and your own efforts. The top sellers online invite others to refer and sell their products on a 100 percent commission-only payment plan.

Your free sales force. Invite resellers, called "affiliates" online, to become part of your Affiliate Program and watch your sales and profits go through the roof! You pay commissions only after sales are made and confirmed. Plus, while it's recommended that you provide your affiliates with sales support, training, and templates, they generally use their own resources, time, money, and relationships to sell YOUR products.

Affiliate control. When using EasyWebAutomation, only several clicks are needed to set up an entire Affiliate Program for all your products. Identify and reward your best affiliate partners by using the automated commission reports to track top performers. Variable commission levels pay out more to your star sales affiliates. Setting up unique affiliate programs for every individual product gives you more flexibility to set commission rates and especially to protect your profit margins.

Sales administration. Track all your sales information. Automation provides dynamic sales administration to monitor your sales from anywhere Internet access is available. All information is real-time data. Tracking reveals how your business is doing. Your automation solution should track various data, such as reports by product, day, and credit card brands used by your customers. When you know which campaigns or products are the most profitable, further concentrate your efforts there and duplicate your success elsewhere.

STRATEGY #6: TEST AND TRACK YOUR ONLINE MARKETING

Testing and tracking bring you extremely valuable data to measure and improve your online effectiveness. For example, ad tracking counts how many click-throughs your links get on the Internet. Links might include Google Ads, or other pay-per-click advertising, banner ads, text links, and affiliate links. Ad tracking determines how many times a banner was clicked and calculates how much revenue was generated from that particular ad. You know how many times a visitor was directed to your Web site from an individual link and made a purchase. Many systems evaluate the cost of each click related to the revenue generated. It also includes a "Split Testing" tool to compare three variations of the same Web page, like your home page, to get real-time market research on what works best. Each time a new visitor comes they're cycled through Page A, B, or C. Assess your marketing and make any necessary changes to continually improve your online sales results.

CONCLUSION

The Internet is extremely competitive. The right strategy combined with powerful and practical systems gives you an edge over your competitors. You'll attract more customers and spend less time, money, and energy winning them over. By automating your sales and marketing processes online with a system like EasyWebAutomation.com, you'll see big profits sooner and more often! Automation services and software leverage the best technology available to make you money day and night, whether you're there or not!

10

JIM BLACK
BUILDING YOUR BUSINESS USING AUDIO, WEB, AND VIDEO CONFERENCING

JIM BLACK is the president of AccuConference.com. He is revolutionizing how business is done on the Web by bringing people together through innovations in audio and Web conferencing technologies. He is a major force in Internet communications. This is the technology that will position you and your company out front and ahead of the competition.

FOR MORE INFORMATION: http://www.easyliveconference.com

In This Chapter You Will Learn:

- The Most Powerful Trends Influencing Today's Businesses

- How Audio and Web Collaboration Are the Next Frontier

- How to Build Your Business through the Power of Audio

- How to Cultivate the Full Sensory Experience through Web and Video

- How to Build Your Business through the Power of Web and Video Conferencing

THE MOST POWERFUL TRENDS INFLUENCING YOUR BUSINESS TODAY

Today we can't imagine dealing with a company or organization that doesn't have a Web presence. In the near future, the public will think the same thing about companies that are not using audio, Web, and video conferencing technologies to interface with their customers. Prospects will want to hear audio testimonials, listen to and see live product and service presentations, or even have the opportunity to test-drive products online and in real time. Today, these technologies are available to you. They're easy to use, cost-effective, and a necessity if you want your business to be a success.

There are several key trends that are affecting not only how we market our products and services to consumers, but how they buy from us. As a current or future business owner, understanding these trends, and aligning your business model with them, will make all the difference in your future success:

- *Technology will continue to be the central platform for building businesses.* Understanding it and utilizing it in innovative ways to capture interest and to cultivate customers will quickly separate out the winners from the losers.
- *The world is growing smaller.* No longer are we selling just to local or even national markets. With the advent of the Internet and innovations in telecommunications, we can easily and effortlessly sell to a global marketplace.
- *The right relationship is* still *everything.* Building and maintaining a strong customer interface is growing even more important as competition continues to increase in virtually every business sector. Presale relationships are just as critical as postsale relationships as the cost to capture each new customer continues to skyrocket.
- *Online commerce continues to expand at unprecedented rates.* More and more people are engaging in and interacting with technology to make buying decisions. This is a boon to online marketers as well as brick-and-mortar establishments who can promote any aspect of their business online.

- *Consumers are opting for more multisensory experiences.* New customers and increased market share await companies who can quickly embrace and implement audio, Web, and video technologies to showcase, market, and deliver their products and services.

AUDIO, WEB, AND VIDEO COLLABORATION: THE NEXT FRONTIER

What do these powerful trends mean to you? In order to be considered among the competition going forward, your company will need to adopt technologies that will further your reach and expand your net work by bringing more of your business to the eyes and ears of your clients, whether at home or at the office.

Competition is fierce and it isn't going away. With the average consumer inundated with over 4,000 marketing messages per day, how are you going to stay one step ahead of the competition? How are you going to be seen and heard above the fray? In fact, one step ahead of the competition isn't sufficient anymore.

Today's small and large businesses must take one leap ahead by employing cost-effective strategies that will save them time, money, and energy while reaching their potential and current customer base. Audio and Web solutions are the answer.

Audio, Web, and video provide a more effective way to communicate with consumers than through traditional, one-dimensional, marketing methodologies. Essentially, consumers "learn" through three different ways—through visual, verbal, and auditory means. If your marketing tunes into only one of these particular channels, you may not be reaching all the prospects you could, not to mention the fact your marketing dollars will not be well spent. However, by incorporating tools that support all three learning styles, you'll increase your opportunity to convert prospects to customers.

Providing a multimedia presence brings people together. Business leaders, located on seven different continents, can easily meet face-to-face, without anyone leaving their offices; sales vice presidents can meet and train hundreds of sales reps with merely a telephone call; and sellers of software can demo products live in front of participants spread worldwide, even giving them the opportunity to try the product themselves with the seller maintaining complete control over the underlying product. What does this mean to you? It means a world of marketing opportunity, and all at your fingertips.

BUILD YOUR BUSINESS THROUGH THE POWER OF AUDIO

Just a few years ago, "solo-preneurs" and small businesses couldn't hope to compete with larger companies when it came to selling and distributing their products and services. Cost structures were prohibitive. There were no economical ways to reach niche markets. Then, the Internet boomed. As more and more people purchased computers, and engineering processes were perfected, the costs of technology plummeted. Everyone was gaining access to this virtual world. Suddenly, many businesses, large and small, were put on an even footing, with the cost of entry being the price of a domain name. Small businesses found themselves playing in a bigger game, in head-to-head competition with the very best.

And, the bar continues to be raised. Your competitors are learning and implementing technologies as quickly as they're being developed and released. Today's companies are implementing everything from audio conferencing technologies to Web and video capabilities—anything to deliver their products and services to prospects—more easily, more quickly, and more affordably.

Audio conferencing is one of easiest and most cost-effective technologies available for you to use. If you're not already using it in your business, you need to be. It's a cost-effective solution to building your business, while boosting profits. This easy-to-implement technology that takes merely seconds to set up, even for first-time users, can leverage your business in unique ways.

THE BENEFITS OF USING AUDIO CONFERENCING

Audio conferencing, on a fundamental level, is all about reaching customers and clients through telephone bridge technology, specifically one that allows many users to be on the telephone line at the same time. The benefits of using this technology are phenomenal, not only for you as a business owner, but for your potential and current customers as well.

- *Extends your reach to the global marketplace.* While not everyone has access to high-speed Internet, most everyone has telephone access. Whether you're at the office, at home, or even driving in your car, you can participate in voice communications.
- *Increases your visibility and credibility.* Companies who are early adopters of today's technology are perceived by potential customers as market leaders. In the minds of consumers, this level of visibility naturally associates with it a high level of credibility. Visibility and credibility combined with your dynamic marketing message are critical to your online success.
- *Lowers the costs of doing business.* The costs of travel continue to skyrocket. With audio conferencing, you eliminate the need for commuting. Not only does it save you money, but it saves time and energy as well. Through audio conferencing, no one is burdened with the inconveniences of long commutes or dealing with inclement weather. No longer do you need to go to the customer, or the customer, to you; everyone can meet in the middle, on the telephone.
- *No reservations required, anytime.* Imagine you just received a call from a client who has several interested buyers, located worldwide, who want to hear about your latest product or service. How fast could you pull together a meeting? And, at what cost? If you need to plan and execute a conference ASAP, audio conferencing can be coordinated in a matter of hours. Imagine the implications of being this responsive to a potential customer or client. You're already half of the way to making a sale.

USE AUDIO CONFERENCING TO BUILD YOUR BUSINESS

Consider some of the many possibilities of using audio conferencing to build your business:

- Offer free or fee classes, seminars, or workshops to a global audience.
- Conduct sales meetings with your distributed sales force.
- Train your personnel on your company's latest products, policies, or services.
- Offer Q & A sessions with new clients or customers around a product or service they've just purchased from you.
- Showcase your latest book or publication by hosting a live, virtual "meet the author" tour right on the telephone.
- Record your calls (for free) with the touch of a button for archiving and future playback. Also, download them for free.
- Upload your own recordings to your Web site for playback at the user's convenience.

Audio conferencing is more than bringing people together through technology; a number of unique features allow users to adapt and customize the technology to serve their business needs.

No matter what business you're in, audio conferencing offers a professional, innovative, and cost-effective approach to reaching consumers. It's a great way to extend your products and services by offering alternative ways to communicate your marketing message. It brings the large company look and feel to even the smallest business through simple, easy-to-use technology, and most importantly, promotes your visibility and credibility, which are critical to staying one step ahead of your competition.

WEB AND VIDEO: CULTIVATING THE FULL SENSORY EXPERIENCE

How would you like to beat your competition by taking a giant leap forward? Web and video conferencing provides the latest tools to deliver and cultivate a memorable and sensational experience for your customers. And multisensory interaction is, indeed, what today's consumers are looking for. They want to make decisions on their own terms, at their own convenience, with as much information as possible, right at their fingertips.

Using cutting-edge technology, you can reach out to your markets, bringing your products and services right to the consumer's computer desktop. This audiovisual collaboration is delivered easily and effortlessly through the Web. So why is this important to your business success?

In 1967, a Professor named Albert Mehrabian carried out a study on communications. The results showed that a person's response to a message is 55 percent visual (primarily facial expressions), 38 percent vocal (volume, pitch, etc.), and 7 percent verbal (the actual words that make up the message). What are the implications of this widely quoted study in terms of how you're marketing your products and services today? What difference might it make to your bottom line if potential customers could see your face and your product, in real time, on a computer screen, while they listen to you describe its functions and features?

Instead of marketing your product solely through a one-dimensional sales newsletter posted on your Web site, why not add the power of Web and video conferencing? If you're selling a product, there's no better way to communicate than through combining audio with visuals. With 55 percent of the message being communicated through the means of a visual interface, what impact might this have on your sales?

Web conferencing is a truly unique tool. It's the perfect solution for any online marketer whether they sell a tangible product or an intangible service. By combining Web with video, you can deliver media-rich presentations that include engaging interactive video, images, animations, sounds, and other effects. With unique branding options, interfaces can be created that match your organization's look, feel, and identity.

Through application sharing features, you can allow users to "test-drive" software or Web-based products right from their desktop, without relinquishing control of the underlying product.

Imagine this: You're an online marketer and you sell a unique product that allows anyone to design customized logos in ten minutes or less by inputting some data, selecting text, color, style, and design options from menus, adding some special effects, and, finally, pressing a button to create the final result. Not only can you demo this live to a viewing audience, you can temporarily turn over control of the product to an eager participant, have them go through a similar exercise, providing a visible and credible testimonial to the truth of your claim. Powerful, indeed.

The more you can involve the prospect with the product, the higher your chances of closing the sale. Could there be a more effective way to market?

USE WEB AND VIDEO CONFERENCING TO BUILD YOUR BUSINESS

Consider some of the many possibilities of using Web and video to build your business. These options can be conveniently bundled with audio conferencing to create the atmosphere of a live, in-person conference.

- Present a Microsoft PowerPoint presentation to your audience, without them needing access to the software themselves.
- Show charts, diagrams, and pictures with ease.
- Demonstrate the features of your software application and even give conference participants an opportunity to "test-drive" the product right from their own computer.
- Explain complex, technical products with ease by utilizing video so that users can see and understand each component.

Extend the value of your marketing message by utilizing innovative tools like Web and video. Similar to audio conferencing, you and your company will cultivate visibility and credibility by building relationships through multiple interfaces. Successful businesses are built upon strong customer relationships.

CONCLUSION

Many companies say they listen to their customers. Customer-centric audio, Web, and video tools can leverage your company to a new level of play. Whether you're new to the business or an established online marketer, productivity tools like these are a critical and necessary addition to your marketing tool kit. Using them today will create your business of tomorrow.

JOHN PAUL MENDOCHA
SPEED SELLING
ON THE INTERNET

JOHN PAUL MENDOCHA, Dr. SpeedSelling™, has set out to do nothing less than revolutionize the way sales professionals sell, and his extraordinary track record as a master salesman, entrepreneur, and consultant says he just might do it. He has spent 30 years of his life in sales, marketing, and consulting, including starting several companies from scratch. John Paul is a sales trainer and sales coach teaching his SpeedSelling™ Boot Camps nationwide, and has helped his clients increase their sales and incomes by two to four to more than six times.

FOR MORE INFORMATION: http://www.speedselling.net

I n   T h i s   C h a p t e r   Y o u   W i l l   L e a r n:

* Speed Selling Techniques

* How to Dramatically Improve Sales

* The Linear Sales Process

* How to Close and Get Someone to Make a Commitment

FROM MARKETING TO SELLING

I want to talk about the tremendous marketing power you have when you use certain techniques, tactics, and strategies to convert leads into sales. SpeedSelling is a way for you to sell faster, easier, and with less stress. Find out how to disqualify those prospects who aren't ready to buy so that instead of spending 80 percent of your time qualifying prospects who aren't ready to buy, you spend 80 percent of your time closing, which is where the money is.

OVERVIEW OF SALES

"Sales" has a bad name. We can all think of negative experiences we have had with salespeople. As a result, most people feel uncomfortable about selling. And this fear (and in some cases loathing) is the source of many of their problems when trying to create success in their business.

The most important activity for any business to thrive and flourish is sales. You can have the greatest products in the world, the most advanced ideas, the highest quality Internet experience, the best customer service, but without sales, it all goes to waste.

Everything in your business is tied to sales and marketing. Everyone in your organization is in the sales and marketing business. Everything you do, from your Web site, to your order fulfillment, to your customer follow-up, is part of your sales and marketing program.

The irony is that most people fear sales and dread the very thought of making a sales call. The reason is that when you sell, you are on the line. There is no place to hide. Sales are a binary event—you win the sale or you don't, it's that simple. Add to this a lack of sales training and fear of rejection, and you have a formula for mediocrity, or even worse, abject failure.

Here is the frank truth: Most people (i.e., your competitors) are terrible at sales. Now here is the good news: They are not getting any better! What that means is if you can become just slightly better than your competitors, you will increase your sales. Just a slight improvement can make or break your business. If you become very good at sales, your sales will increase dramatically and you can dominate your market!

Buying Resistance

Let's look at the data. In the 1970s you had to ask for the order five times before someone would buy. That means someone would tell you no four times before they would say yes to whatever it was you were selling. The interesting thing is that the average salesperson would ask for the order an average of 1.5 times. Do the math. Most salespeople were doing a lousy job.

Fast forward to today. Today you have to ask for the order nine times before someone will buy and the average salesperson is still only asking 1.5 times. So buying resistance has almost doubled but the skill of the salesperson has not changed! Most people are terrible at sales and they are not getting any better!

Why is this important? You have an *incredible* opportunity in your reach to dramatically improve the sales from your Web site and destroy your competition. Why aren't you doing it? How many times are you asking people to buy on your Web site? Don't hesitate; the time to act is now!

There is one additional point that is very important for you to know: People buy on emotion and justify with logic. That's right; they buy on emotion and justify their purchase with logic. Many people like to think that they make their buying decisions based on logic. Nothing could be further from the truth. Logically we would assemble all the facts, determine what is best to buy, and then we would all be shopping at the same store and driving the same car. People buy on emotion. And this is even more true in businesses.

The Four Big Questions

What this means is you must make sure that you are marketing and selling with emotion and then have the facts to justify logically why this is a good choice. Just watch any ad on TV or look at any ad in a magazine or newspaper. The ads utilize four major benefits that create a buying environment. Your marketing information must answer one of the big four questions: Will this product make me healthier, wealthier, sexier, or save me time? All humans seek these four big benefits. Start thinking in this way and you will improve your sales dramatically.

My goal is to give you techniques that are actionable, relevant, and give you the biggest bang for your efforts. The rest of this chapter will give you an overview of sales and marketing, the biggest problems when selling on the Internet, using the telephone for follow-up, the negative assumptive close, and two easy ways to handle objections.

SALES VERSUS MARKETING

The place to start is at the beginning. Before we get into the specifics, you need to know the role of marketing and the role of sales. When you understand what each of these roles are, only then can you maximize your use of both to make your Web site more effective and ultimately put more money in your pocket.

One of the important aspects of marketing is to generate leads—to capture the attention of a suspect and give that suspect enough information so they can determine whether they have an interest in what it is you are selling and then identify themselves to you. This makes them a prospect and, if you apply the correct marketing principles, a qualified prospect.

The role of sales is to gain commitment—to take that qualified prospect and convert them to a customer. This commitment may be in the form of opting in, requesting more information, or actually placing an order for your product or service. It is important to understand that a sale is about gaining commitment. This importance will become more apparent later in the chapter.

Sales and marketing are inexorably linked. You cannot have one without the other. You need to have a way to identify qualified prospects (marketing) and then gain commitment from those prospects to purchase your products or services (sales). They work together hand-in-hand.

SALES IS A PROCESS

Sales is a process and there are several different models of how this process works. The most common is the Linear Sales Process. This is diagrammed in Figure 11.1.

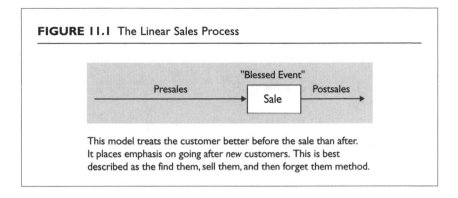

FIGURE 11.1 The Linear Sales Process

This model treats the customer better before the sale than after. It places emphasis on going after *new* customers. This is best described as the find them, sell them, and then forget them method.

Sales is considered to be a straight line process and everything before the blessed event ("the sale") is considered presales and everything after is considered postsales. This model treats a sale as an isolated event.

Figure 11.2 views sales as a circular event where presales flow into the blessed event that flows into postsales, which naturally flows into presales again. I prefer this model because you want to keep having sales events on a continuous basis with your customers, with one sale flowing into the next. Now you are in a state of continuous "pre-post-sales." This

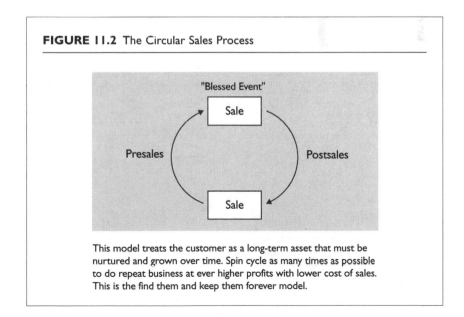

FIGURE 11.2 The Circular Sales Process

This model treats the customer as a long-term asset that must be nurtured and grown over time. Spin cycle as many times as possible to do repeat business at ever higher profits with lower cost of sales. This is the find them and keep them forever model.

results in incredible repeat business that nurtures the growth of raving fans—your repeat customers.

DEFINING YOUR SALES PROCESS

Lay out your sales process. You must know what your sales process is before you design and build your Web site. Most Web sites are designed backwards—Web site first, sales process second, or never. If you are unsure of your sales process, however, let's learn to diagram it now. It doesn't have to be perfect from the start. But you do have to start.

Ask yourself these questions:

- Is what you are selling a one-step, two-step, or multistep process? See Figures 11.3, 11.4, and 11.5.
- How can you give your prospects the opportunity to buy at every step of the process?
- At what point(s) do prospects buy now?
- What are the percentages for each point?
- What information is needed between each step in the process to move the sale along?

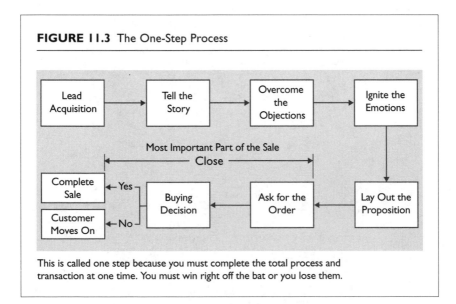

FIGURE 11.3 The One-Step Process

This is called one step because you must complete the total process and transaction at one time. You must win right off the bat or you lose them.

FIGURE 11.4 The Two-Step Process

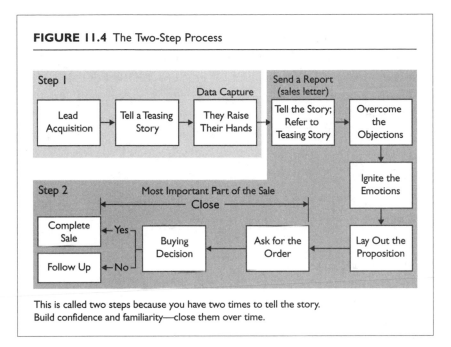

This is called two steps because you have two times to tell the story.
Build confidence and familiarity—close them over time.

FIGURE 11.5 The Multistep Process

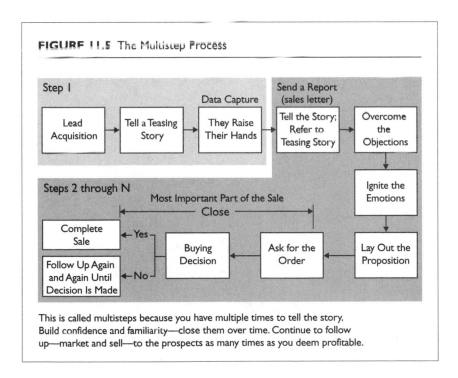

This is called multisteps because you have multiple times to tell the story.
Build confidence and familiarity—close them over time. Continue to follow
up—market and sell—to the prospects as many times as you deem profitable.

When you have the answer to these questions you are well on your way to understanding how you sell your products. As time goes by you can refine the process and combine steps, but take your time! Too often when people come up with a process that works, they get impatient and try to reduce it based on one or two sales. Sales is all about effectiveness, not efficiency.

Once you understand your sales process you can address the problems you have when selling on the Internet.

BIGGEST PROBLEMS WHEN SELLING ON THE INTERNET

Everyone is obsessed with having a great Web site. They spend countless hours and thousands (if not tens or hundreds of thousands) of dollars to come up with cool, slick graphics that dazzle the eye and boggle the mind. They forget that the whole reason you have a Web site is to produce sales. Slick does not equate to sales. If it did, the dot-com bust would never have happened.

If you think you need to have a slick Web site to make money, go visit Google.com. Google has 32 words on their Web page. It is very simple and they are one of the most successful Web sites in history.

The following five areas present the biggest problems when selling on the Internet. Understanding each point will enable you to shift your online sales approach from one of "I hope somebody buys something" to one of actively doing everything to capture and qualify your prospect and make it easy for that prospect to buy from you.

1. *Creating a Web site without knowing your sales process.* How many steps are in the buying process? What information does your prospect need to make a buying decision, or do they need personal contact? Otherwise you will experience the next problem which is . . .

2. *Trying to accomplish too many steps too quickly with the Web site.* Too often we try to one-step the prospect: "Hi, I just met you—buy now." In other words, someone visits your Web site and you try to get them to buy immediately. If it takes seven steps before your prospect buys your type of product, then make sure your Web site

supports this process. Have the necessary steps in place to support your sales process.

3. *Does everything on your Web page move prospects closer to the sale?* Remember, if you have a seven-step sales process, you are gaining commitment (i.e., making a "sale") at every step. Make sure you do that.

4. *Not conveying benefits.* This is a major problem in any sales situation but it is amplified when selling on the Internet. Too often people talk about the features of their products or services and leave off the benefits. Remember, people buy on emotion and justify with logic. Your marketing information must answer one of the four big questions: Will this product make me healthier, wealthier, sexier, or save me time? Make sure the sales copy on your Web site conveys the benefits of using or owning your product/service. Make the benefits tangible and cover the five senses—sight, touch taste, smell, and hearing—keeping in mind the big four.

5. *Forgetting that sales is information collection not information distribution.* The Internet is the most incredible information distribution mechanism ever invented. You can find out about anything, and I mean anything, on the Web. Unfortunately, people who have Web sites feel they must distribute information just like everyone else and don't think about information collection. You have to collect information on your prospects so that you can market to them. This should be one of the first steps in your sales process— get the prospect's e-mail, name, address, telephone number, fax number, their permission to market to them, and any other data you require. You owe it to your prospects, and you owe it to yourself.

SALES PROCESS EXAMPLE

An example that illustrates the points of knowing your sales process is the Web site I created called EasyInstantLeads, http://www.easyinstantleads .com. This is a service that helps people get their Google AdWords on the Internet quickly and easily.

The sales process has three steps: 1) initial exposure, 2) understanding of the value, and 3) decision to buy.

When people first visit the Web site for EasyInstantLeads, there is an education process that occurs. Our approach gives exciting information about the service, uses an attention-grabbing headline, describes the three value propositions available to the prospects, and culminates with a buying decision. If prospects decide not to buy, we offer a free report that captures their contact information. If they still don't buy, we have their contact information and their permission to continue to market to them.

This multistep process is much more effective than trying to one-step the prospect into buying right off and maximizes our selling options and opportunities. By knowing the buying process a prospect goes through, we are able to design a Web site that helps us accomplish our goal each step of the way. That doesn't mean that we don't get lucky and have someone who wants to buy immediately. What it means is that we have a Web site that supports our sales process and maximizes our effectiveness in every situation.

FOLLOW UP

Follow-up is very important but, unfortunately, most people fall down on the job here—they either don't do it or they do it wrong. It's really very simple.

Ask people how they want you to follow up. "Tell me, would you rather me follow up in two, three, or five weeks?"

"Is the morning or the afternoon a better time to call on you?"

"Do you want our next meeting at 8 AM or 10 AM on the 31st?"

These are simple, nonthreatening questions and your prospects will appreciate you for asking them.

One of the most popular ways to sell to people is the hard sales method of hammer them, hammer them, hammer them. Today, people are bombarded by marketing messages. You may decide to back off on continuing to contact the prospect because you don't want to annoy the customer. But you will lose out by not following up. Do the smart thing and ask them how they want you to follow up and then do it!

USING THE TELEPHONE TO IGNITE YOUR INTERNET SALES

Personal contact using the telephone is a very powerful tool for igniting your Internet sales. It is unexpected, your competition is probably not doing it, and it gives you more opportunity to gain feedback from and present benefits to your prospects. Space is limited but here are a few tips:

- Decide why you are making the sales call before you dial the number. What do you really want to accomplish? Develop a script.
- Group your calls to be more effective. You will be in the zone when you make a series of calls.
- Use teleconferencing. This is a powerful use of the telephone. I do live teleconferences with Dr. SpeedSelling at specific dates and times. These I advertise on my Web site.
- Time your calls. Set a kitchen timer and when it dings the call is over and you go to the next call. Set shorter times, not longer. You will get more done in less time.
- Smile when you are on the call. The smile can be "heard." The telephone is one of the most powerful tools in sales. Use it and you can elevate your Internet business to an entirely different level.

CLOSING THE SALE

Mention closing and everyone freezes up. The gut-wrenching terror happens when you are going to ask someone to make a commitment and give you money. The average person feels uncomfortable about asking for a commitment in the form of money. It doesn't need to be that hard or anxiety ridden for you. What you need to have is a straightforward process that is easy for you to use and has a logical flow.

There are whole books and courses on closing. In this limited space, I will give you one of the most powerful closes you can use, the Negative Assumptive Close. This close is very smooth, natural, and easy to script and works with anything. Technical people and nonsalespeople love using it and find it easy to use!

The Negative Assumptive Close is a close that is used very, very effectively in cases where you are asking people for a decision because it takes them through a process, and that process will then drive them to a decision point. This works especially well if you're going for a job interview, if you're asking a banker for money, or if you have someone with a lot of questions.

Most closing techniques require the prospect to say yes in order to buy. Many prospects have their guard up, especially when you are getting them to say yes many times in a row. The Negative Assumptive Close works because it requires the prospect to say no to buy and catches them off guard.

The close starts very innocently by asking the prospect the following question: "Do you have any more questions?"

If they have more questions, then you cannot ask the next question, which is the close. You have to answer those questions and objections first. Answering those questions and objections is absolutely critical at this point.

By the way, don't be surprised if they come up with other questions because often they will do that. You continue to answer all their questions and ask them if they have any more questions. At some point they will run out of questions. At that point in time, you then go to a transition that leads you to the close.

The transition is:

"Do you have any more questions?" They answer "No."

Now we go right into the close.

"Do you see any reason why you wouldn't proceed today?" If they say "No," they just bought. It's that simple.

If they say "Yes," then ask, "What haven't I shown you?" They will give you more questions or objections. You answer these and then go right back to: "Do you have any more questions?" You continue through this cycle over and over until they buy.

The importance of this technique is we step them right into the close and we use these words exactly. Just a note here, whenever you're putting together a close, it's important that you say the words exactly. Make yourself a script and use it. The reason is that many people will vary how they ask the close and they will botch it. What you want to do is make sure that you get the close right the first time. You only have one time to close them. Everything else is just gravy. You don't have a second shot at it.

Remember, we're not playing tiddlywinks; we're playing sales—real, hard-nosed sales—you've got to ask them for the money.

You may be wondering how many times you have to go through this cycle. The answer is: As many as it takes! I just had a coaching client use the Negative Assumptive Close in a job interview. He was interviewing with the president of the company. After one hour and forty-five minutes, the president said, "We are going to hire this person." His staff said there were other candidates flying in to interview and the president said, "This is the best person for the job, we are hiring him today." He got the job.

This is a very powerful close. Use it. Create a script and practice it. Become proficient and you will find it easy to use and, more importantly, it will put money in your bank account!

HANDLING OBJECTIONS

What is an objection? An objection is a reason given by a prospect for not making a decision (commitment) to move to the next step in the sales process. They can range from money issues, color, availability, timing, not the right fit, or "I have to get approval from my spouse, boss, or banker."

Objections are very valuable in giving us the feedback we need to evaluate our products, services, marketing, and sales information from the perspective of the customer and helping us craft our sales and marketing materials to increase sales. The feedback method and the benefit restatement are two of the easiest ways to handle objections, find out the real reason they aren't buying now, and move them toward the sale.

1. *Feedback method.* This works when someone says, "I don't have the money." You respond by simply feeding their objection back to them: "So you don't have the money to go ahead today? What if we split it into payments?" "Well, I really don't want to make a decision." What has happened is that we have now smoked out an objection that is not related to money. Money was just being used as a smoke screen. The Feedback method is easy to use and highly effective.

2. *Benefit restatement.* "I'm looking at two products." Say, "Let's look at all the things you like about my product." Then restate all the

benefits so that it is benefit statement/objection answering. Have at least four to five benefit statements. Give them a fill in the blanks form to restate the benefits.

These techniques can be used whenever you are in a sales situation. You may be wondering how you apply these techniques to your Web site. The secret is to take your list of common objections and evaluate your Web site to see if you address each of them in your sales letter. For example, go to the Web sites of any of the authors in this book and you will see how they handle objections as part of their Web copy.

Nothing happens until you sell something. This applies doubly to the Internet. If people are stopping at your Web site and not buying—it's worthless.

Selling is a skill and sales takes practice. Just because you read this once doesn't mean you have become an expert or that you are proficient. You would not expect to read a chapter on Web site development and then start charging big dollars to build Web sites. You need practice and experience. Have fun with sales. Use these techniques whenever you can, even in non-sales situations. Give yourself permission to test yourself in the real world. That is how you are going to get good at sales.

Speed selling is a comprehensive methodology that allows you to sell faster, easier, and with less stress. It focuses on closing and getting someone to make a commitment to become a customer, then a client, and then a raving fan. It focuses on the conversion of high-quality leads, which the rest of this book is dedicated to, into closed sales. Without converting leads into closed sales, they are nothing but names on a sheet of paper or blips on a screen. Make no mistake. You must sell. Without selling, your Web site is just something you can show your friends. If you can't convert those leads into closed sales you can't build a business, because building a business is based upon transactions.

Chapter

12

CHRIS MURCH
EBAY—THE WORLD'S
ONLINE MARKETPLACE

CHRIS MURCH is an eBay PowerSeller, which means he consistently sells over $1,000 a month on eBay. He has been selling on eBay for over seven years, currently has two seller accounts that include two eBay stores and is the proud producer of eBay's official talk radio show, "eBay Radio" with host Jim "Griff" Griffith, on his Internet talk radio station, wsRadio .com. Jim Griffith wrote *The Official eBay Bible* and contributed to this chapter. Over 450,000 individuals and small businesses make a living on eBay as even large companies have added eBay to their sales and marketing channel. The good news for individuals and small businesses is, for the most part, eBay is still a level playing field that translates into a real opportunity.

FOR MORE INFORMATION: http://www.wsradio.com/listingtips/

In **T**his **C**hapter **Y**ou **W**ill **L**earn:

- What eBay Is

- Five Steps to Selling on eBay

- Ten Strategies to Gain Visibility for Your Listing

137

WHAT IS EBAY?

Some people are under the misconception that when they are purchasing something from eBay, it somehow gets shipped from the "eBay  Warehouse." Simply stated, eBay is a unique online platform that connects buyers and sellers. Buyers pay nothing to eBay when they place bids and purchase items from sellers. It is the sellers who pay eBay listing fees and final value fees, (a small percentage of the sales price). eBay has done a superior job of setting up the guidelines and rules that make it a safe environment to buy and sell from.

BACKGROUND OF EBAY

Over Labor Day in 1995, Pierre M. Omidyar created a simple auction site and posted it to various bulletin boards. As the site slowly but steadily grew in popularity, it has always been the "eBay Community" that has contributed to and made the site truly "The World's Online Market Place." Over the years as the Internet and the technology supporting the Internet improved, eBay, with the vital input of the community, kept pace. Over 96 percent of online auctions are done through eBay. eBay has expanded into eBay Stores along with "Buy It Now" options to augment their very successful auction model. eBay is truly a great business success story and probably one of the most successful online success stories.

QUICK FACTS ABOUT EBAY

- eBay has over 125 million registered users.
- A global presence in 28 international markets, including the United States.
- Over 20 million items on sales at any time, with 2 million added daily.
- eBay members have left nearly 2 billion feedback comments regarding their eBay transactions.
- 1/100th of 1 percent of transactions on eBay result in confirmed cases of fraud.

TEN TIPS TO UNDERSTANDING EBAY

Following are ten tips for getting started and becoming familiar with eBay.

1. You can browse on eBay without having to register, but to bid, buy, or sell, you need to be a registered user. It only takes a few minutes to register and select your "user name." You do require a validated e-mail address. eBay.com has a "register" link on every page of their site.

2. Computer and connection requirements recommend that you use at the minimum Windows 98 or higher. For your Internet browser, the latest version 6.0 is most efficient. You will also need at least a 28K connection to the Internet, with 56 or higher recommended. eBay does use what are called "cookies," which are small files placed on the hard drive of your computer. Cookies are used to save the information you have previously entered on a site, making it run more efficiently for you. You will need to set your browser to accept cookies. eBay respects your privacy and does not use any "cookie" information from your computer. To learn how to enable cookies, you can log onto this page on eBay: http://pages.ebay.com /help/welcome/help-with-cookies.html#accept.

3. eBay has a wonderful "learning center" that includes audio tutorials that walk you through several aspects of using eBay. As long as you can listen to audio on your computer this is a great place to start: http://pages.ebay.com/education/index.html.

4. eBay also has a "Help" link on all of their pages along with another great feature, "Live Help," where you can use "instant messages" to communicate with a customer service representative from eBay. Because eBay has millions and millions of users each day, they are not able to provide any telephone support.

5. With over 20 million items listed on eBay, using the "Search" feature requires a little practice to find what you are looking for. When using the "basic" search, for whatever words you list, only those listings that contain all of the words will appear. If you type in "New CDs," hundreds of thousands of listings will come up. If you type "New Ghana Gospel CDs" in the search field, only a few will show up.

6. Keep in mind you are mostly dealing with individuals on eBay so it is up to you to do your homework. To get started, try bidding on low-cost items first. Before placing a bid, read all the information provided by the seller including shipping information and payment methods. It is also highly recommended that you check out the "Feedback Rating" of the seller carefully. Do not place a bid, because it is legally binding, unless you are comfortable with the seller along with knowing all the costs and condition of the item. Other options include "Buy It Now" for the price listed or purchasing items within the eBay Stores that require a special eBay store search.

7. Pay with a credit card or, if you plan on being a regular buyer or seller on eBay, sign up for a PayPal account, which allows you to pay through your credit card or bank account. The majority of sellers on eBay prefer PayPal and for qualified sellers, you can receive up to $500 in payment protection from eBay. *Never* pay with a wire transfer. This is where the very few bad guys that do take advantage of eBay buyers get their money.

8. Use the feedback system. eBay continues to be a safe place to buy and sell because of their feedback system. After all transactions it is recommended that you leave feedback for the rest of the community to see.

9. To sell on eBay requires a seller ID along with additional verification information. It does require effort to provide detailed descriptions and good clear digital pictures, along with collecting and shipping the items you are selling, but once you have bought a few items on eBay and are comfortable with the buying process, there is no better way to clean out your garage or attic or possibly start up a side business.

10. Never respond to any e-mails that appear to come from eBay requesting account information, passwords, or bank or credit card information. The few problems that do occur in dealing with eBay are what are called account hijackings, where the "bad guys" obtain a user's (mostly sellers') user name and password by sending spoof e-mails that look very convincing but ask for your user name and password. They then use the seller account and good feedback ratings to sell items and collect the money, but never deliver the goods. eBay is constantly monitoring these "bad guys"

and work with law enforcement agencies around the globe. The challenge for eBay is many of them are offshore in other countries that do not have aggressive law enforcement agencies to work with. If you do receive a spoof e-mail, it is recommended that you forward it immediately to Spoof@eBay.com as the eBay Trust and Safety team does an excellent job of following up.

FIVE TIPS TO SELLING ON EBAY

There is no magic formula for selling on eBay. Successful selling on eBay requires the combination of a proven track record (high feedback ratings from the eBay community); superior, professional listings that stand out from the competition; along with trial and error. One of the reasons eBay has been so successful is buyers essentially set the price they are willing to pay. The end result is rarely are retail prices ever reached on eBay.

1. *Obtain positive feedback ratings.* The feedback rating system has proven to be one of the key ingredients to eBay's success. Both buyers and sellers are able to leave positive, neutral, or negative feedback. This feedback is linked to your user ID and stays visible for as long as that user ID is active. It is critical for sellers to have both a high percentage of positive feedback (over 98 percent) and a track record as well. In other words, when you first start selling and your feedback rating is zero or one or two, there is very little for a buyer to judge you on. With that in mind, it is highly recommended that you start by purchasing several items on eBay, low cost if you prefer, to build up your feedback rating. We recommend obtaining at least ten or more feedbacks, which need to be positive, prior to selling.

2. *Set up a PayPal account.* If you are serious about being a regular seller on eBay, besides opening up a seller account, make sure you have a PayPal account as well. Over 70 percent of the buyers on eBay prefer to pay with PayPal. You can open up a personal account that allows you to accept up to $500 a month in funds. If you exceed that amount, you will need to sign up for a business PayPal account. PayPal is a great service and, although their trans-

action fees tend to be higher than traditional online credit card payments, it is well worth it. PayPal can also be used to pay and accept funds outside of eBay as well.

3. *Start selling something—anything.* Start selling by cleaning out your garage or by getting rid of unwanted items. It is true that you can sell just about anything on eBay. You can either start your price out at the minimum selling price you are willing to accept or a better recommendation is use the reserve price option. This means you start the item off at a low price to attract bids but if the bids do not reach your reserve price, you are not obligated to sell and the buyer is not obligated to buy. Make sure you do a little research on eBay to see what the current price is for similar items you want to sell. Use the "Completed Auctions" option of the advance search to see what some items actually sold for.

4. *Clear and precise item description and picture.* Put yourself in the buyer's shoes and provide everything they will want to know about the item you are selling including condition, exact dimensions, and shipping price. It is also recommended that you offer a money-back guarantee. It is critical that you include a clear picture of the items.

5. *Listen to eBay Radio.* eBay Radio is a weekly Internet talk radio show that wsRadio.com broadcasts live via the Internet every Tuesday from 11:00 AM to 1:00 PM Pacific time. The show is hosted by Jim "Griff" Griffith. Griff is eBay's original customer service representative, Dean of eBay Education, and eBay's official spokesperson. As previously mentioned, eBay does not offer telephone customer support, but eBay Radio does have open call segments during the live show where you can call in via a toll-free number and ask Griff any question you wish. The show also has a great resource directory and is archived for listening on demand 24/7 by topic segments. To listen, log onto http://www.wsradio.com/eBayRadio.

Tune In
Host Jim Griffith
Dean of eBay University

TEN TIPS AND STRATEGIES TO GAIN VISIBILITY OF YOUR EBAY LISTINGS

Once you start selling on eBay, the most successful selling comes through experience and plain old trial and error. One of the keys is to be a little more effective than your competition on eBay. Make sure you track your results.

1. *See what your competition is doing.* It is always a good idea to see what your competition is doing on eBay. Use the advanced searched option "Completed Auctions" to see how your competition sold similar items. Chances are you will always learn from your competition. Take what you think is working for them and put it in your own words to add to your competitive edge.

2. *Make sure you have good keywords in your item description title.* For the most part, buyers find your listing through the basic eBay search feature, which keys on the item description title. A listing appears when all of the key words the buyer places in the search feature are included in the item description. As an example, if you are selling a car wax, make sure your listing includes the words "car wax." If your listing says "automotive wax" without the word "car" in it, and the buyer searches for "car wax," your listing will not show up because you did not have "car" in it. It is imperative that you have all the key words listed in the title. If you don't, buyers will not be able to find what you are trying to sell. The item description allows for up to 55 characters. Use all 55. Add a hit counter to all of your auctions and test different key words in your listing title and descriptions to see if some auctions do better than others.

3. *Try one or more Listing Upgrades.* See http://pages.ebay.com/sellercentral/tools.html.
   - *Home Page Featured.* The eBay.com home page receives tremendous traffic and listing your item as a home page featured item can be a real bargain and is worth testing.
   - *Featured Plus.* Your listing is placed within the featured items located in the top section of the listing and search results pages that buyers see first. Your item also appears in the gen-

eral listings and search results for double the exposure. Featured listings are 28 percent more likely to sell!

- *Highlight.* Employs a colored band to emphasize the listing in the search results. If you're listing in a crowded field, anything to make your item stand out is helpful.
- *Bold text.* Draws additional attention to a listing by bolding the text when the listing is part of search results. Bold listings are shown to increase final price by an average of 25 percent.
- *Gallery.* Attracts attention by adding a thumbnail photo next to your listings on the Category Listings or Search Results page. Gallery listings are shown to increase final price by an average of 11 percent.
- *List in two categories.* Occasionally, buyers only search by specific categories, so by adding an additional category, it will provide additional visibility. Use the hit counters on all of your listings and keep track of the traffic to determine if adding more than one category is helpful.
- *Gift Services.* Some buyers are looking specifically for gift services, which may include direct shipping to a gift recipient, gift wrapping, or express shipments. By adding the gift icon to your listing you are suggesting that the item for sale makes a great gift and you as the seller may be willing to provide some extra services as well.

4. *Use "Subtitle" feature to indicate special offers like free shipping or "No Reserve."* The subtitle is a great feature that shows in the eBay buyer search. It provides additional information that increases the chances a buyer will click on your item over others that do not use this feature

5. *Open an eBay store and cross merchandise your store items in your nonstore eBay listings.* See http://pages.ebay.com/merchandisingmanager/. The eBay Store showcases your listings in one customized, searchable showcase with a unique URL. With an eBay Store, buyers can only search within your items. The store offers listings in multiple quantities for longer durations and the ability to create custom categories. It also comes with advanced merchandising tools that allow you to control which of your items are displayed on key buyer pages. The basic eBay store is only $9.95 a month and lists auction items as well as "Buy It Now" items.

Once you have your eBay store in place, promote the store and individual store items in your auction listings. Because each eBay Store has its own unique URL, it can be used as a possible "on-line shopping cart" for your current Web site; however, buyers need to be eBay registered users to purchase and bid.

6. *Add your eBay Store listings to other third-party vendors or search engines* at http://pages.ebay.com/help/sell/contextual/export-listings.html. Set up partnerships with third parties, such as product search engines, to drive traffic to your eBay Store listings. This capability provides your partners with up-to-date information of your listings and their URLs. If you choose to do this, eBay can make a file of information about your Store Inventory listings available for your partners to download.

7. *Gain banner placement on keyword search pages with eBay Keywords.* See https://ebay.admarketplace.net/ebay/servlet/ebay. By purchasing keywords, a banner is created that brings more buyers to your listings through keywords matched to search terms. Buyers see your banner and text ad when they search on a term you've selected.

8. *Co-op advertising program.* See http://www.ebaycoopadvertising.com/. This is an advanced program created to provide Power-Sellers and Trading Assistants with a scalable marketing tool to grow their business. As a qualified co-op participant, eBay will reimburse 25 percent of print advertising costs each quarter up to $8,000. Certain conditions apply, but if you qualify it is an excellent program that could provide tremendous exposure through a wide range of traditional print media options.

9. *Bundling of complementary products and accessories.* Because it is perfectly legal to cross promote items within auction listings, Buy It Now and eBay Store items offer as many complementary products and accessories as possible. If you sell cameras, offer camera bags, batteries, photography books, or any accessories that make sense. Make sure these complementary products or accessories are fully cross-promoted. Another example is if you are selling gold-plating equipment, offer some gold-plated items with full cross-promotions from those items that state, "If you wish to purchase gold-plating equipment to gold-plate items yourself, visit our eBay Store" or link to appropriate auction listings.

10. *Sell Popular items at http://www.Pulse.ebay.com.* Selling the most popular items viewed on eBay is made easier with a feature called Pulse. At pulse.ebay.com, you will be able to see the most viewed items that are obviously in demand. These lists are based on actual buying activities and are updated every day. The eBay marketplace is always changing and growing.

ADDITIONAL RECOMMENDED RESOURCES

- *The Official eBay Bible.* To put selling on eBay in high gear, purchase *The Official eBay Bible,* by Jim Griffith. Griff was very helpful in assisting with the content in this chapter.
- *eBay Turbo Lister.* This feature is a desktop download that is highly recommended if you are listing the same type of items over and over, or you wish to develop a template that contains your basic information that does not change. Turbo Lister is free and can be downloaded via the "download" links on the bottom of any eBay page. Simple to use, this program will save time in quickly changing and uploading listings to eBay.
- *Nine-Segment Listing Tips Audio Series.* A free nine-segment audio series available at http://www.wsradio.com/listingtips. This audio series takes a product never sold on eBay before and over a three-month period, with the mentoring of Griff, gives advice and insight on tweaking the listings, creating an eBay Store, and incorporating many of the mentioned tips into a successful eBay sales campaign. Each segment is about ten minutes long and is available in Windows Media Player, Real Player, and MP3 downloadable formats.

JON KEEL
MASTERING PAY-PER-CLICK: GOOGLE, OVERTURE, AND MORE

JON KEEL has developed a local, national, and international reputation as a performance-based online marketing expert, having been actively involved in this arena since January 1997. In addition to working with Improved Results, he codeveloped the Xavier University MBA e-Business program, where he taught online marketing and e-commerce for over three years.

FOR MORE INFORMATION: http://www.improved-results.com

INTRODUCTION

Pay-Per-Click (PPC) search engines came on the scene in early 1998 with the advent of GoTo.com (now known as Overture.com). They caught on as a method of quickly generating targeted traffic to your Web site. Today there are well over 500 PPCs on the market, although Overture and Google AdWords are the two major players.

HOW DOES PPC WORK?

With PPCs, you bid on keywords that are relevant to your Web site's content. Along with each keyword on which you bid, you create a title and description (think of this as a classified ad headline and description).

In general, your position on the PPC is determined by your bid price (the exception is with Google AdWords, where your position is determined by a combination of your bid price and your click-through rate, which is the percentage of times that people click through on your listing compared to the number of times people type in your keyword term). You pay only when a visitor clicks through on your listing, hence the term, *pay-per-click*.

You can generally change your position upwards or downwards by changing your bid price. This provides a real time auction type of format in that you can quickly adjust your position by modifying your bid. As noted above, with Google AdWords, you can also affect your position by varying your title and description to obtain a higher click-through rate (it's actually possible to pay less than advertisers listed below you if you have a higher click-through rate).

To control your advertising expense, you can fix the amount of money you want to invest by setting a daily budget amount. This prevents you from overspending for your PPC advertising.

Depending upon which PPC you use, you can increase the exposure your listing has for a much greater viewing audience than those that just use the particular PPC on which you're bidding. As an example, Overture and Google AdWords have both done great jobs at getting their results syndicated across the Internet. In other words, if you generally are in the top three positions for a given keyword at both Overture and Google, you have immediate presence across many other search engines and Internet properties, places where people are going—places where people will see your search engine listing.

TRAFFIC VERSUS CONVERSION

While PPCs were originally envisioned as a way to obtain high volumes of targeted traffic, over the past several years they have proven to be an accurate method of determining which keywords will actually convert for your Web site.

What is conversion and why is this important? Conversion is the number of "calls to action" that visitors take as a percentage of the total visitors who visit your Web site. For example, if you're selling a product and 1 out of 100 visitors purchase your product, your sales conversion is 1 percent.

WHY IS THIS IMPORTANT?

If you send nonconverting traffic to your site, you'll only have traffic, you won't have new business. In other words, the Web site traffic "game" involves not only getting the right kind of visitors to your site (targeted traffic), but getting those visitors to do what it is you want them to do (take a call to action as noted above). Examples of calls to action are: 1) to buy what you're selling, 2) to opt-in to your prospect follow-up process, or 3) to give you their contact information for your subsequent online or offline follow-up, etc.

If you can determine which keywords actually convert to calls to action on your Web site *and* you know the value of those calls to action, you can determine the return on investment for those keywords. It is important to know which keywords don't convert for your Web site. This is a businessperson's dream—to know which advertising actually works and which doesn't work, and then to know the return on investment for the advertising that works.

A friend once said it this way, "If you knew that for every $1 you invested in advertising you'd get back $4 in revenue, how much would you invest in advertising?" Conversely, if you knew that for every $1 you invested in advertising, you received less than $1, why would you continue to spend money in that kind of advertising?

One other serendipity that results from determining the converting keywords is tied in to organic search engine marketing, or optimization. Historical search engine marketing has paid no attention to keywords that actually convert for a Web site, probably because a method never existed to determine those keywords. It has focused solely on the most popular keywords and the competitive nature of those keywords on the organic search engines. However, if you knew the keywords that actually converted to calls to action for your site, why wouldn't you use those same keywords in your organic search engine marketing efforts?

HOW TO DETERMINE
THE CONVERTING KEYWORDS

How do you determine which keywords convert to your desired calls to action?

Think of each keyword as an individual advertisement for your Web site. You can use special ad tracking software that allows you to put tracking code on your Web site. When a visitor clicks on a specific keyword and then clicks on the desired call to action on your Web site, the software measures this action. You then know that the specific keyword led to the desired call to action.

Following this thought, for each keyword in a PPC campaign, you can determine four metrics:

1. Cost per visitor (the cost per click)
2. Cost per prospect (the cost of an opt-in)
3. Cost per customer (the cost of an order)
4. Value per visitor (the value of an order divided by the number of visitors it takes to get the order)

Once you know the value per visitor and the cost per visitor, you can answer the question my friend asked, and you can do it for each individual keyword on which you're bidding.

HOW DO YOU DO IT?

What is the PPC process? Understand that this process works regardless of which PPC you use. At the same time, I recommend beginning the process with both Overture and Google as they represent at least 90 percent of the available PPC traffic on the market. Additionally, they both draw from different types of audiences given that their results are shown in different search engines. You may find, as our experience shows, that you'll achieve different results (or metrics) with Overture and Google, or you will find that different keywords convert differently (I believe because of the different audiences that see their results).

Here are the eight steps you want to follow to ensure you get the best results from PPCs and are able to determine the individual keyword conversion for your Web site:

1. Set your goal. Think of your PPC campaign as a test. What results do you want to achieve? How much money do you want to invest to determine the converting keywords for your site? I generally recommend that you generate at least 2,000 to 3,000 click-throughs to your site to get statistically relevant results. Depending upon the number of keywords you're testing, this should give you enough traffic to determine how your Web site converts and which keywords are working for you. Note that if you use a large list of keywords you may want to generate more traffic to get reliable results.

2. Select your keywords. I recommend starting with a list of at least 100 keywords. If you can develop a larger list, that's probably better. Why? At the beginning of your PPC "test," you don't know which keywords will convert for your site. You may think you know, but the only way of actually determining which keywords "work" for your Web site is to generate traffic and measure the results. Your opinion really doesn't count.

Your chances of determining the correct keywords are much better the larger the list you have. Some free resources you can use to build your list include: Inventory.Overture.com and GoodKeywords.com. Google AdWords also has a useful tool, although it's better for determining similar keywords to those you're considering.

3. Set up your individual keyword tracking. Both Overture and Google AdWords give you free tools with which to track individual keywords. One limitation of both of their systems is that they allow you to track only one call to action; however, you may have two or more calls to action for your Web site.

At the same time, it's a good method to get started. As you gain more experience with individual keyword tracking, consider other paid alternatives. When you get to the point of wanting more robust tools, search on Google (or your search engine of choice) for "ad tracking software" to look at alternatives that might be appropriate for your situation.

4. Set up your bids. The easiest way to do this is to develop an Excel spreadsheet with the following columns: Keyword, Overture title, Overture description, Google title, and Google description. Google and Overture are separated in the spreadsheet as they allow different character limits (this means you can't necessarily use the same title and description for a keyword at Google that you can at Overture. Overture gives you a little more flexibility as of this writing. I always recommend you review both Overture and Google for their latest information and guidelines).

Set up your accounts at both Overture and Google. For Overture, go to http://www.overture.com and click through to "Precision Match" (Overture offers various advertising solutions and Precision Match is where you'll want to start). For Google AdWords, go to http://www.adwords .google.com.

Once you open your accounts, submit your bids. Start at $.10 per click at Overture and $.05 per click at Google (at the time of this writing) to get started. You can always adjust your bids later. With Google, your bids will be live in several minutes. With Overture, it will take several days, because Overture's editors want to review your bids for compliance with its bid policies.

5. Measure traffic and individual keyword conversion. Overture and Google give you reporting tools to measure your traffic by keyword. Presuming you're using their keyword conversion tools, start seeing which keywords are beginning to convert. Depending on the per-click pricing you're seeing, I recommend you check several times a day for the first several days so you stay on top of things. You'll probably find that you need to adjust your bids upwards in order to gain your desired position and click-throughs.

Here's an important note: So that you don't spend more for advertising than you've budgeted, initially set your daily bid amounts conservatively. It's much better to have your traffic stopped because your account has zeroed out than to spend hundreds of dollars (or more) in advertising before you know which keywords are converting.

6. Eliminate your nonconverting keywords. After you've seen several hundred click-throughs to your site, you should be able to see which keywords are and are not converting. Rather than continue to spend advertising dollars on keywords that don't convert (you may be surprised at which keywords convert and which don't convert for your Web site), eliminate or disable the nonconverting keywords. You can always go back and retest nonconverting keywords, but for now you want to focus on the keywords that do work.

7. Optimize your click-throughs. This is one of the real advantages of Google AdWords. You can run several ads side by side to see which title and description give you the highest percentage click through.

As noted above, this is particularly important with Google AdWords as your final per-click price is somewhat determined by the click-through percentage. There are several good paid courses available that will give you terrific information on how to complete this process. Search at Google for "Google AdWords course" for the latest information.

8. Optimize your bids for converting keywords. Once you know your converting keywords, you can optimize your bid position (by changing your bid price) to see if a higher or lower position gives you a higher conversion or more traffic, or both. You'll ultimately find that for each individual keyword you'll find an optimum bid price and position that gives you the highest return on investment (ROI) or net profit possible.

To tie all of this together, let's review an example. To simplify things, we'll assume you're only using one keyword. The analysis is the same regardless of how may keywords you use.

Your testing has shown the following results for your selected keyword:

- 200 click-throughs
- Total click-through cost of $60
- 20 opt-ins (for example, visitors who have given you their name and e-mail address in exchange for a free report that you offer at your Web site)
- Two sales with total revenue of $200

You determine your site metrics as follows:

- Cost per visitor is the click-through cost / click throughs = $60/200 = $.30/visitor.
- Cost per prospect is the click-through cost / number of opt-ins = $60/20 = $3/prospect.
- Cost per customer is the click-through cost / number of customers = $60/2 = $30/customer.
- Value per visitor is the total revenue (or other financial measure you use) / Click-throughs = $200/200 = $1/visitor.

Let's assume you've previously decided that you'll invest up to 50 percent of your revenue to acquire a customer.

With your testing results, you now know that you can vary your bidding between $.30 (the bidding results you've found so far) and $.50 to either make it tougher for your competition or to try to maximize your position to get more orders.

Here's another thought. Let's say that with the same data from above, you want to set up an affiliate program or go to potential joint-venture partners to generate additional business. The fact that you know through actual testing your value per visitor is $1 makes you a much more attractive potential partner than someone who doesn't know their metrics.

You can state with assurance to these potential partners that you might be able to pay them up to $.50 for each visitor they send you, presuming the visitors they send are similar to the visitors you've seen from your PPC results. The fact is that most people on the Internet today don't know their metrics; you've got a potential significant competitive edge on your competitors who might want to talk to the same potential partners.

SUMMARY

Pay-per-click search engines offer you a method not only to quickly attract targeted visitors to your Web site, but a way to determine the metrics for your Web site. Properly used, PPCs can tell you if your product or service offering will be attractive to your target market. And, if your preliminary results aren't what you want or need, they allow you a way to make whatever changes need to be made to your Web site and continue to quickly retest until you achieve your desired results.

They also allow you a method to determine which keywords "work" for your Web site. Armed with this information, you can expand your online advertising to organic search engines, which, in the long run, can give you consistent volumes of targeted traffic.

The process I've outlined is the same eight-step process I've used with over 200 clients to help them use PPCs to generate targeted traffic to their Web sites and define their individual keyword metrics.

And by the way, every test doesn't lead to results that warrant further use of PPCs. Sometimes the numbers just don't work. Even after you retest and retest. If this happens for you, understand that it's still a successful test . . . the numbers just didn't work. It's the same in any business; every idea doesn't always work.

Given the time-sensitive nature of business today, you need to be able to move fast, to make decisions quickly. You'll find that using PPCs will let you determine the economics of your online venture in just weeks. If PPCs show that your site metrics work, you can expand your efforts "now" and gain a competitive advantage. If PPCs show that your site metrics don't work, you can move on to explore other alternatives and let your competitors waste their time exploring ideas that you know don't work.

At the end of the day business is about just that—gaining a sustainable competitive advantage. Armed with the knowledge you gain from PPCs, you'll always be making informed, business decisions.

14

DEARL MILLER
ADVANCED TRAFFIC STRATEGIES

DEARL MILLER is creator of the *7 Most Powerful Web Traffic Creation & Conversion Tactics* and editor of the Web traffic industry journal, *Trafficology*. He has spent the past eight years helping small businesses, entrepreneurs, and nonprofit organizations use the Internet to compete with (and triumph over) even their biggest competition. Currently, Dearl specializes in using "The Science of Web Traffic" to transform money-losing sites into million-dollar profit centers in 60 days or less.

FOR MORE INFORMATION: http://www.onlinetrafficnow.com

In This Chapter You Will Learn:

- The Science of Traffic

- The Four Types of Web Traffic

- Seven Online and Offline Traffic Strategies

WEB TRAFFIC IS A SCIENCE

Web traffic is a science. It is not magic; it is not a trick; it is not a secret. There is a set of fundamental laws and underlying principles that govern why people visit a site and make a purchase online. We call that science *trafficology*, and the sole purpose of OnlineTrafficNow.com is to teach you that science.

Let's evaluate the alternatives to learning the art of this Web traffic science:

- You could use "tricks," but most new tricks cease to work a couple weeks after invention, and many will actually hurt your business.
- You can hire someone or "buy" traffic, but if you don't hire the right person or buy the right traffic all you have done is thrown your money away—plus you still have to convince your visitors to buy.

If you want people to come to your site and buy your product or service, you need to know who they are, what they want, and how to effectively communicate why they should purchase your product or service.

No program or trick can do that. And most "experts" have no idea how to do it either!

You can do better, you can use Web traffic science!

When you start to look at things from a scientific perspective, you begin to understand why things work and how to do things better. Think about other sciences. When you have a heart attack, do you see a hocus-pocus witch doctor or a highly-educated medical doctor? You go to the hospital and see someone who understands what is happening and what you need to do to survive.

It's the same way with Web traffic.

You can't risk your financial future on tricks and gimmicks. You must use sound Web traffic fundamentals to build a consistent flow of traffic, apply time-tested Web conversion techniques to complete the sale, and create another satisfied customer.

It is up to you—science or voodoo? Choose, but choose wisely!

THE FOUR TYPES OF WEB TRAFFIC

1. *People who found your Web site by mistake.* They have no desire for what your product or service does. For these people, the only way you can help them is by clearly stating what you do have, so that you do not waste their time or your money. Also, by clearly stating what you offer, you plant in their mind your "brand." So, if they ever have a need for your product in the future, they will come back.

2. *People who have a desire, but don't know what fills it and may not be ready for a solution.* It is your job to grab their attention and clearly explain what your product or service does to fill their desire. Not only do you have to sell your brand of the product, but you also have to explain how this type of product actually does what they want.

3. *People who have a desire, know what type of thing fills it, and are evaluating alternative solutions.* These are people who know that your type of product is what they want, but are comparison-shopping the different brands. It is your job to clearly explain why they want your brand more—and how you do a better job at filling their want.

4. *People who have a desire, know exactly what fills it, and have their credit card in hand.* These are people who are already sold on your product. You just need to make everything easy to find and help them check out as quickly as possible. We call them "Targeted Web Traffic."

Of this last group, targeted traffic (people who know exactly what they want, have their credit card out, and are ready to spend online), still only completes the sale 30 percent of the time.

Seven out of every ten people who want to spend money on a product you are selling leave your site unsatisfied.

Unbelievable, but true.

HOW TO FIND THE CUSTOMERS THAT WILL GIVE YOU MONEY

So now you are asking, "How do I get people to buy my product online?"

It is not hard. Now that we know the different types of Web traffic, we know where to concentrate our efforts:

- Bring more targeted traffic to your Web site.
- Improve your sale processes to increase conversion (turn browsers into buyers).

We next review seven easy ways you can draw massive amounts of targeted traffic to your Web site in record time.

ONLINE TRAFFIC STRATEGIES

1. Getting Your Site Listed in the Search Engines

Search engines are a powerful traffic creation resource. It's estimated that 85 percent of all online sales start with search engines. Furthermore, people who find your site via the search engines are already interested in what you sell and are actively looking for more information on your topic.

Bottom line: Search engines are the biggest pool of the highly targeted Web traffic you will ever find. But, I am sure you have already found that getting them to send you traffic is not an easy chore.

It used to be that a legitimate business could make a good living by putting up a nice site and submitting to a few search engines. Somewhere along the way, spammers got involved—the same people who are filling your e-mail box every day with offers for drugs and other services you don't want. These shady characters realized they could make money by tricking the search engines and the people using them.

The search engines fought back. In an attempt to stay ahead of the spammers, they constantly change how they rank Web sites. Now it is harder for everyone to optimize their site. You have to be very careful not to do something that will get you penalized, and every time the search engines change you need to reoptimize your site.

Additionally, the big companies saw online sales opportunities and hired full-time search engine optimizers. Many small companies are also having their site professionally optimized. This means there is more competition for the best keywords and that optimization is even more difficult for the "little guy."

The #1 key to search engine optimization. The number one factor in search engine optimization is the keywords you choose to optimize for. You need to focus on what I call the "best keywords."

The best keywords are the emotional, benefit-filled terms that have such things as the following: the most number of searches; the least amount of competition; and that draw targeted traffic that is ready, willing, and able to spend money on your product or service.

To find the best keywords, you need to:

- Focus on the wants and desires of your customers.
- Research the terms using the free tools found at http://www .trafficology.com/research/.
- Test your keyword conversion using a small Google AdWords campaign.

This process helps you determine the exact phrases that draw the most visitors to your site who will buy your product or service. These are the terms you need to optimize your Web site for. Using others will be a waste of your time and financial resources, and will hurt your ranking for the terms that do draw targeted traffic.

I cannot emphasize the importance of keyword research enough. Do not continue until you have found at least 20 to 30 of the most popular, least competitive phrases that relate to your product or service.

Keywords are the foundation of every online marketing technique. Taking the time now to find your keywords will mean the difference between success and failure online.

You may be asking, "Now that I have my keywords, how do I optimize my Web site for search engines?"

There are two things you need to understand about search engines:

1. They all have a different way of ranking the exact same page.
2. They don't want you to know what their way is.

As a result we must rely on testing (trial and error) to find out what works and what doesn't. When you combine this with the fact that all the search engines constantly change the way they rank pages, it is very difficult to keep up.

The first step in search engine optimization should be building good pages that your visitors will like. This is not rocket science, just common sense. If you build a page that users want to see, then the search engines will find you and rank you. This is why keywords are so important.

If you know what keywords people are typing in who want to buy your product, then you are more than halfway done.

Here is another thing to remember about search engine optimization: Other than picking the best keywords, there is no single thing that you can do to dramatically improve your ranking.

The search engines use many factors when ranking your site. The key is to understand what those factors are and then tweak your content-rich "good pages" for those factors.

Look at it this way—half the work is getting the best keywords, the rest is creating good pages and tweaking them for the different search engines. Sure, there are many tricks out there—but tricks don't last. And as every search engine optimizer has found out, it is only a matter of time until the search engines make your trick useless (or worse).

You can't build a sound business on the traffic from tricks. If you are serious about being successful, take the time to learn the methods of how search engines rank your site. Then build a quality site that provides good content and takes into account the many different factors search engines use to rank your site.

So what are the factors?

The search engines keep their criteria a secret; each search engine has different criteria, and they all change their criteria on a regular basis.

Here are the ten most important factors to focus on when optimizing your Web page:

1. Have a unique title for every page.
2. Make your title something that describes the benefits you provide and the wants you fulfill.
3. Use keywords in your title (not repeatedly).
4. Get a domain name with your keywords in it.
5. Use the <h1> & <h2> tags and put your keywords in them.
6. Put your keywords in the text that is linked to your subpages.
7. Use your keywords in the copy text on your Web site, and make them bold in a couple of places.
8. Include your keywords at the very top and very bottom of your Web page.
9. Include your keywords in the ALT attribute of your <IMG> tag.
10. Include your keywords in the TITLE attribute of your <A> tag.

If you have the right keywords, if you have created a clean Web page with good content, and if you have followed the other things listed above, you will do fine in the search engines.

Here are seven things you must make sure you *never* do:

1. Do not try to trick the search engines.
2. Do not repeat your keywords over and over again. Use your keywords in a natural sentence and where it seems appropriate. Overusing keywords is called "spamming" or "stuffing," and the search engines hate spam, too.
3. Do not try to hide your keywords.
4. Do not use frames.
5. Do not use flash for your whole site (some flash is ok, but not for your entire site).
6. Do not include words in your images.
7. Do not use too much JavaScript (put it in an external file if you do).

You may ask, "Ok, now that I have optimized my page, how do I get into the major search engines?"

Before we address that question, we need to identify who are the major search engines. An estimated 95 percent of all Web traffic originates from the following handful of sources:

- Google
- Overture
- Inktomi
- AltaVista
- Open Directory Project
- AlltheWeb
- Lycos
- Yahoo
- LookSmart
- AskJeeves
- MSN

How to get listed in the major search engines. The best way to get listed in the major search engines is to have a link from a site that is already listed. When the search engine checks the links on that site, it will visit your site and include you in their search results.

If you have a site that sells a good product or has some good content, it is very easy to get someone to link to you. Just go to your favorite search engine (like Google) and search for something related to your product or service, or your town. Then e-mail them asking for a link exchange.

For example, say you sell golf equipment. Do a search for golf courses in your area. Then e-mail or call the Web master and offer to put a link on your Web site if they put your link on their site. Then in 30 to 60 days you should see your site in the search engines. (Note: You no longer have to wait 30 to 60 days. By using an advanced strategy known as RSS, you can get your site listed in both Yahoo and Google in less than 48 hours).

Some search engines charge fees to be included, for example, Overture. They are completely pay-per-click, so you will only be included if you pay. Sure, you will be listed within days, but it will cost you cash.

Other search engines have what they call the "express inclusion service." Basically you pay them a fee, and they will make sure you are listed within a week.

The search engines are a powerful Web traffic tool. As we have shown, they are an important part of drawing paying customers to your Web site. With a little bit of effort and a lot of studying, you can make the search engines work for you.

2. Links

Quality inbound links help you in two ways. First, they provide a way for Web traffic to find you while surfing online, and, second, they improve your search engine rankings.

Here are a few tips on how to rapidly increase the number of links to your site:

Approach sites that link to competitors. If a site is currently linking to the site of a direct competitor, there is a very good chance they will also link to you. You just have to ask them and agree to link back.

To find Web sites that link to your competitors, do the following:

1. Go to http://www.google.com.
2. Enter: link:www.competitor.com (the URL of your competitor).
3. Press the search button.
4. Contact these Web sites.

You can do the same thing faster if you use a linking tool such as Zeus, Arelis, or Link Spider (http://www.Axandra.com, http://www.scamfreezone.com/spider/).

Enter the URL of your competitor and the software program will present you a list of all pages that link to that competitor. You can also e-mail these Web sites directly from Arelis.

If you set aside an hour or so every week for this traffic technique, it will certainly increase the traffic and the search engine rankings of your site dramatically.

Easy way to quickly boost your link popularity. Most of the major search engines are tracking the link popularity of the sites they list. One particular search engine might find 500 links to your site and another one might also find 500 links, but they are *not necessarily* the same 500 links.

Link popularity is especially important at Google. It is very important that Google be aware of all sites linking to you. One way to do that would be to resubmit to Google all the sites that link to you, one at a time, but that would take forever.

Here is a trick: Search for links to your site at AltaVista and HotBot using this query: link:www.OnlineTrafficNow.com *and/or* link:http://www.onlinetrafficnow.com (make sure you insert your own URLs, of course!).

Set the preferences on each search engine to list as many links per page as possible. Copy the URL of the search results page and paste that entire URL into the Google site submission page.

Then click the "Next" button on the search engine results page to get another page with sites that link to your site. Copy and paste that URL to the Google submission bar. Repeat until you have submitted the URLs of all the search results pages from AltaVista and HotBot to Google. Google will spider those pages and find all the sites linking to your site.

You can find out how many links to your site Google is aware of by searching for "link:www"(your URL).

I've used this technique successfully several times and one reader who tried it reported, "I had 626 links at Google two weeks ago. After submitting those search engine pages, I now have almost 1,500!"

3. Promoting Your Online Business Using Articles

The ultimate traffic creation method for someone on a shoestring budget is online articles.

The idea is to write an information-packed article on a topic that directly relates to your product or service. In the article you explain how to do something or provide a list of tips. At the bottom of the article explain how your product or service is connected to the topic of the article with a link to your Web site.

Next, disseminate your article to various online and offline newsletters and magazines that are related to what you have written. A way to get your articles in the hands of publishers is by submitting your writings to free online articles sites. You can use software that will send articles to e-zine editors directly or you can hire a service.

Hiring a service is very inexpensive, often sending your article to more than 1,000 e-zine publishers and costing you less than $20.

If your article is interesting and well written, newsletters and magazines will publish your article. Their readers will visit your site and purchase your product.

4. Use Your Sig File

Your Signature File, or Sig File, is a few lines of text that is automatically added to the bottom of every e-mail you send. This is a simple, effective, and free way to tell people about your Web site.

Your sig file should be as short as possible, creating a sense of curiosity and encouraging people to visit your site. One technique is to ask a question that can only be answered by visiting your Web site. Here are a couple of examples:

Free Report—Top Ten Web Traffic Tips
http://www.OnlineTrafficNow.com

How to Get Ranked First in Google
http://www.OnlineTrafficNow.com

Use your top keywords and give a compelling, benefit-filled reason why the reader should visit your Web site.

This simple yet effective marketing technique is very easy to set up. Every e-mail program is different, so check out your program's help section for exactly how to set it up for your e-mail.

Note: One advanced technique is to add a graphic to your sig file. This can be anything from a little smiley face to a full-blown banner-ad–like graphic. Doing this will cause your sig file to stand out and has been proven to increase the traffic from sig files.

5. Discussion Boards and Newsgroups

Discussion boards and newsgroup participation can produce a steady flow of highly-targeted, no-cost Web traffic.

If you are on a tight budget but have some spare time, this is a good way to essentially trade your time for money. All you do is find the online groups that best match the topic of your site. Then you make intelligent, useful contributions to the group. It can be anything from answering other people's questions on topics you are an expert on, to providing your opinion on the future of your industry.

There are thousands of newsgroups on virtually any topic imaginable. To find the group that best matches the topic of your Web site, just do a search online or visit GoogleGroups at http://www.google.com /groups.

Now, the way to get traffic from these groups is with your sig file. Many discussion boards have an automatic sig file option similar to the one described above. If you find a discussion board that does provide you with an automatic sig file, just add yours in by hand.

A word of warning: Do not just post a link to your site or an advertisement for your company in the newsgroups and discussion boards. That will get you banned and possibly spammed by other disgruntled group members. The point is to provide an intelligent contribution to the group's conversation. If you have something useful to add, by all means post your comments and add your sig file at the bottom.

Note: You may want to focus your efforts on the most popular groups related to your site. Fortunately, Google has added an "activity" bar that lets you know just how much traffic each newsgroup gets. That's enough to keep you busy for a while!

6. OnlineTrafficNow's Tell-a-Friend Script

Fifty-three percent of online visitors went to a site a friend or relative told them about in the past 30 days. You can increase the chances of someone telling their friends and relatives about your site by implementing a "tell-a-friend" script.

My "refer-a-friend" script *is* one of the best marketing tools I've ever used.

The basic idea is that visitors will enter the name and e-mail address of friends and relatives they think will be interested in your site. Then, the script automatically sends a personalized e-mail promoting your site to all their friends from the visitor.

To get the best results from your tell-a-friend script, you'll want to make your visitors an offer like this: "If you'll refer our site to your friends, we'll give you a free. . . ." (You have to fill in the blank, of course).

It's an amazingly simple tool, but it's a terrific way to virally grow an e-zine or other online business.

If you want to spend a few hours setting up your own tell-a-friend script, you can easily find one for free by searching online. If you'd rather just spend $5 a month, the following sites offer an easy to use tell-a-friend service (and they both have a free trial):

- http://www.tell-a-friend-wizard.com/
- http://www.tell-a-friend-king.com/

7. Unused Real Estate—Thank-You Pages or Confirmation Pages

Do you have a contact form on your Web site? You know, one of those fill-in-the-box forms where people leave their comments or ask you a question. After visitors click on the "Submit" button, they are usually taken to a thank-you page. And this page usually just says "Thank you. . . ."

Foreclose on this piece of property and post some useful information. You could ask people to sign up for your newsletter, you could post affiliate links to other sites their customers may be interested in, or inform them of a product that you have on sale.

What about the order confirmation page, the page that people see after they have placed an order?

It is a fact that people who have just ordered are the hottest prospects you can get. Use that space on the order confirmation page to promote a related product—either yours or an affiliate link for someone else's products.

CONCLUSION

The single most important factor in the success of every online business is your ability to draw a steady flow of highly-targeted traffic to your site. At first, bringing visitors to your site may seem to be a trick or a secret, but it's not. Trafficology, the science of Web traffic creation and conversion, is the proven way to create traffic that is ready, willing, and able to buy your product or service online.

I hope you take a few minutes today to apply the lessons you've just discovered. When you are ready to learn more Web traffic tips, tactics, and techniques, check out http://www.onlinetrafficnow.com. There you will find over 500 innovative and unique ideas to help you create a massive amount of Web traffic in record time.

15

MARTIN WALES
PUBLICITY FOR YOUR
ONLINE SUCCESS

MARTIN WALES has been helping organizations and sales professionals get more customers and close bigger business for more than ten
years. Through his vast experience as a corporate marketing executive
and respected radio and television personality, Martin has advised thousands through training, private coaching sessions, and media. Martin's
business columns are published internationally and as curriculum content for several MBA programs. He also hosts the very popular Entrepreneur e-biz show on wsRadio.com.

FOR MORE INFORMATION: http://www.customercatcherradio.com

In This Chapter You Will Learn:

- How to Start Your Free Media Blitz

- How to Win Expert Status

- The Power of Online PR

- How to Create Your Own PBS

PUBLICITY FOR YOUR ONLINE SUCCESS

You can get millions in media exposure *without* spending $5,000 per month and up on a public relations (PR) agency or even more on advertising. If you want your online business to prosper and profit, then master publicity. With publicity, you can easily position yourself as the expert in your market, win public recognition and respect, and turn the almighty credibility you earn into cash! By modeling proven techniques, all these benefits and more can be yours without spending thousands of dollars on riskier forms of marketing. Being in the press, while also producing your *own* media, attracts the best customers who seek you, trust you, and buy from you!

Online consumers buy from someone they believe is trustworthy. To gain that trust you should position yourself as a recognized industry specialist and recommended resource. It's the *combination* of effective online and offline public relations and publicity that rapidly creates and continuously affirms your credibility and buyers' confidence.

Beyond the mass media of TV, radio, and newspapers, think of the Internet as *your personal media machine.* The Internet lets you cheaply and quickly produce your own far-reaching, broadcast network. Your communications develop what I call "Media Magnetism." With this, you acquire that level of trust to decrease buying resistance, close more sales and larger transactions, and increase customer confidence and loyalty. And like magic, your media efforts gain momentum to attract additional exposure. For example, many TV producers find guests by scanning the newspapers and online media.

MEDIA MEANS MONEY!

While some pay huge sums for media exposure and advertising, I've obtained literally millions of dollars in *free* marketing for myself and my clients by using a combination of online and offline tactics. You can too! Free PR and publicity multiplies Web traffic and e-commerce activity. Companies pay $5,000 to $40,000 for full-page ads, as listed and sold from magazine rate cards. Why not occupy that same space without spending a penny? When you master PR, you accomplish two objectives: You save money *and* you control the message and your positioning in your industry or market.

The public (your prospect pool) form opinions, positive or negative, based on what they hear and see in print, on television, and on the radio. When you recognize the importance of media attention and harness PR power, you'll boost recognition and revenue. Using positive media is a potent competitive advantage in the digital world. I repeat that it's the credibility and social proof of the media, when presented throughout your online sales process. Done correctly, you proactively make media work for you to increase site traffic, conversion rates, and sales, while also saving a ton of money!

How do you start your free media blitz? The possibilities are endless, but these recommended tactics are quick and effective:

- First, don't wait around for the media to find you. Produce your own media. Creating your own newsletter, e-zine, and audio and video material help the traditional press find you. To begin, it's easiest to be quoted in or write articles for lesser-known and smaller industry-focused trade magazines. I call this "shooting rabbits while you hunt moose." Apply to be listed as an expert through PRNewswire .com or similar services that media members use to source comments and analysis of current events.

- Take the names of local reporters and columnists and send them an e-mail or call them. Compile an e-mail broadcast list for sending digital releases.

- Exhibit your expertise by writing articles for online publications and upload them to automated, e-zine syndication sites such as EzineArticles.com. Seek advice at Ezine-Tips.com and EzineQueen .com. A bonus from syndication sites is distributing content full of hotlinks back to your sites to build site traffic and search engine ranking!

- In your article's bylines include an e-mail address, preferably to an autoresponder (visit EasyWebAutomation.com) that *automatically* captures information and sends a series of e-mails with content and strategic links. Always ask to have your picture included. Online, e-zines allow readers to click your URL instantly. However, print maintains an edge for "perceived" credibility.

- Get yourself on radio, TV, and in print. An immediate yet overlooked tactic is to just *call* talk radio shows and mention your URL while introducing yourself. Seek invitations to guest by calling the shows' producers with your pitch.

- Be prepared. Have articles ready and a list of interview questions for the media written ahead of time. My producers and I often book guests right up to show time, when others fail to appear.
- A fast growing media format online is Internet radio. While I host a "traditionally" broadcast business talk radio show in one city, I also host two Internet radio shows, *CustomerCatcherRadio.com* and *The ENTREPRENEUR Magazine E-Biz Show,* which are available around the world! The journey to being a host began with offering a business article to a magazine that also had a radio show. *Tip:* Pick your media strategically. Hosting is not for everyone but the payback is tremendous. Having your name linked to radio shows, with your picture, name, and brand displayed in full-page magazine ads and aired on numerous commercials every week (that you don't pay for!), provides immense credibility and positioning.
- Internet radio (like wsRadio.com) is excellent for niche markets that couldn't feasibly support an audience for traditional radio in any single city, like motorbike enthusiasts or pet fish owners. Plus, your customers can listen any time and click on links to your site or directly to online order forms *while they listen!* A live feed on radio or TV is heard only when it's live and is not clickable. Internet media you produce empowers your market to pick when and what *they* want to listen to. This gives you additional leverage by extending the geography of your audience, and recycling your content and lengthening its "shelf-life" and marketing effectiveness.
- With the growth of Internet and satellite radio (as the public avoids advertising) your content could be syndicated to promote your business! Internet radio won personal recognition for me from the author of *Permission Marketing,* Seth Godin, and a page in his book, *Bull Marketers of 2004.*
- You might consider hosting radio or TV "segments." These minute-long fillers on regional business shows make perfect Web content, too. See segment examples at http://www.CustomerCatcher.tv taken from my television spot called *Business Break.* You'd pay a fortune to produce this professional video and buy the airtime, but if you volunteer to host you don't spend any of your own capital.
- Hosting gives you *access.* Phone calls are returned and you get to speak with top management, business gurus, and even celebrities! You have PR agents and publicists calling *you* to set up conversa-

tions with your best prospects! My role as a radio host exposes me to fantastic contacts, major centers of influence, celebrities, and larger corporate clients, all while heightening my public profile and personal branding.

- Produce content for your Web site when you speak at a seminar or workshop by capturing it on audio and video. Place clips on sites to add to your credibility and trust building. This personal media is powerful for substantiating your positioning! At events, use PowerPoint presentations and handouts to showcase your Web pages and direct attendees to your sites.

- Recognize alternative methods for exposure, aside from media. *Tip:* Host a chamber of commerce panel and get your picture and URLs included in all event marketing. Even the people who do not attend are introduced to you!

- For the full story on *How You Can Get $4 Million in Free Publicity in a Single Year—Without Writing a Single Press Release!* send a blank e-mail to PR@CustomerCatcher.com.

Gaining both online and offline exposure for yourself and your URLs starts relationships with highly-qualified prospects. Media is a powerful endorsement, with implied third-party credibility, and it legitimizes your expertise and what you offer.

EXPOSE YOURSELF!

Free media coverage is a great way to get your name out to the public and build your credibility. There are no agency fees if you do it yourself, but it does require an investment of your time, focus, and effort. There are many tactics to generate free media coverage, aside from getting arrested by the FBI for embezzling company funds and doing the "handcuff march" on the evening news. Paying a professional PR agency can be appropriate if there's a budget for it and if they have industry relationships and immediate access.

The more positive and frequent your public exposure, the more prosperity you'll claim. People love the familiar so accumulated and continuous exposure, no matter how small, enhances your profile. Use your published articles, screen captures of your TV appearances, and audio clips of your radio interviews (or entire shows) as Web content. Turn your media copies into direct mail pieces to send with your latest promotion or downloadable Adobe PDFs from your Web pages. Weave them all into concrete credibility in your target market.

Finally, while using media to convert prospects is effective, you can also face competition and protect your market share. Remind current customers that their decision to work and stay with you was the right one. Reinforce this by sending them copies, or links, to your latest media attention.

HOW TO WIN EXPERT STATUS IN YOUR MARKET

Positioning yourself and actually becoming an expert in your market requires time, patience, and personal confidence. Knowing you're an expert in your field isn't enough. You need to let the public know that you are! Use these tips and tactics to successfully reach expert status:

- *Use the media to build a personal brand.* Act as an "ambassador" for your industry by participating in associations or lobbying the government.
- *Build a PR campaign* not only around your product or product features, but related to current events, community support, unique marketing campaigns, and awards you win.
- *Publish your knowledge.* Publishing your knowledge, already covered above, has several advantages for your online positioning strategy. It puts you in the position of industry expert merely by your presence while contributing to your personal brand recognition. Keep in mind magazines that have both offline and online publications are excellent for inviting prospects to your Web site.
- *Be daring and take risks.* Take a stand, or opinion, in a respectful debate to win recognition and respect for your leadership.
- *Finally, don't always stick to convention just because the business market dictates certain protocols.* Check out Raleigh Pinskey's book, *101 Ways to Promote Yourself,* at PromoteYourself.com, and George McKenzie's site called PublicityGoldmine.com.

Remember, it's the *combination* of media and marketing that really communicates the benefits and unique aspects of your business and attracts customers to your Web site.

ONLINE PR POWER

Public relations online is powerful for three reasons:

1. *Accessibility.* The online population is massive and still growing. They use the Internet for research and you can easily provide valuable, relevant content. Your Search Engine Optimization (SEO) is important here.
2. *Affordability.* Using free press release services online works within any budget. Select small, tightly targeted releases within a niche or industry.
3. *Internet leverage.* The Internet deals with facts and information without focusing on the size or prestige of your company. Potential customers are using the Internet for research and obtaining knowledge.

Consider using an online press release service, such as www.PRWeb .com to garner interest. Your press release, whether printed, faxed, or digital, must be well written and distributed appropriately for it to work. Most companies alert the public about a new product or new service they offer. These releases, while informative, are dry and quickly ignored. In fact, the bottom line is "If it's not *news*-worthy then you won't be selected for attention." Think of what each media channel's audience wants to hear, see, or read.

While composing your online releases, keep in mind the value of using highly relevant keywords often to benefit from SEO. Including live links stimulates more traffic and higher Page Rank (PR) in the search engines. Your publicity and PR shouldn't rely solely on press releases. If you want more help with your digital press releases, I refer you to B. L. Ochman at WhatsNextOnline.com.

Place a "media room" in your site's menu to serve reporters, columnists, producers, and editors. Utilize audio or video clips for variety.

There is so much written word on the Internet, try other formats to ensure your messages get delivered.

YOUR OWN PBS

The Internet *is* media! You possess the power for your own Personal Broadcasting System (PBS). Cultivate the mindset that all Web sites are media channels and you can offer them content (with your links), because everyone is looking for fresh content and expert advice every day.

Pump up your sites by using audio and video effectively. Give your clients a reason to return and do business with you. Pull out all the stops by broadcasting quality content, timely information, and unique experiences while providing ease, simplicity, savings, and other advantages. A couple of suggestions to improve your PBS include:

1. *Interactive media.* Present your own media that visitors can interact with and return for more! Offer incentives by showcasing featured products or promotions. Use innovative Internet technology, such as video and audio, to create a unique, exciting experience. For the latest innovations and easy-to-use and affordable tools, head over to MyInstantVideo.com and AudioMarketingOnline.com.

2. *Social proof.* Just being in the press or media is a testimonial. Again, this comes back to familiarity. The more people see your face and hear your name, the faster your credibility grows and your business will see the results. Use customer, industry leader, and celebrity testimonials to promote the quality and reliability of your site's services. The strongest and most effective sales assistance comes from direct testimonials. I strongly recommend using audio and video testimonials, as well as printed quotes on your Web sites. Testimonials have increased response rates from 10 to 234 percent and it'll work for you! If you want to easily collect them, visit www.MoreCustomerTestimonials.com for a complimentary minicourse.

The success of your online publicity strategy relies on combining all of the above tactics for maintaining successful online positioning and presence.

SIGNING OFF

Would you enjoy doubling your personal income just by acquiring the mindset outlined here? It doubled mine every year for four years straight! Remember that your Web site is your own PBS and media tool. Use it to promote yourself and your company. Take advantage of the millions of dollars in free publicity available in the media. Dare to move beyond the textbook methods of standard marketing and publicity courses. The leverage that you get from combining your online and offline media and marketing is your ticket to sensational sales and online success!

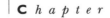

16

DECLAN DUNN
MASTERING
AFFILIATE PROGRAMS

DECLAN DUNN is CEO of Dunn Direct Group, home of the break-through Right Now Marketing system that shows you how to power your own business in plain, simple English. Developed through years of testing with companies ranging from Fortune 100s to small businesses, this system combines instructional technology and direct marketing to drive results.

FOR MORE INFORMATION: http://www.dunndirectgroup.com

In This Chapter You Will Learn:

- What an Affiliate Program Is

- How to Test the Market

- The Importance of Knowing Your Customers

- How to Use the Right Tools

WHAT IS AN AFFILIATE PROGRAM?

Affiliate programs, sometimes referred to as "associate" programs, are simply online reseller channels.

I like to use a retail analogy: If I've got a retailer who has a store and I have a product, and I want the product to be in his store, I am going to go approach him and say, "Hey, I've got this product and I want you to put it in your retail store and I will pay you X percent for every one you sell." It is very, very simple.

The affiliate program does the same thing. It says, "Hey, I've got a product, I want you to put this in an ad either on your Web site or in an e-mail." These two options, on a Web site or in an e-mail, are the best ways to do it. When that ad generates a sale, you get paid a percentage (or a "commission," if you like) as the affiliate for the sale of my product on your site or your e-mail list.

It's the same thing as a reseller saying, "Hey, I will take your product," and then you say, "Well, if I sell so many, how much money can I get per unit?" They might just do a free registration thing, or just decide, "Hey, I just want to get a bunch of interested people." Take mortgages, for example: I want people to fill out a form. I will pay you per form and I will call them myself. The affiliate is the one who has the Web site or the e-mail that encourages those people to fill out that mortgage form, so I pay them per form.

Basically, I'm paying for an action that a customer takes, whether it's a purchase (which is most often the case in an affiliate program) or a lead, or, let's say, their name and mailing address. And this is, to go back to the retailer scenario, truly simple. I want to be able to go into this Web site (my retailer) and say, "Gosh, I don't only want to put this on your Web site, I want you to feature it." It's like when you walk into a store and the end cap has the most amazing product you've ever seen! It's featured; it's the first thing you run into.

We do the same thing in the affiliate network. We want to get people to feature it on their Web site so we send a solo e-mail with the message "all this for only . . ." and we pay them when that generates an action, be that a purchase or a lead.

A good affiliate program is like a great joint venture. There's no mystery to it: "Hi, I have a product. You've got customers I'd like to reach. Let's make a deal."

It's a wonderful way to test whether your offer is working, to see whether people are purchasing and what sort of category they are purchasing. An affiliate network is a very smart way to test your offers. We use it at Adnet, my company, to test all the offers that we have. The real beauty of an affiliate program is we're paying on the performance of the ad, we're not paying for them to show the ad. So, instead of paying them to show what's called an "impression" (in other words, one person sees an ad), we're paying them when that ad creates an action. And this is so critical, with small business especially, as we're trying to figure out what works well. We send out an offer to develop an affiliate program and say, "Well, great, these people will do this, and will only get paid when that person takes an action." Our job is to make sure they've got great copy. Their job is to get us in front of people interested in that product or service.

TESTING THE MARKET

What's really brilliant is we'll test our ad copy and we'll test our headlines. We test all these in the affiliate program and then when we know how many people actually buy that product or service subject to our advertising, we will buy ads on sites that don't do "cost per action." Take the big sites like Yahoo!, for instance. You're not going to get Yahoo! to do an affiliate deal with you. They are pretty huge. They like to sell their ad space. Well, if I use my affiliate network to test all my ads I can then go to Yahoo! and say, "Hey, I will buy an ad because I know what numbers I need to reach to make it worth paying for that ad." So, it's a 100 percent sure-fire way to develop the return on investment (ROI) of your campaign without necessarily paying dollars up-front.

I've seen some really brilliant things done online. People have tested offers or seen headlines and then gone out to the real-world stores once they've determined what attracts buyers online through the affiliate program. They then go into the real world and feature that same offer. And it's in the real world they will say, "Hey, you're at our store. You didn't buy anything. Give us your e-mail; we want to get you on our e-mail list so that we can give you an update." It's a way to make the online and offline world feed off each other.

SMART MARKETING

I encourage most people to have their own products. If you are just a reseller for someone else's products, you fall into the problem of having to deal with a lot of different products. It's a great idea because if I have a product, I can go to your site and you might say, "Hey, if you want to add your product to my list and I want to add my product to your list, we can exchange."

And an affiliate program is a smart way to keep your marketing costs to an absolute minimum. To build on this, we take the customer and think about how a normal coach works; for example, how old they are, how much income they have, do they own a house, etc. You know, the basics: Know your customer. Then we want to know where they go on-line. What is their normal behavior? Do they read a newspaper? Do they rent business services such as a Web hosting service? We're going to those places where customers are already working. It's like an old Mark Twain saying, "The key to success is to find out where the customers are meeting and get there first." That's how we operate. We start really different. We assume we're the customer and we search the search engines; we don't work too hard. We watch what the customer does and we visit all those sites because the Internet shows you all the information you'll ever need. If you go to Google, for instance, they turn a keyword like "Web hosting" into more Web services than you can shake a stick at. We then contact these service providers with just a simple proposal. They fill in the supplied form and instantly place a little link on their site. This has all been automated, and the software is very inexpensive. Very easy, it's really not rocket science. It's direct marketing.

SETTING UP AN AFFILIATE PROGRAM

If you're a smart direct marketer, you will also set up a free chapter. This is so that you have something to give away for those who won't buy your e-book that first time. It's just like offline; we're talking probably a 2 percent gain for making an initial sale with our first contact. You go out and you create the product.

Second step: You go out and buy the affiliate software. We recommend a company we have, called DirectTrack.com. It's about a $1,000 and takes three to four days to set up. There are more expensive programs, and there are cheaper ones, but this one is about the middle range. When you set it up, the software has all the links within it. All you do is create your ads, whether it's a banner ad, a big display ad in other words, or an e-mail. You give the program all the creative stuff and the links are coded so they can be tracked. Everything is built into the software so you don't need to worry about any of this. Once you have everything set up, you go and contact a Web site and say, "Hey, I have an e-book on direct marketing. You have a site with an e-mail list of 50,000 people who are interested in direct marketing."

LET YOUR AFFILIATES DO THE WORK

Let me give you two examples of how I did this with an active marketplace. There was no business behind this beginning; I just had an e-book. I went out and contacted the top people in direct marketing on the Internet and said, "I will pay you $30 per book on a $97 book if you show this to your customers." I called up the three leading people. (I should say here that this is all about partnership. If you don't want to go crazy, you really want to pick up the leaders in the industry that you're targeting.) Alan Gardyne's associate program was one that I selected. He sent out these lists to 60,000 people. He ended up generating close to $15,000 in his first month just from that! A lot of people now find him to resell their books. It started spreading like wildfire because not only was the book good, but the copy and conversion were good.

The bottom line: Affiliate links make lots of sales. They are a sales force waiting for you. Put your e-book in their hands. A lot of people read Alan's work and want to resell a book. We find them and are able to sell the books, and we just keep watching our numbers. We say, "Hey, it worked for Alan Gardyne. Here are a couple of other people like him. Let's contact them." Doing this is a very, very simple way to contact others and show them how to do it. All they have to do is pay for the link to some copy on their site or in their e-mail, schedule the campaign, and you're on your way!

FEES FOR AFFILIATES

Standards are tricky. I'll give you two examples. The first is if you are selling a physical product. If you're a real reseller, you know your margins are around 5 to 10 percent, and that's going to be tricky to sell to anybody like Amazon. If you pay me 10 percent to sell a $20 book, it would make $2. You would have to sell a lot of books to make a couple of thousand dollars. What we tend to do with an e-book is up our margins. Because it's an e-book and it costs us nothing, we up our margins to $30 or we would do a 50/50 split with major barters. For example, if you sell 100 books, I will pay you 25 percent; if you sell 100 to 500 books, I will pay you 33 percent; if you sell over 500 books, I will pay you 50 percent. The really good sellers are going to want to know how to do it. With an e-book it's efficient to be able to play with margins, especially if you're smart.

My second scenario is if you have a back-end product. I have a friend, Marlon Sanders of AmazingFormula.com, who is a reason marketer. He gets a 60 percent margin from a $50 product. People sell it like crazy and Marlon has a back end of anywhere from $500 to $5,000 to $10,000. Because of this, Marlon has funded advertising up-front so he can then funnel into a back end that is much bigger, his virtual business.

I could tell you the real journey of the e-book marketing world. I don't sell a $29 book, I sell a $97 piece of information with ideas you can't find anywhere else. We had a lot of people sell $29 products. I sold a $97 book, an e-book. We sold over 1,000 units at $97 in the first month. If we had sold them for $29 we would have made $29,000. Our $97 e-book equated to $97,000 and my affiliates got paid from a third to a half of this. We paid out $35,000 to $50,000 in commissions. That's a great people generator.

BOOKS AND E-BOOKS

My e-book is called *Winning the Affiliate Game* and you can find it at ActiveMarketplace.com, which was one of the very first e-book sellers on the Internet. Most people were selling physical books so we decided for those who want the physical book, we will charge you $20 to $30 shipping and handling. Still, a third of the people ordered the physical book!

In doing this, we avoided throwing away a third of our sales. Most of my friends still only write e-books because they are so much easier to work with than sending out a physical book. But they are throwing away a third of their sales.

SUPER AFFILIATES

A super affiliate is really a name I invented. This is somebody who can go out and sell to a large amount of customers. Alan Gardyne has an associate program called the little niche, which has a very good list. He can do a tremendous amount of sales by word of mouth. An affiliate might do 1, 2, or maybe 10 or 20 sales. Super affiliates can do hundreds. They are the really good resellers—the people who know how to move products or services in your niche.

BUILDING A STRONG NETWORK

In the old days everyone bothered about quantity. My advice is to handpick your best resellers. I come from a tradition of setting up reseller channels for computer hardware. I pick the partners who are in front of enough customers. I ask, "How many customers do you reach? What percentage of those will actually look at my ad and click? And what percentage of those will convert?" That's how I do my numbers, and that's how I determine the top partners. I begin with each individual customer. I find out who is the best in the business. Nine times out of ten you find the same three people. I then contact those people and try to make a deal with them.

Consider it like a partnership business development. The new wave of marketing, affiliate marketing, is to really focus on a small number of partners. You know if you have 100 or 200 really good resellers, you should be happy. You might have 10,000 affiliates but that doesn't mean they are doing anything. In fact, what we discovered in the early days is that of the 10,000 affiliates probably only 5 percent of them are doing anything!

It's only a good idea to offer a general affiliate program if it's a large mass media product that anyone, anywhere, anytime, would want. Then it's not a bad idea because you can get out to the masses, but the more specific you get in the targeting of your specific audience, the more you want to handpick. It's not an "either/or" question. Amazon still has over half a million affiliates that sell books. They do a great job. But I don't think most of us will be in the Amazon boat.

MAKING MONEY ON THE INTERNET

The key to success is really threefold. Number one: Focus on your niche. Know what you know very well and become the expert, or the leading credibility resource. The biggest problem online is the question of whom do you trust? Who are you? You are nobody, even if you've got a bit of a name; remember, it's a fast Internet. So why should they trust you? Always start out with "How can I develop trust?" and I mean in the product, testimonials, guarantee—things that give reassurance.

Number two: Direct market books. This is totally about direct marketing. Hundreds of years of experience go into it, the only genius in direct marketing are the numbers that result. It's not you, it's not genius, it's the customer responding to your offer. Act like a direct marketer. Forget that you're an Internet business. Don't call yourself a marketer; call yourself a human being marketing product. *And make sure* you really focus on that.

Number three: Focus on developing a lead product. As you do this, remember that people want to have a back-end product, if possible, because it's very important.

The last thing I would suggest is that you must have an e-mail address. Let's say someone comes to your affiliate program and sees your book but doesn't buy it. You want to have some way to say, "Hey, if you give me your e-mail address, I will give you a free chapter," or "If you're leaving this site, let me give you a free $10 certificate toward your purchase." E-mail and repetition of messaging is tremendously successful. And to make this non–rocket science, I use a company called AWeber .com. It costs me $20 a month to automate everything completely, the e-mail acquisition and all the follow-up. I follow up seven times in 14 days. If you can cut and paste and write good copy, you can use this service.

It will amaze you to see just how easy it is to have all the stats, and that everything is built in, so you can carry out a marketing campaign.

You don't just sell something that might just be a 1 or 2 percent gain, you build a list of interested customers that you can go to over and over again and build an ad that grows all along.

TESTING FOR SUCCESS

Your affiliate program has all the numbers you really need, figures such as how many people click onto your site and how many people purchase and take the action. The nice part is actually the affiliate program.

When I buy an ad I use my affiliate software and I put a code on it so that when I go out to see how many people I'm paying for that ad, I see how many people have seen that link and bought from it. This is how I measure my ROI. I use my affiliate software to track every ad I do, every ad tracks a complete ROI. It's such an easy way and most people totally ignore it. They just sit back and use the offline world where you have no way of tracking your ROI.

On the Internet everything is accountable. Everything is accountable! It's scary; we know how advertising works and how advertising doesn't work and that's the beauty of it. You just have to be able to use the tools. As far as testing mechanisms go, the affiliate program is, in fact, a giant testing pool.

17

JIMMY D. BROWN
MASTERING E-MAIL MARKETING

JIMMY D. BROWN is the Web's leading authority on e-mail marketing. His eight-hour home-study course is considered by many to be the most complete course available on the subject. He is a prolific writer, highly-respected marketer, and is frequently a featured expert at the top Internet conferences in the nation.

FOR MORE INFORMATION: http://www.masteringemail.com

In **T**his **C**hapter **Y**ou **W**ill **L**earn:

- How to Create a Deep Foundation
- The Five Kinds of E-mail Marketing
- The Five Kinds of Tightly Targeted Sublists

YOUR BUSINESS IS A SKYSCRAPER

I've used this illustration before and continue to use it; an online business is much like a skyscraper, and certainly building an online business is similar to building a skyscraper.

So that's what I want you to do. Think of your business in terms of a skyscraper.

Each floor of your skyscraper is made of different offices. Offices like joint ventures, newsletter publishing, automated follow-up, article distribution, free reports, autoresponder messages, e-courses, networking, traffic generation, conversion, relationship building, and so forth.

They are all part of your business, this skyscraper that you are building. All are important, but none of them is as important as the foundation.

Every single level of your e-business is tied to the foundation. And that foundation is e-mail marketing. *It is impossible to be successful online* without *some form of marketing via e-mail.*

Nothing else comes close to the power of a good list and an understanding of how to use it.

It's your foundation. It's the base upon which you build your e-business. Everything about what you are going to do online is directly related to your list. And everything you do online should, in some way, work toward building and perfecting your list.

Now, I don't know how familiar you are with foundations, but let me share something about them with you: the deeper the foundation, the taller the building.

Your success online revolves around that same principle. You don't just need a list—you need a DEEP foundation of e-mail marketing.

And I use that acronym to describe e-mail marketing, DEEP. That's D-E-E-P. And each letter represents something that I feel is absolutely critical to becoming a successful marketer online. Certainly the formula that I'm about to share with you has enabled me to earn a lot of money since I began using it.

I call it the "DEEP" formula.

The DEEP Foundation of E-mail Marketing

- *D = Diverse.* "D" equals "diverse." You need more than just a newsletter list. That's only the tip of the iceberg of e-mail marketing, just a drop in the bucket, so to speak.

- *E = Effective.* The first "E" stands for "effective." It's one thing to have 50 different lists; it's another thing to know how to use them. And use them to your maximum advantage.
- *E = Educational.* Here's the big key to e-mail marketing—to educate your subscribers.
- *P = Proactive.* The "P" represents "proactive." Your e-mail marketing needs to be proactive. You need to aggressively build your lists. You need to frequently provide your readers with rock-solid content. You need to put those offers in front of your readers so they can buy from you.

THE POWER OF SUBLISTS

As we focus on sublists, we're going to talk about one important aspect of the DEEP foundation and that's diversity—building multiple lists and sublists, all with a specific purpose and function.

It's important that you understand this concept from the beginning. E-mail marketing isn't just an e-zine; it's not just about publishing a newsletter. That's a good beginning, but that's really all it is, a beginning.

E-mail marketing is about starting, growing, nurturing, and profiting from a wide variety of lists and sublists that all work toward building your DEEP foundation and your business online.

As you build your lists, there are five rules that you should always follow.

1. Work Toward Multiple, Tightly Targeted Lists

Like I've already mentioned, you want more than a newsletter list, you want lots of lists and sublists. So, that's the key here, work toward multiple, tightly targeted lists.

That simply means, develop an entire family of lists, each one of them focusing on a tightly targeted niche.

Let me give you an example. Let's suppose I wanted to promote a handful of reprint rights licenses to a new product that I just developed. I'm preparing to place an ad in a newsletter. Which do you think will sell more licenses for me?

- A daily joke list with 500,000 subscribers.
- An Internet marketing list with 25,000 subscribers.
- A reprint rights announcement list with 325 subscribers.

I use these examples because it's an actual scenario that I faced. At first glance, you might think, "well the list of 500,000 subscribers would pull more results just because of the sheer number of subscribers."

Wrong answer. It's an extremely large list and the wrong target audience. Try again.

"Ok, then it must be the Internet marketing list with 25,000 subscribers. After all, Internet marketing folks are interested in selling products, so a large majority of them would be interested in a reprint rights license. And 25,000 must outpull the 325 subscribers, right?"

Wrong again.

The smallest list, by far, with only 325 subscribers, outsold a 500,000 nontargeted subscriber list and even a 25,000 slightly targeted subscriber list.

Why? Because it is a tightly targeted list. Every single member, few though they are, specifically asked to receive information on new products available with reprint rights. They want new products to sell and want to know when there is something available for them to buy.

Now, that's a list!

It's a small list. But, it's a loyal list. And it is tightly targeted. Any mailing to that list produces immediate results, because it's exactly what they are looking for. The more targeted your lists are to a very specific niche, the greater response rate you'll have when you send out an offer. I've had offers on some of my lists that had a staggering 76 percent conversion.

So, look beyond the standard e-zine and focus on tightly targeted lists, also known as sublists. In just a few minutes I'll be explaining about different kinds of lists to create and how to profit from them.

2. Build Only 100 Percent Opt-In Lists

Translated, that simply means, only put those on your list who requested that you do so. The phrase "opt-in" means just that, the people opted (optioned) to be included in your list.

Never, never, never—trust me, you'll thank me later—never put them onto a list without their permission or send out any kind of mailing to them without their permission. That is considered spam and will get you into hot water faster than you can say, "Oops, I messed up."

Spam is also known as "unsolicited commercial e-mail." It's a "no-no." Don't do it. I promise you, there are much, much, much better ways to use e-mail marketing and build lists.

Your purpose is to make money with your sublists. You'll always make more money with your lists by sending your offers to those who are interested enough to have requested joining your list than those who have never expressed any interest at all.

3. Remember Quality Is More Important Than Quantity

I've sent advertisements to lists of 500,000 subscribers that didn't pull nearly as good responses as the ads I sent to lists that only had 500 subscribers.

Quantity isn't nearly as important as quality. A large list isn't nearly as important as a loyal list. I'd rather have 500 "eager beavers" who can't wait to read my mailing than 5,000 that won't ever lay eyes on my e-mail messages (the majority of which submitted a Hotmail e-mail address).

Many, especially in the Web marketing/business market, sign up to every new list they come into contact with. They use an e-mail address they rarely check and get dozens, even hundreds, of newsletters each month.

Do you really think they are going to read them all? Or, even any of them? Not likely.

And yet, they are included in a list, probably a large list. Is that list useful? Not nearly as useful as a list of those who really do read the e-mails they receive.

That's what you want to go after. A list of people who really do read the e-mails you send them. A list of those with whom you can build relationships. A list of those who will come to trust you and rely upon your recommendations.

A quality list.

Don't get caught up in the numbers. The numbers will take care of themselves in time. Your list will grow if you use the techniques I'm going to share with you. Don't worry about getting a huge list, that'll work itself out in the long run.

Work on building a loyal list of those who actually read your messages, in fact, who actually look forward with anticipation to reading your messages.

Even if the list is small, that list is going to make you some money. A loyal list equals a profitable list. Let me say that again, because it's important: A loyal list is a profitable list.

I make more money from my small lists than I do my large lists in a lot of cases, and that's because they were built to focus on very specific niches where folks anticipate the information when it is sent to them.

Quality is more important than quantity. Don't ever forget that.

4. Take Your Time and Do It Right

You're building a foundation, remember? Do you think foundations are built overnight? No. They take time. And the bigger the foundation, the more time it takes.

One of the problems that most list builders face is their own impatience. For some reason, we have this belief that we can build a huge list overnight.

Sorry, but it just doesn't work that way.

List building is often a slow process. At least, if you're going to do it right. Remember, you're looking for quality subscribers to build a loyal readership of those who look forward to hearing from you. The point I want to make here, and please pay careful attention, is to simply take your time. Don't get so impatient. Impatience usually is the forerunner to quitting.

Did you catch that? Impatience is usually the forerunner to quitting. Most folks who get impatient get discouraged. And then they quit. Don't do that. Take your time and do it right. Build a high-quality list and I promise you it will earn you a nice profit.

5. Think "Viral" in Everything You Do

Here's the big key in building lists: setting off a marketing virus that automatically brings in new subscribers on remote control.

In everything you do in e-mail marketing you want to use it to launch and continue to spread your marketing virus. You want others to bring in subscribers for you. And you want that cycle to continue to spread all over the Web until there are hundreds and thousands of people bringing in new leads for you.

THERE ARE FIVE TYPES
OF TARGETED SUBLISTS

1. Announcements

The first kind of tightly targeted list that I want to mention is announcement lists. An announcement list is exactly what it is—the members subscribe to receive new announcements relating to a particular topic, subject, or theme.

When I released *Profit Pulling* e-books about two years ago, I decided that I would make it available with reprint rights. I also decided that I would create additional products in that line in the future and that I would likewise make available with reprint rights.

So, I decided to create a tightly targeted list, an announcement list. I began offering the "Profit Pulling Updates" list. This list has a very simple purpose. Anytime I release a product that has reprint rights available, I send an announcement to the list members.

I simply let them know that the new product is available and I provide them with a link to check out the offer. That's all it is. There isn't any content. I don't share information. No tips or tactics. It's an announcement list. When there is a new product I have available with reprint rights, I e-mail the announcement list.

At last count, I have 712 members on the list. It's not an incredibly large list. But it is an incredibly profitable list because of the function of the list itself. Those who subscribe to it want to buy products. You can't beat that. They want me to let them know when I have a license available so they can buy it.

I earn around $10,000 in profit every single month because of building that list. That's $10,000 in money I can spend, every single month, that comes in from a list of just over 700 subscribers.

Like I said earlier, *quality* is more important than *quantity*.

That's a small list that's worth its weight in gold.

The idea is to build an announcement list where people request that you provide them with certain announcements.

Let me share some specific ideas here on announcement lists you should consider building:

- *E-zine articles.* Do you write and distribute e-zine articles? If you allow other publishers to reprint your articles in their newsletters, then why not create an announcement list for them to join? Anytime you have a new article ready to be published, you simply send out a mailing to the list. Can you imagine the power of such a list? Even if it is only 50 publishers, what kind of market reach could you have if 50 publishers reprinted your article in their e-zines? We're talking about the potential to reach hundreds of thousands of subscribers. That's a list worth creating.

- *Customized e-books.* Do you put together e-books that can be customized with affiliate links, either for free or as a paid service? These are in-demand products and I am positive a highly profitable list could be built to announce when new customized e-books are available. And, even if you don't create the e-books yourself, you can be on the watch for affiliate programs that create them; and let me tell you, many affiliate programs are now offering customizable e-books. So, you focus on two-tier affiliate programs, those that pay commissions on two levels of referrals, and you announce anytime a new customizable e-book is available from one of those two-tiered programs. Then, when others obtain their customized e-book through your referral link, if anyone buys a product through their coded e-book, you earn a commission as well, and all you did was announce that the e-book was available. Again, we're talking about a very profitable announcement list.

- *Free trials.* Here's another great announcement list idea. How about one devoted to "free trials" for a specific niche. Let's say, for example, it's about Internet marketing. One of the ways that many marketers introduce their products to customers is by offering a free trial, or a very low-price trial, like $1. The customer joins the service to check it out at little or no risk, and if they remain an active customer, the marketer begins charging their full price. So, here's where you can make some money. You set up an announcement list that notifies subscribers anytime there's a free or very low-cost trial to an Internet marketing–related product or service. This could even include free chapter giveaways, free demo versions, free "lite" versions, etc. You send your announcements with your affiliate link included in the mailing. Your subscribers go to the site, they join for free, and if they continue as a paid member, you then receive the commission. And again, it's all because you announced the free trial to a list of those who requested the information.

2. More Information

Another type of tightly targeted list is what I call the "more information" family of lists. Basically, these lists consist of additional information. In other words, you provide content and if the reader wants more information, they request it from you through your autoresponder or e-mail address.

Again, let me provide you with a case study.

When I recorded the live teleseminar, "E-mail Strategies Explained," several times during the ten hours of that call, I mentioned that I had specific resources available that the listeners could use, but because they contain lengthy Web site links, I didn't have time during the call to give the specific URLs. I told the listeners if they would like to obtain a copy of the resources to simply send an e-mail to a specific autoresponder address.

In other words, if you'd like more information, here's a tightly targeted list that you can send an e-mail to in order to obtain the information.

Out of those who requested the resources, 41 percent joined My Lead Center, which is an autoresponder and mailing list service that I own and promoted in the information sent out. Every one of the 41 percent who joined pays me $14.97 per month to use the service.

And that's just one use of the "more information" tightly targeted list. The idea is to provide some information and have the reader (or the listener, as it was in the example above) request additional information from you at a predetermined list address.

And another list is born.

How about a few more examples?

- *Part two of an article.* A great way to create a "more information" list is by writing a part two to any e-zine article that you write and distribute. You write the article in two parts and then distribute the first part to e-zine publishers and content directories. And in your resource box at the close of your article, you mention part two of the article and how the reader can obtain a copy of it. And just like that, you've created another list—interested parties who are requesting the second part of your article. Another idea for this is to create a full e-course, consisting of five or more articles, and then publish part one of the article, and then you mention the remaining lessons in the course in your resource box. Either way works great and is perfect for creating new sublists.

- *Expanded details from a sales letter.* Here's another idea that only a handful of savvy marketers are using. Inside your ad copy of your sales letter, mention some detail that you aren't willing to share in the public and will only hand out to those who request the information. For example, you might talk about the fact that you lost 35 pounds and mention that you used a specific technique that very few people are using. And you're willing to share it with those who request more information through an autoresponder. Imagine the subscription rate on this one. Someone is reading your sales letter about a weight loss product and you mention some outrageous benefit like losing 35 pounds and right there in your sales letter you mention that you'll share the technique if they ask for it. Do you think many will request it? You bet.

- *Free information.* How about an information list that focuses on any kind of free information? Whether it's a set of resource links or a download link to some free tool or a free password to a member's only site, here's another opportunity to build a list. I use these kinds of lists to collect hundreds of new subscribers every month to just one of my sublists. When someone arrives at my eBookCreator.com site they can download a fully functional copy of my e-book compiler software, but they have to request the download link by sending me an e-mail to my autoresponder. By doing this I have a record of every person who downloads my software and am able to convert a staggering number of them into paying customers.

3. Registrations

Another tightly targeted list would be what I have dubbed "registrations." The idea is to have folks register with you before they are able to fully use your content.

Again, let me refer to an example of my own. About two years ago, I created a nifty little e-book that I called *Traffic Virus*. Yep, I actually came up with that title before Terry Dean created the e-book *How to Start a Traffic Virus*.

Traffic Virus had several different traffic-generation tools listed in it. It was basically a resource tool for submission sites, traffic tools, etc.

What I did was to have each person who downloaded the e-book register with me as an official "traffic virus partner." In order to register as a partner all they needed to do was to send me an e-mail to trafficpartner @123webmarketing.com.

At last count, there were 22,000 registered users of the e-book. Do you think you could earn any income with that list?

Again, it was all done through what I call "viral" marketing. I had them register via the e-book itself. That's the only method of building that list that was used. I automatically built a list of over 20,000 members in a year and a half with absolutely zero work doing it.

So, use registration lists. Here are some ideas you can consider using for this type of tightly targeted list:

- *E-book registrations.* Give away a free e-book that allows all readers to also begin giving it away and have folks register in order to access the content of the e-book.
- *Partner registrations.* If someone wants to become an affiliate in your affiliate program, or wants to become an authorized distributor of your free e-book or wants to become a member of your e-zine list-building co-op, or any kind of partnership, have them register.
- *Prelaunch registrations.* Are you planning on launching some kind of product or service in the future but aren't ready yet? Why not

create a registration list that allows those to become a part of the project before it's available? A prelaunch registration list is another great list. You could have thousands of members ready to become active even before your project is completed.

4. Partners

Another favorite tightly targeted list that I use, and certainly you can use too, is a "partners" list. This list consists of those who either: a) are your partner in some kind of project, or b) would like to become a partner with you.

I mentioned it briefly as a type of registration list, but it's so powerful and profitable that I actually include it as its own kind of sublist.

I use these kinds of lists for a variety of reasons, generally for joint ventures. For example, a few months ago, I released a new product entitled, "Get Web Profits Fast." It is a course on creating and profiting from joint venture partnerships. It's also a viral marketing tool because every person who buys a copy has master reprint rights to continue selling it themselves and authorizing others to do the same.

Inside the e-book, I listed ten different kinds of joint venture projects, and gave the basic details of how to set them up. And, in the following chapter, I mentioned that I would be putting together similar joint-venture projects in the future. I invited anyone who wanted to become involved in one of the projects to e-mail me at profitsfast@profitsvault.com.

Do you see what happened here? I don't even have the projects put together yet. I'm not exactly sure when I'll get to them. But, when I do, there will be plenty of people who are waiting in line to participate. I used the viral marketing tool to automatically build a list of partners well before I am even ready to launch the joint ventures themselves.

Partners are a great kind of tightly targeted list to build. At the same time you establish relationships with those who will help you build your business, you help them build theirs. You get to tap into their resources and their sphere of influence.

So, let me quickly share some kinds of these "partner" lists . . .

- *Joint ventures.* As I mentioned earlier, joint ventures are a great type of database to build. Compile a list for those who want to participate in various joint-venture partnerships related to your field.
- *Affiliates.* If you are selling a product or service, then you absolutely must have an affiliate program and a database of affiliates you can contact on a regular basis.
- *Customer databases.* If you aren't following up with previous customers, then you are missing out on some easy money. Research shows that 92 percent of satisfied customers are likely to do business with you again. So, it's important to have a list of your previous customers and their buying patterns. For example, I have sold 208 copies of a viral report entitled the "No Cost Marketing Report." All 208 of those people who purchased it did so because they wanted a report to give away as a lead generator that they could customize with their affiliate link to earn back-end commissions. I'll be releasing a new viral report in the next few days—who do you think I'll contact first?

5. Bonuses

The last kind of tightly targeted list that we're going to talk about is what I refer to as "bonuses." This one doesn't require a lot of explanation. It's simply a list of people who respond to a bonus offer.

Here is a classic example. Every member of *Profits Vault Monthly* receives a new product each month to sell and keep every penny they earn. These are e-books. Inside each new e-book is an "unadvertised" bonus—a free copy of the seven-day e-course, "The Mathematic, Scientific, This-Is-What-Einstein-Would-Have-Done Approach to Earning Income Online." Voila! A free bonus builds a new sublist.

This one is especially profitable, because it not only builds a list, but it also automatically follows up for seven straight days of lessons.

Again, I love to use e-courses. They are an absolutely invaluable part of my online business, and are critical to e-mail marketing success.

The idea here with this type of list is to give away some kind of free bonus and have those who are interested sign up in order to receive the bonus. Whether it's a bonus report inside an e-book, a free bonus for joining your newsletter, a bonus software program after someone has bought your product, a bonus resource on any of your content pages, or a bonus for completing a survey, you've got another kind of sublist you can build to ultimately use to create income on the Internet.

So, these are the five basic types of sublists that I build and I certainly recommend that you begin building as well. There are dozens and dozens of tightly targeted lists that you can work on from these five categories.

As an afterthought, I'll be attending an upcoming seminar and I'm hoping to put together a brainstorming session with some of the other speakers to come up with some unique sublists. If you'd like a free copy of the ideas we come up with, send an e-mail to sublists@profitsvault .com.

See how easy this is? I just created an announcement list.

The ideas are limitless.

C h a p t e r

18

CRAIG PERRINE
PROVEN LIST-BUILDING
AND PROFIT STRATEGIES

CRAIG PERRINE is known as the "List Profit Coach" for his track record of helping clients build huge, highly responsive lists, totaling over 7 million subscribers to date. Craig speaks at exclusive seminars about his list profit secrets and e-mail copywriting. He offers a free e-course on how to quickly and easily build a list.

FOR MORE INFORMATION: http://www.listprofitsecrets.com/OMS/

In This Chapter You Will Learn:

- How to Build a List of Targeted Subscribers

- How to Build Your List Quickly and Easily

- How to Pull Repeat Profits from Your List

PROVEN LIST-BUILDING STRATEGIES

On August 17, 2004, my friend John Reese set a record for marketing an information product online. He sold over $1,080,000 in one day via e-mail marketing when dozens of people with responsive lists promoted his brand-new home study course.

Now everyone wants to know how he did it.

It's clear that the most important factor was the power of e-mail promotions that drove all the buyers to his site. The true power was the ability to direct all those people with nothing more than e-mail to take action and buy a $1,000 product all on the same day.

Without the lists of subscribers, there would not have been a million-dollar day. Similarly, without a list, an online business is unlikely to be profitable.

The fact is, to make any real money online, as I'm sure you've heard, you need to build your own list. Here's why . . .

Getting new visitors to your Web site takes time, money, and effort. Convincing first-time visitors to your site to buy from you is even harder. Studies have shown that on average it takes between five and seven exposures to you for a prospect to consider buying. By their very nature, first-time visitors have not built up a level of trust with you, in most cases, to be comfortable enough to buy from you.

When you can get someone who visits your Web site to give you their name and e-mail address with permission to contact them again, you've got a potentially valuable prospect. So, instead of trying to sell to first-time visitors to their Web sites, savvy marketers now create Web sites for which the only purpose is to get you to enter in your name and e-mail address and ask for more information.

Why? Because every person who gives you their name and e-mail address becomes your subscriber who you can follow up with and build a relationship with. Once you've proven yourself, they'll trust you and will be much more likely to buy something from you over and over again. Done correctly, your own list of subscribers can be like having your own license to print money every time you click "send."

Perhaps most important, in an age when your prospects are bombarded by advertising from all directions, having a relationship with your subscribers is one of the few ways to truly stand out and get their attention. When you build a list in the way I'm going to describe, your subscribers will bond to you and they'll open your e-mails first instead of all the others that flood into their inboxes every day.

The good news is that there are many different low- and no-cost ways to build a list, and some very powerful ways to "buy your list" if you have more capital. Remember, once you have your own list, you can instantly roll out your new-product promotions, or do joint ventures selling other people's products for hefty commissions. What you are about to discover is that even with the rise of spam and other challenges that e-mail marketers didn't have to deal with in the "early days," having your own list of subscribers is still, hands down, the most powerful and profitable way to market online today.

Of course, there is more to making money with a list than simply clicking "send" on "any old e-mail." That is why I'm going to lay out in this chapter the same list profit secrets that I use every day for myself and my clients. You're going to benefit from what I've learned helping customers and clients build lists totaling more than 7 million subscribers. So read on and find out how you can build a profitable list in minimum time and for minimum investment.

HOW TO REALLY BUILD A LIST OF TARGETED SUBSCRIBERS ONLINE THAT WILL MAKE YOU MONEY

The fact is that most people struggle to build a list of any size at all. Why? Because most marketing "how to" materials are pretty vague about how to build a list. Once you know the simple step-by-step system I am about to teach you, building a good size list can actually be quite easy.

Here's is a proven, step-by-step way to build your list.

Step 1. The first step is to find a target market that is ripe with prospects for what you have to sell. If you don't have that, the rest of your list-building efforts will be a waste of time and money. You have to find a group of people who want something specific and focus on selling them exactly what they want.

No one needs movies or chocolate or a Hula Hoop or a Pet Rock or Gucci shoes or a Rolex watch, and yet consumers make the companies that produce these products into profit machines because the desire to have them is greater than logic. There is also no greater expert on what your target market will buy than real people in your target market.

So your next step in building a list is finding out what keeps your prospects from getting what they want. As I've just shown, they will go to great lengths to get what they want, which includes paying you a lot of money over and over again if you are positioned correctly.

If you can come up with products and services that solve problems and help your prospects get what they want, you'll make money. It's that simple. People spend a lot of money to overcome their problems and get what they want. It doesn't matter if you create the products or partner up with companies that will pay you a commission for referring customers to them. Your job is simply to identify what your prospects would pay money for and let them know you have solutions to their problems.

This is exactly what my friend John Reese did. He spent the better part of two years being around people online and in person at seminars so he could hear firsthand what was keeping people from being successful making money using the Internet.

He identified that getting traffic to their Web site was a recurring theme and that most people went about it all wrong. This made "generating traffic" a perfect topic for John to offer a solution for because there were a lot of people who would spend good money to solve this frustrating problem.

As it so happens, John was already an expert in this topic and was able to put together an easily digestible multimedia course that could show exactly the successful methods he used to get traffic. Once he put together a product that directly answered their need and gave them what they wanted, he produced over a million dollars in sales in one day.

At this point, you know the right way to build a list. Start with a viable target market that wants something and has money to spend and then find out what they want. Sure, there is a little work to do in the beginning, but I can tell you it sure beats jumping in to a new business only to find out later it's doomed because no one wants what you're selling.

Now that we've laid the foundation, let's look at ways to tell your target market that you have what they want so they can come and join your list.

Step 4. Tell your target market you have what they want. The key to getting the attention of your target market is to stand out from all the noise and hype that your prospects see every day and show them that there is genuinely something in it for them to take the time to get to know you.

Let's be clear about one thing: Your mission is not to "outhype" your competitors or have a bigger ad budget for glitzy jingles and slogans. Far from it. Your mission is to prove that you have something of value to offer them and demonstrate that you understand their problems. By far, the best way to do this is to create attractive bait that will lead your prospects to you just as a bloodhound will follow the scent of a delicious dog bone. We'll get into how to do that in the next section.

HOW TO BUILD YOUR LIST
QUICKLY AND EASILY

When I say build a list, I mean gather people who are high-quality prospects for what you are selling and get their permission to e-mail them. Why would they give you permission to e-mail them? If you followed the earlier steps by carefully identifying your target market and what they want, here is where that effort pays off.

Now that you can offer them a credible solution that eliminates the obstacles in their way and helps them get what they want, you will have no problem getting people on your list. Your solution to their problems is your bait that will attract subscribers like bees to honey.

That said, if you have what they want, you're in good shape to select ways to reach out and start getting the word out about your bait. There are basically two different ways to do this: 1) you can build your list on your own by directly adding subscribers, or 2) you can find other people who already have lists and find ways to get access to them in what are called joint ventures.

Let's talk about how you can build your list first.

Write articles. Even if you are not a writer, you can use informative articles to attract very positive attention to yourself and get subscribers to your list. Whatever niche you're in, you will take the information on what is keeping your prospects from getting what they want and write articles about solutions to their problems. You'll have no problem finding e-zines and Web sites that will publish your articles because you are addressing issues that are truly important to your target market. To find e-zines in your niche, all you have to do is type in your niche and the word e-zines into Google.com. For example, type in "nutrition" and "e-zines" and you should get a number of ideas for where to publish your articles.

Once published, your article should paint a favorable picture of you and your company, even if indirectly, so that your readers will want more information. The beauty of this is that you can offer more information at your Web site at the end of your article and that is a very natural way to get people to visit your site, which of course will ask them for their name and e-mail address in exchange for the additional information. Presto, you have a new subscriber!

If you are not comfortable writing articles, you can simply list out the number of problems facing your target market and how your products solve those problems. Then hire writers on Wlance.com or locally to write your articles for you. You can also record yourself talking about your product and how it solves these problems as if you were talking to a prospect, and have that recording transcribed at Idictate.com and use that as another article.

Write an e-book. Once you have enough articles, you'll probably find you can put them together to create an e-book or a report that you can either sell, or even better, offer to your niche market for free to get publicity. E-books have perceived value and establish you as an author. If your e-book is all about solving the problems that keep your prospects from getting what they want, they will want to get a copy and will likely share copies with their friends.

Your e-book, of course, should offer reasons throughout to visit your Web sites or talk about products that you offer and their benefits. In reality, your e-book will act as a long sales letter for your business while it is informing your readers about how to solve their problems.

In a minute we'll get into an even more powerful way to use your e-book to build your list.

Write an e-course. Instead of combining your articles into an e-book, you can break them up into e-mail "lessons" that you can send to new subscribers who visit your Web site. For example, if you were interested in how to get more subscribers and build a list, and I told you there was a free e-course available at http://www.listprofitsecrets.com/ecourse .htm, you'd want to go subscribe.

I would then send you a five- to seven-part e-course that you would get every few days in your inbox and it would deliver on my promise to tell you how to build a list.

Once you had completed the e-course, I would stay in touch as long as you are a subscriber with the latest information on list building and how to make money with e-mail marketing.

Those are all strategies you can use to go out and build up a list of subscribers. Once you have an e-book or some articles or an e-course to offer your target market, you can use some even more powerful ways to joint venture (JV) with people who have lists to reach a large number of prospects very quickly.

Other people who have lists, even competitors, are always looking for more information to offer their lists. Let's say you have an e-book or e-course on a powerful new technique for list building. If you were to contact me, there are several ways that we could work together that would help me give something of value to my list and, at the same time, add targeted subscribers to your list.

Of course, you have to lay the groundwork for doing JVs by creating the e-book or e-course, but in exchange you have access to other people's lists and can grow your list very quickly.

With a little bit of capital, you can use paid advertising to buy subscribers. Through a method called "coregistration" you can buy subscribers who request information from you in ads you place on Web sites that already have traffic. Typically, you would offer a free subscription to your e-zine or newsletter, which would be offered to visitors on the Web sites you advertise on and you'd pay anywhere from $.05 to $1 or more per subscriber. The advantage here is that you can determine how many subscribers you will get and how much it will cost you. It is important to make sure that the subscribers you are buying are targeted to what you offer and that you get proof that they "opted in" to receive your newsletter. Typically, the time and date they requested your e-zine and their computer's IP address are included with the name and e-mail data that you get with each subscriber.

You can literally get hundreds or thousands of subscribers for a relatively small cost. More importantly, because you pay for each subscriber, you are not renting a coregistration list, which means you can mail to them on an ongoing basis to build a relationship.

Another advanced strategy that allows you to leverage vast resources is to use the power of the offline and online media to spread the word about what you have to offer. If your e-book has news value and you take the time to learn how to do a press release, the radio, magazine, and TV media can get you more subscribers than you could possibly pay for in a short period of time. This strategy alone could occupy an entire chapter, but I want to open your mind to the possibility.

Of course, you should also consider the vast world of offline marketing to drive targeted traffic to your list. You can offer the same e-books and e-courses through ads in magazines, direct mail to rented lists, and articles in targeted publications, and get new subscribers when they give their name and e-mail address at your Web site. Don't overlook the offline market because it is a lot bigger and has a vast array of choices for all budgets. The main objective is to build your list so you can follow up with them by e-mail and that is what we are going to talk about next— profiting from the follow-up.

HOW TO PULL PROFITS FROM YOUR LIST OVER AND OVER AGAIN

The first step to making money with your list now that you have used the step-by-step methods to get new subscribers is to build trust with them. Just as you have to know what your target market wants before you can know how to entice them to subscribe to your list, you must build trust with them before you can expect to sell them anything.

The good news is that by following the list-building steps I've outlined, your subscribers already think you are an expert because they've read your articles or your e-book or e-course.

They may have even heard you interviewed on a teleseminar, so you are in pretty good shape already. From here, what you want to do is build on that tenuous connection you have and turn it into a strong bond so that whenever you offer something to your list, whether it is your own product or someone else's, they will buy if it meets their needs.

To get there, I recommend that you position yourself as a celebrity with your subscribers and build a list of fans. If you write your e-mails to your list from the heart and inject your own personality into what you send them, and you always deliver value to your list, and they will learn to respect and admire you.

Because your entire model from the beginning has been to help them get what they want and solve their problems, this is going to naturally occur as you go along. Once you have a list of fans, you can pretty much count on your list being very profitable if you've done the previous steps correctly.

Here are five steps that you can take your new subscribers from just getting to know you to taking actions that make you money:

Step 1. Give them more value once they subscribe. If you plan on at least seven to ten e-mails to your new subscriber that offer articles, cool resources, teleseminars on topics of interest, and goodies they can download free, then you will have laid the groundwork for an important psychological response.

Robert Cialdini, in his excellent books on persuasion and influence, has explained that people have a tremendous need to reciprocate when someone gives them something. So, if you give your list great value and help them get what they want, you will find that when you ask them to take a look at a product or service that you offer, they will be predisposed to do what you ask.

Once you have established that bond with your new subscribers, you are in a position to make sales and you will be in a much stronger position than all the other marketers out there who have simply been blasting out hype in their ads trying to get attention. Make sure that when you send your new subscriber e-mails that your reply address is always the same so they recognize that it's coming from you. You will also want to make sure that you write "subject lines" in your e-mails that generate curiosity so your subscribers almost have to open your e-mail to find out what you've got in store for them.

Step 2. Review other people's products and make recommendations. A powerful way to make money online is to register as an affiliate for companies who sell products that offer true value to your subscribers. You can then tell your subscribers about these products and when they visit the special Web sites that you send them to, they have the ability to give you credit for any sales that result from your referral.

Typically you will get anywhere from 10 percent to 50 percent commission on each sale you refer, depending on the program, and this can add up to serious money once you have enough subscribers.

With higher ticket items your commission could be $100 to $500 or more, so even a few sales can add up quickly. The advantage to offering reviews of other people's products and referring your subscribers is that you can further build goodwill by telling them about great products while not directly selling them anything of your own. This positioning reduces the natural resistance new subscribers have to being sold and allows you to make money while you build up the relationship. Make sure that you give honest reviews based on your own personal experience with these products and don't just send out marketing materials for those products if you want this strategy to work. Remember, you are building trust with your subscriber and your honest, objective opinion about products and services that you recommend is what they expect from you.

Step 3. Once your list trusts you as an expert, eventually they will want to buy a product from you. The very nature of the bonding process will demand this and you can see that when you have a list clamoring to buy products from you there is hardly a better situation you could ask for. And, all you really need to do to produce products that your list will buy from is to survey them and find out what they want or what they are having problems with. Then, you can either create a product that gives them what they asked for or you can hire someone at Elance.com to do it for you to your specifications.

Step 4. A natural progression from creating products is to offer a limited amount of your time for consulting and coaching with your subscribers. You will get requests for one-on-one time with you and, if you position yourself correctly, you will be able to charge a high rate per hour and work only with the clients you choose. This can be a fantastic income stream and can lead to more product ideas as you get to know your subscribers better and find out what they want at a deeper level.

Step 5. The biggest payoff will come when you organize live events, such as retreats and seminars, where you can bring together a large group of your subscribers to hear you and other speakers talk about subjects they are interested in. There is a huge opportunity to charge admission for these events as well as to sell more products and consulting from the speakers themselves.

IT'S TIME FOR YOU TO GO BUILD YOUR LIST

I've shown you a system for building a list that can be summarized as follows. You now know how to find out:

- Who you want to target when you build your list
- What they want
- What problems they face so you can offer them solutions
- Where they can get what they want and solutions to their problems
- Why your subscribers should get these things from you

This is the foundation of e-mail marketing and will help you follow a step-by-step process that is proven to work. So many people fail to build lists because they don't target a niche and instead try to reach everyone. Or they have no idea what their niche really needs and thereby offer bait and products that are uninteresting to the people they want to attract.

And still more people get subscribers and then fail to build a relationship with them because all they want to do is sell, sell, sell. Build your list as I have shown you, and you will have a loyal band of subscribers who can literally provide you with income streams beyond your wildest dreams.

19

PAUL MYERS
THE PERILS OF
THE INTERNET AND
WHAT YOU CAN DO
TO PROTECT YOURSELF

PAUL MYERS is a copywriter, consultant, and the publisher of *TalkBiz News,* one of the Internet's oldest e-mail-based business newsletters.

FOR MORE INFORMATION: http://www.talkbiznews.com

In This Chapter You Will Learn:

- What Spam Is

- How to Avoid Blocklists and Content Filters

- How to Avoid Scam Attempts

- How to Protect Your Computer

- Time Wasters

THE PERILS OF THE INTERNET AND WHAT YOU CAN DO TO PROTECT YOURSELF

It's a jungle out there. And in the middle of the Internet jungle is a swamp, just crawling with nasty critters you want to avoid. That's what this chapter is about. The perils and pitfalls of doing business online.

Just keep in mind that this is an introduction to the problems, not a complete explanation. Whole books could be written on each of these topics. The goal here is to make sure you're aware of the nastiest hazards and to help you protect yourself from them with a minimum of time and expense.

The good news is that all you need to protect yourself from some of these is to just finish reading this chapter!

Before we get into the specifics, I'd like to point out something that may not be obvious. Every kind of person who exists offline also exists online. That part you knew. What you may not be aware of is that the nasty kinds of people are out there in much larger numbers on the Net than you're ever likely to see in real life.

There are a few reasons for this. The first is simply that you'll "run into" more people online than offline, and from more parts of the world. If you're new to the Net, you'll see this soon enough.

The second reason is based on the technology itself. It's easier for people to be anonymous online. That gives an incentive to the crooks to prowl the virtual byways looking for inexperienced victims. Long before you know enough to track them down, you'll know enough to avoid their scams.

A third reason is that it's simple for one person to use automated systems to hit millions of people with spam, cons, and virus infection attempts, nearly all at once.

In short, the Internet is a magnet for the bad guys. And that's without even considering the problems from the technology!

The good news is, with a surprisingly small amount of effort, you can protect yourself against most of these problems and go happily about your business.

Let's get started.

BLOODY VIKINGS!

Spam. You've seen more than enough of it, I'm sure. At the moment estimates vary wildly, setting spam and viruses at anywhere from 50 percent to 90 percent of all e-mail traffic.

The scourge of e-mail got its name from an old Monty Python script. Two customers went into a restaurant that served spam with every meal. After they'd read a few of the choices, a group of Vikings in the background would begin to chant "Spam, spam, spam, spam" so loudly that they couldn't hear each other speak.

One of the customers looked over her shoulder and yelled, "Shut up, you bloody Vikings!"

Mindless noise that drowns out meaningful conversation.

Spam.

So, how do spammers get your e-mail address in the first place? No matter how tempting it may be to believe, it's almost certain that your ISP did not sell your e-mail address to spammers—even if you got spam to it within hours of creating the address.

Sometimes spammers use old lists of addresses, and someone else may have had that address before you. They may have scraped it from a post or a Web page or an e-mail that got forwarded around by someone you know. They may have gotten it from a machine that was infected by a virus, yours or a friend's. Yes, some viruses will grab your entire e-mail address book and ship it off electronically to a spammer, who will usually sell it to other spammers on top of sending mountains of his own junk to it.

Sometimes they just guess.

Yes, really. Spammers have software that can very rapidly try enormous numbers of combinations of words and numbers before the "@" sign. They track what is refused and what's delivered, and keep the addresses that are valid. This process is called a dictionary attack. It's one of the most common ways for spammers to get addresses that may not be available publicly.

It's close to impossible, as you can see, to keep an e-mail address totally free of spam. But there are steps you can take to cut down on the amount of it you get, and how much of it gets to your e-mail box.

First, if your ISP or Web host offers SpamAssassin or another dependable spam filter, use it. Check the spam folder at least once a week to look for real mail that got inadvertently caught in the filters (called "false positives") before emptying that folder. No spam filter will ever be 100 percent reliable, but the better ones can save you from wasting an awful lot of time.

Warning: If you're using your mailbox for business, I recommend against using what are called "Challenge/Response" systems. Those reply to anyone who e-mails you the first time, requiring them to go to a Web site and type in some password or phrase.

Many people will refuse to jump through hoops to help you keep your mailbox clean. They have enough trouble dealing with their own spam. And you will lose customers if you try to make them do it.

If your ISP or Web host doesn't offer spam filtering, you may want to put a program on your own computer to reduce the amount that gets through. There are a lot of these programs available, and they are introduced or updated so often that between the time I write this and the time you read it, the whole market could change.

To get a sampling of programs you can use, go to Google.com and search on the name of your e-mail program and the phrase "spam filter program" (without the quotes.) When you find one you're thinking of installing, search on the program name and the word "review" to find out what others think of the software.

I recommend having two separate e-mail addresses, too. One that's used publicly, and one that's harder to guess that is only given out to family members, friends, and business associates. There are lots of other things you can do to cut down the amount of spam you get, but these will take care of the majority of it with a very small amount of effort.

The next step is scarier.

WHO ARE YOU CALLING A SPAMMER?

Believe it, unless you're fond of being hated by the majority of the world and having to literally hide from your customers, spamming is not something you want to do. It will get your site shut down, your domain blacklisted, your ISP accounts closed, and cost you a lot of business.

Most people would never dream of spamming, of course. But a surprising number end up doing it because they don't understand what it is and how to avoid it.

The simplest definition of spam, as most people talk about it, is "unsolicited bulk e-mail." The fastest way to get into trouble is to try and play with the definition of one of those words. It's hard to get around what "e-mail" means, but you'd be surprised at the rationalizations some people have for the other two.

For example, you'll hear some people claim that it's either not "bulk" or not "unsolicited" if it's "targeted." By targeted, they mean, "We think they'll be interested in it." It doesn't matter why you think they'll be interested. If they didn't ask for it, and it's bulk, it's almost certainly spam.

That leaves the question of what "asked for it" (solicited) means. It means they asked for it directly, knowing what they'd be getting it before they got it. It does *not* mean:

- They asked for information on your product and got signed up for your newsletter.
- They signed up for a contest and you bought their e-mail address.
- They e-mailed you at some point.
- You had their postal address on your customer list and some company "matched" that with an e-mail address they think belongs to your customer.
- You bought a list.

People who try to play games with the definition of permission are going to get into trouble for it. Don't fall into that trap, as tempting as it might seem.

Another common trap is to believe a company when they tell you they can e-mail your ad to huge numbers of people who supposedly asked to receive ads about products like yours. In virtually all cases, this is a lie. Until you have a lot of experience and have done a ton of reading and research into the issue, don't even think about dealing with people who make claims like this. It's not worth the headaches, I promise you.

In the beginning, build your own list of prospects, one person at a time. This may sound like a slow and tedious process. It will seem that way at first, but what you'll learn from it is important to your long-term success. You'll learn how to fine-tune your e-mails so that they create better results and fewer headaches. You'll find out what's really needed to build credibility with your prospects and subscribers. And, most importantly, you'll learn a little bit about how e-mail really works.

Those are the kinds of lessons that you won't get properly from a book. Just be patient while you learn and pay attention to what your subscribers have to say, and you'll get there much more quickly than you might think right now.

WHAT'S A BLOCKLIST, AND WHY AM I ON ONE?

Building a list of prospects or subscribers is no good if you can't get your e-mail delivered, right? You'll probably hear horror stories about legitimate businesses that end up getting their e-mail blocked at various ISPs. Many of these people brought the problems on themselves.

Let's first look at the two things that most commonly result in your e-mail not getting delivered to those on your list.

BLOCKLISTS AND CONTENT FILTERS

A blocklist is pretty self-explanatory. It's a list of servers and/or domains, which are believed to be sending spam, that is used to block e-mail from those sources.

A content filter is a little more complex. It's a system that "reads" your e-mail before delivering it, and checks it for words and phrases that match patterns commonly found in spam. It also checks for various technical criteria that usually match e-mail from spammers.

Getting on a blocklist can happen in a number of ways. The most likely is that you spammed, whether deliberately or not. If your ISP or Web host allows spammers to use their services without shutting them down quickly, your e-mail might get blocked along with e-mail from the rest of their customers.

If enough of your subscribers don't remember asking for your e-mail and complain, you could end up blocked.

Or you could get blocked because a competitor (or some random "whacko") subscribed to your list and reported you for spamming, just to create trouble for you. This is pretty uncommon, and not something you'll probably ever need to worry about, but it does happen.

And, like so many other things online, there are other factors that can gum up the works. But there are steps you can take to all but eliminate your chances of ending up in a blocklist.

Never add anyone to a list yourself. Let them do it. Be very clear at the point where they sign up about what they're getting, how often they'll get it, and who they're getting it from.

Require that they confirm their subscription. This just means that when someone asks for a subscription, an e-mail is sent to the address they used, telling them to reply or click on a link to show that it was them who asked. This one step will remove nearly all the potential for problems, and also tends to ensure that the people you're e-mailing are actually reading your mail.

Make your e-mail address and subject lines clear, so they know the e-mail is something they asked for.

Send on a regular basis; weekly or twice monthly is about right for most lists. Lists on extremely specialized topics can have longer intervals between mailings, but it's best not to go more than a month in most cases.

Make sure there is always a way for people to unsubscribe easily. And make sure it works.

Keep your lists clean of bad addresses and addresses that regularly can't be delivered to. If you're only mailing to a few hundred people, this isn't as big an issue as it is for larger lists. It's called "bounce handling," and it's something you need to pay attention to no matter how big your list.

Use a responsible host for your e-mailing, and never send large amounts of e-mail through your ISP's servers.

That's really almost all you need to do to make sure you don't end up in a blocklist, and that you can more easily get out of it if you do.

The best way to handle the technical end of things is to use a responsible and established list hosting or autoresponder service for your mailings. They have the experience and connections to do it right. And believe me, if you're sending e-mail to a lot of people, you are going to want to do it right. There are a lot of good e-mail list and autoresponder providers on the Net. The one I use is http:www.//lists.aweber.com.

CHECK THAT!

The way to deal with content filters is to check your copy against a good content checker. One that's easy to use is at http://www.lyris.com/contentchecker/. You'll get an e-mail back showing any problem language. It's simple to make the necessary adjustments. There's one thing you need to watch out for, though.

The checker will tell you that you're okay if your score is below five. Do everything you can to drop that score below four, or even three if you can, because there are things the filters check for that aren't included in the body of the e-mail.

Do that, and you should be fine.

"CON-NECTIONS"

It's quite likely that you'll be exposed to more scam attempts online in one week than offline in your entire life. Seriously.

The most common examples are the e-mails from strangers in foreign countries who want you to help them bring millions of dollars to the United States to invest. They promise you a share, and assure you the entire transaction is safe. You'd be surprised at how many people fall for this and end up losing thousands of dollars in the process.

Another common example is the forging of e-mails from financial institutions (or your ISP) claiming problems with your account and asking you to log in and correct them. The URLs in those e-mails invariably lead to sites owned by gangs who specialize in stealing credit card information. Go there and give them your details and they'll clean your accounts out faster than you can say, "Where'd my money go?"

Another con, and much less obvious, is the e-mail that comes in with an attachment asking you to look at the screensaver, or open the Word doc, or run the patch for Windows.

These can install any number of viruses or "Trojans" on your system. The "payload" (the installed program) can:

- Record every keystroke you enter at any financial Web site, and send them off to the thief who monitors the destination.

- Send your entire address book to a spammer. Ever wonder how you end up getting spam to addresses you only gave to your friends?
- Allow a spammer to use your computer and ISP connection to send spam directly. Yes, another way you could be spamming and not know it. Give a hacker complete access to everything on your computer. Wonderful.
- And many other fun and exciting adventures.

Once upon a time, viruses you got were only a threat to you. Now they're not only a threat to you and your family, but to everyone whose e-mail address or information is on your computer, or whose Web site you visit, or whose e-mail address is on the list of the spammer who takes control of your machine.

Here are some simple steps you can take to dramatically reduce the risks from these virtual nastics:

- Always run a virus checker and update it weekly. Take your pick. On any given day, any virus checker is likely to be as good as any other.
- Never open files sent by e-mail, from anyone, unless you were expecting them. Many viruses and Trojans are sent from machines belonging to friends who don't know they're infected.
- Turn off macros in Word and other MS Office programs. (You can find this under the security settings menu option.)
- Do not download pirated software.
- Do not click on any link in a spam. Don't even open them. Yes, if you have certain features enabled in some e-mail programs, even previewing them can allow your machine to become infected.
- Never buy anything from a spammer. Ever.
- Install and use a firewall. If you don't know how to do this, have your favorite techno-geek do it for you. A very good one, called Zone Alarm, can be had for free from http://www.zonelabs.com.

Those steps won't prevent all possible problems, but they will keep out the vast majority of them, without a lot of time or expense.

To keep up on the latest scams, go to http://www.scambusters.org and subscribe to their newsletter. It's run by some friends of mine who've been monitoring this stuff since 1996. They run the newsletter and site as a public service.

While you're there, look through the archives. It's a good way to get familiar with the landscape quickly. And it's all free.

A REAL CRACKER

Those of you who've been around the Net a while probably noticed that I used the word *hacker* a few times incorrectly.

The correct term for someone who takes over other people's machines for malevolent purposes is "cracker." A truc hacker might break into your system to poke around and see what they can see, but they don't mess things up, and they aren't trying to steal your virtual stuff.

Crackers, on the other hand, are truly nasty people.

They'll scan the Internet for computers that are exposed. A good firewall will help cut your risk of being compromised this way. This is a good idea no matter what kind of connection you have. It's absolutely critical if you're using an "always on" connection, like a cable modem or DSL line.

More direct targets are the servers that your Web sites reside on. Unless you're an ubergeek, you can't do much about security on those machines. About the best you can do here is to ask your Web host about their security efforts, and hope the person you speak with there is knowledgeable and truthful enough to answer you accurately.

It's a very good idea to keep sensitive information, as much as possible, on machines that are not connected to the Net in any way. The prices for decent computers have dropped to the point that it makes a lot of sense to keep your financial and business information on a separate machine.

For processes that must be on connected machines, use the services of companies that have extensive experience in their fields. Trying to save a few dollars on hosting sensitive information could end up being a very expensive proposition in the long run.

DUDE, WHERE'S MY DATA?

One of the biggest problems of using computers is that they can break without warning. This can sometimes involve losing some or all of the data your business depends on.

Make backups. Make them regularly, and keep copies in your office and in a separate location that would be safe if your business computer and everything near it burned or was hit by lightning.

The price of DVD drives is low, and they make very reliable and reasonably fast backup systems for large amounts of data. There is no excuse for not backing up your data. You should backup all business documents, customer and subscriber lists, e-mail addresses books, your e-mail archives, special software, your Web site(s), and anything else that would be difficult to re-create.

If you have proper and current backups, a hard drive crash is just a serious annoyance. If you don't, it can be devastating. Over 90 percent of businesses fail within one year of a catastrophic data loss. You should back up your data at least once a week. If it changes frequently enough, you may want to use an online backup service, like http://www.xdrive .com. They'll give you five gigabytes of backup storage for $9.95 a month. Just make sure you have the software and your passwords backed up separately. And keep local backups anyway. It's not a question of *if* you'll need them, just *when*.

NET OF THE LIVING DEAD

There are a variety of ways to get distracted online. Web surfing, checking your e-mail every 30 minutes, chat programs, and who knows how many others. You need to be careful of all of them.

But the easiest pitfall online can be the "Time Vampires," also occasionally referred to by the less generous as "The Brain Suckers from Mars." These are people, usually very nice, who want free advice. You know, the sort that you usually charge a lot of money for and that takes a lot of time to give properly.

It's easy to say yes. After all, it's just doing something nice for a stranger, right?

Sure. But you'll soon see that there are more strangers out there who want your product free than you can possibly accommodate. And while you're thinking of their welfare, most of them have no concern whatsoever for your family and their needs.

Put specific and severe limits on how much time you'll spend pro bono, if any. And stick to them.

Yet another of the nastier time-sinks you'll run into are those who think that they can get anything they want by waving around their lawyers. (Note: These "lawyers" are usually nonexistent. People who really intend to sue don't normally bash you over the head with it. They file suit.) If someone even hints that they're thinking of any form of legal action, I usually give them my lawyer's contact info and tell them that we are no longer able to communicate except through our respective attorneys.

Please note: This is what I do. This is not legal advice. I am no more an attorney than the imaginary friends most of these people call lawyers. Talk to your own lawyer about this. It's an enlightening discussion that can save you a lot of headaches and lost sleep later.

I won't get into a description of the sorts of weirdness that these folks will claim to have grounds for suit over. Suffice to say, there are a lot of them, and they usually aren't real coherent. Just expect it. If it doesn't happen, consider that a bonus. But don't freak out just because someone says they're going to sue you. That is exactly what they're expecting.

Oh yes, and watch how you spend your time on discussion boards and lists. They can be tremendous time-eaters.

BE THE GURU

There is a huge amount of information you'll need to assimilate over time. That's the bad news.

The good news is that you can become an expert on most things Net-wise in a lot less time than you'd expect, if you make a habit of learning just one new thing per day. The interesting thing about the Net, like any other system, is that the parts are all connected. Everything you learn makes everything else you might want to learn easier.

Don't panic if it seems like you don't know everything you think you should. No one else did when they got started.

And here's a secret: No one else does now, either.

20

ANDY WIBBELS
UNDERSTANDING BLOGS
AND RSS FEEDS

ANDY WIBBELS is a blogging evangelist and creator of the "Easy Bake" Web logs seminar that has helped hundreds of small businesses leverage blogs to increase profits and save time. He is also an expert in helping entrepreneurs use news feed and podcast technology to increase visibility, develop new products, and monitor their competition.

FOR MORE INFORMATION: http://www.blogsandfeeds.com

In This Chapter You Will Learn:

- What a Blog Is

- How to Make Money with a Blog

- What a Feed Is

- How to Get Started with a News Aggregator

5,000 HITS IN ONE DAY

I was stunned. In the midst of the 2004 U.S. Presidential Elections, I posted an irreverent political cartoon on my Web log. It was just something I had cooked up with an old graphics editor—a little animation of John Kerry morphing into Herman Munster (see Figure 20.1). A couple friends and fellow bloggers saw it and laughed.

Then something strange happened.

Over the next three weeks more and more people started linking to my little cartoon. Gradually more and more people found the link and more and more people started visiting my Web log. Then some high-traffic political Web logs caught on and my Web site was blitzed with traffic for five days solid. I was getting thousands of hits from people searching Google for "John Kerry Herman Munster." I received comments from all over the country and all over the world laughing at the cartoon or ranting about it.

That's when I experienced, firsthand, the power of Web logs to reach a passionate audience hungry for information, entertainment, and expertise.

PART I: WHAT THE HECK IS A BLOG?

Here's my definition of a blog: *A blog is an instantly, easily, and frequently updated Web site focused around a topic, industry, or personality.*

FIGURE 20.1 Morphing John Kerry

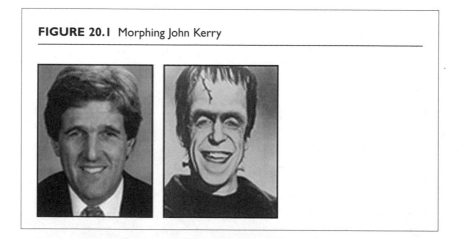

A blog, short for Web log, looks very much like an online diary with the most recent entries—called posts—on the homepage and links to archives of older posts. Often, the posts allow readers to add their own comments at the end to give their opinion or reaction to the post's content.

But, the big deal about blogs is that you can update your blog instantly from any Internet connection anywhere in the world. You use a special type of blogging software called a blog tool to create and update your Web log. You type your latest post into a simple online form. Click "publish" and it is instantly available online for the whole world to see.

How a Blog Works

But how does it work? Why is it easier and cheaper and faster than a conventional Web site? Here's a walk-through.

1. You want to update your Web log with your latest article, update, or announcement.
2. Using any Web browser from any computer, you log in to your blog tool and click the button to create a new post.
3. An online form appears asking for the title of your post. Type in the title.
4. There is also a field for you to write the body text of the actual blog post. Type that in, too.
5. Click "publish."
6. Your Web log is updated in a matter of seconds and your newest post appears online for everyone to read.
7. You go back to your life and remember when you used to pay a Web designer every time you wanted to update your site.

HOW BLOGS HELP BUSINESS

Business blogger Angie McCaig nailed it when she said that a blog is great for business because it provides:

- Fresh content on a daily or at least very regular basis.
- An informal voice that visitors can respond to and get to know.
- Useful information via outgoing links.

Blogging brings back that human voice, that informality that doesn't take things so seriously and enables you to build trust and a deeper connection with your prospects and clients. They're getting to know the real you, not some fabricated brand. Blogs don't aim to seduce the reader into a hypnotic buy-anything trance; they aim to inform, entertain, and create an active conversation.

Get to know your customer. Nobody buys from people they don't know. Blogging allows you to demonstrate your expertise and point of view quickly and easily, and allows the customer to receive your updates in the format they choose.

Collaborate and cross-pollinate. Through skillful partnering, you can create, collaborate, and cooperate in making your own marketing buzz to drive your business to thrive. Many large companies use private blogs to track projects and work groups around the world and report on the latest victories and challenges.

Develop new ideas faster. Web logs are the perfect forums to test out new ideas and get instant feedback. Let them see how you develop your products and services and they can show you how to best serve them.

Reach a mature, affluent, cyber-savvy audience. A survey of over 17,000 blog readers revealed that they are older than the conventional online audience and more affluent. Blog readers buy a variety of items online, click on ads, research purchases online, and are very comfortable with e-commerce.

Fire your web designer. Getting established online can eat up a huge chunk of any starting business's budget and time. You can have a blog ready for traffic tomorrow morning. And all without having to know one lick of HTML. There are 10,000 fewer decisions to make and you're online in the time it takes to watch a sitcom.

Three More Ways a Blog Can Power Your Business

1. *Write your book.* Let your customers help you write your book. Post chapters or ideas and help them help you in researching, testing, and suggesting.
2. *Deliver a Webinar.* Start the Webinar before the call. Use a blog where the participants can get to know each other online before the Webinar. Then after the call-in, move the discussion back into the virtual world to blog learnings and experiences—all recorded, organized, and archived.
3. *Show off your clients.* Invite clients to share their successes with your products and services. It's like a testimonial that never ends. Let clients share their learning and research with your prospects so they can see firsthand how you can help them, too.

Become the Filter

I was in the middle of leading a seminar on blogging when a participant in the audience heckled: "Who reads these things? There's too much stuff online! I don't have time to do all of this reading!"

Neither do your prospects, clients, and colleagues.

Think of all the information that your potential customers and current clients need to know to succeed in their businesses and in their lives. I don't have to read 100 marketing magazines, journals, and Web sites each month to get the information I want. I just find a handful of bloggers I trust to filter the information for me.

What if you can become the filter for your customers? You can provide a digested version of the latest industry trends and news that matters to their businesses and lives. You can become the Web site they can't live without. As you build your reputation, over time, they trust you with their purchases and products. Think of a blog as a sales brochure that never ends.

SIX WAYS TO MAKE MONEY BLOGGING

Here are six ways that you can make blogging pay and help you build your online business:

1. *Sell your own products.* Use a blog to talk about how others are using your products. Enable comments so clients can post testimonials easily for others to see. You'll spend less time managing Web pages and more time making sales!
2. *Develop a members' only blog that requires a membership fee.* Use a public blog to create interest and then a private one for exclusive access to you and your ideas.
3. *Get a sponsor.* Once you've created a dedicated audience you can find a sponsor that needs to get in touch with that audience. Have them underwrite your blog expenses.
4. *Include affiliate sales opportunities.* Writing a book review? Include that Amazon link and suggest related products. Tease the reader with how a product has changed the way you do business and then show them just where to buy it.
5. *Use hosted ads.* Services like BlogAds or Google AdSense can put ads on your blog that are related to your content. PVR Blog, which covers news in personal television recorders like TiVo, pays for its hosting using this method.
6. *Add a tip jar.* Ask readers to send you some dough through PayPal or Amazon if they are finding your blog useful.

Start Your First Blog

Here's a quick guide to starting your first blog. We'll be using a blog tool called TypePad. TypePad provides not only the blog tool software for you but also hosts your blog as well. The tool also has enough flexibility to let you personalize your blog, but not so many options to get overwhelmed. It costs $5–$15 a month and offers a 30-day free trial.

The first thing to do is create your account with TypePad.

1. Go to http://www.typepad.com/ and click on the button for the 30-day free trial.

2. Create an account.

3. Enter your billing information.

4. Choose a Web log name. Something obvious but juicy. You can change your blog's title at anytime.

5. Choose a layout structure for your blog and a design style. Again, you can change these if you want at a later time.

6. Choose a level of Web log privacy. ("Publicized" is fine for right now.)

7. Confirm your registration.

8. You are now registered, logged in, and ready to add your first post to your first blog!

Your First Blog Post

Now let's walk through making your first post!

1. Click on the "Post" link next to the name of your Web log. The "Compose a New Post" screen displays.

2. In the title field, type 'Hello World!' Don't worry about choosing a category for right now.

3. In the post section type a few sentences of text.

4. Scroll down to the bottom of the page and click on "Save." Type-Pad publishes your post.

5. Click on "View Web Log" (located on the right). Your new blog loads in a new window.

6. That's it!

Wash. Rinse. Repeat.

Now that you've made your first blog post, take some time to explore and experiment with TypePad. It is a powerful tool with many features that are great for beginners as well as advanced bloggers.

Say Hi to Google!

You'll also find that blogs are among the top results in search engines. Here's why:

- *Blogs are updated frequently.* Search engines are always scanning the Internet for the latest and greatest, so blogs are updated much more often than a conventional Web site.
- *Blogs are interlinked.* They are also more likely to be linked with many incoming as well as outgoing links. Search engines use this information to rank a page's importance for different search keywords.
- *Blogs are built structurally.* The HTML behind blogs is usually much simpler and more meaningful. Many conventional sites are clogged with pointless tables and graphics.
- *Blogs are better organized.* Along with their structural simplicity, blogs use archives and other architecture to be more readable by the search engines. They are built for "speed reading" by an indexing robot.

The Future of Blogging

Once all the blogging hype is done, what will remain is the notion of personal content management. Large corporations use software to manage the content of millions of pages on a Web site. Blogging is content management on a personal level. Eventually the idea that you can easily edit any page of your Web site from anywhere at anytime won't be any big deal.

Thinking out of the (In)box

Every day, hundreds of people read what's on my Web sites. But more and more, they aren't going to my Web site to read it. They get my articles and updates, as well as the latest updates from all of their other favorite Web sites, rolled up into their own customized newspaper. They do it with feeds.

PART II: WHAT THE HECK IS A FEED?

A feed is a small file on a Web site containing the site's latest updates and headlines, called items. The feed file is updated every time the site itself is updated. Feeds have many different names: news feeds, RSS feeds, Atom feeds, XML feeds, Web feeds, channels, syndicated content, etc. To make things simple, I'm just going to call them feeds.

Just like a word processing document can be in Microsoft Word or WordPerfect format, a feed can be published in multiple formats. Think of them as flavors. Common formats are RSS and Atom. Nearly all feed formats are in a family of formats called XML. That's why sometimes a feed is referred to as an XML feed.

How You Read Them

Similar to how e-mail is read with an e-mail program, feeds are read with a special type of software called a news aggregator. A news aggregator is like having your own research assistant. It periodically scans your favorite Web sites and always knows the latest news, rolling it all up into your own customized newspaper.

How Feeds Work

Here's how a feed works from the perspective of an online marketer:

1. You add the latest article or update to your Web site or blog.
2. You also update your feed file and upload it to your site. If you are using a blog tool or a feed generator, this is done automatically.
3. The aggregator of one of your readers periodically checks your site's feed for any updates.
4. The aggregator notices that you updated your feed and grabs the feed file.
5. Finally, the aggregator combines your feed with the customer's other favorite news and updates into an up-to-date, customized view.

How Feeds Help Business

So let's look at what just happened:

- You added new information to your Web site or blog.
- Your customers were notified that you added new content.
- They read your updates right alongside their other must-read news like *The New York Times* or *CNN*.
- You didn't clog their inbox.
- You didn't fight for attention with the rest of their e-mail.
- No spam filter stood in the way.

Feeds are a direct channel to your customers. You are part of the most important news that they read. Your updates and products are as important to them as their favorite Web sites and news sources. They are committed to receiving your messages. You aren't competing with their personal e-mail or other e-zine publishers.

Getting Started with a News Aggregator

The easiest way to understand the value of feeds for online marketing is to start using a news aggregator your-self. We are going to use the free Web-based news aggregator Bloglines for this example.

Create a Bloglines Account

There are five easy steps to creating a Bloglines account:

1. Go to http://www.bloglines.com/ and click on the link to sign up. A brief message displays with a register link at the bottom.
2. Click on the register link. The registration form displays.
3. Complete the form and click "register." Bloglines sends a confirmation e-mail to your inbox.
4. Go to your e-mail and find the confirmation e-mail. It'll have the subject "Bloglines Validation E-mail."
5. Click on the link in the e-mail to validate your Bloglines account. Your registration is now complete.

Get Familiar with Bloglines

Click on the "My Feeds" tab. The My Feeds screen displays. The My Feeds window is split into two panes or sections.

1. The left pane shows the feeds you are subscribed to. By default you have been subscribed to Bloglines News.
2. The right pane will show the latest updates for that feed.

Click on "Bloglines News." In the right pane the latest updates from the Bloglines News feed displays. Each item includes a linked headline leading to the actual article on the Bloglines company Web log and an excerpt of the news story or article

Next to the name of the Bloglines News feed is an "Unsubscribe" link. Clicking on this link will remove this feed from your list of feeds.

Five Steps to Adding a Feed

1. Click on the "Directory Tab." The Directory displays.
2. Click on "Most Popular Feeds." The list of the most popular feeds displays.
3. Find a feed you like. Click on "Subscribe." The details of the feed display.
4. Don't worry about all the options available right now. Click on the "Subscribe" button. The My Feeds page displays with the new feed added to the list on the left pane.
5. Click on the linked name of the feed and the latest updates display in the right pane.

Finding Feeds

So where do you find all of these feeds that you can add to your news aggregator? There are many places to find feeds for your favorite Web sites.

FIGURE 20.2 Syndication Buttons

XML

RSS

Syndicate this site (XML)

Most sites have buttons or graphics that link to the site's feeds. They usually look something like Figure 20.2.

Look for the words *RSS* or *Atom* or *XML* or *Syndicate.* To get the link of a feed, click on the actual button, link, or graphic. You'll see the link to the feed in your browser's address bar (see Figure 20.3).

Another place to find feeds to your favorite sites is in feed directories. Some of the more popular ones are Syndic8 (http://www.syndic8.com; click on "Categories"), and News Is Free (http://www.newsisfree.com/; click on "Browse Sources"). Once you navigate to a certain news source you'll see the familiar orange-and-white button. Click on it to get the link to the feed.

What to Do with the Feed Link

When you click on a feed button or link it'll look like techie gobbledy-geek. Don't fret about that. All you need is the link in your browser's address bar, the part that starts with "http://." Just copy and paste that to your news aggregator.

FIGURE 20.3 The Address Bar

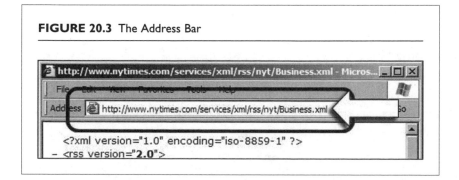

Now you've got all the basic know-how to start using an aggregator to do your online reading. You can customize your daily view of the news and what's new online—and none of it is taking up space in your inbox.

Create a Feed in Five Minutes

So what if you don't want to just read feed but actually publish them? There's three ways to create a feed:

1. *The boring way.* The long, boring way to make a feed is by hand. You can use a text editor and try and cook up your own feed and then upload it to a server. But that takes forever.
2. *The super-easy way.* Use a blog tool or feed generator to create your feed. Reference the blogging tutorial above to get started.
3. *The other easy way.* If you aren't ready to dive into "blog land" but still want to have a feed for your e-zine or site, you're in luck. You can use an e-mail-to-feed service to create a feed from your newsletter's broadcasts. One such service is MailByRSS, available at http://www.iupload.com/. Simply e-mail your newsletter or announcements to MailByRSS and then MailByRSS takes that e-mail and turns it into an item in your feed.

Say Hi to Yahoo!

Another big fat reason to get started with feeds is because the traditional search engines are starting to integrate feeds and their content into their search listings. The prime example is Yahoo!

Until recently, Yahoo! only allowed users to read news sources that they chose. But now Yahoo! has started allowing users to add feeds to their customized news view. And here's the kicker: Once you add your own feed to any Yahoo! search you are added to the searchable database of feeds within minutes. Yes, all you have to do is create a feed and add it to the Yahoo! feed database and be part of Yahoo!'s feed search results instantly!

The Future of Feeds: The Death of the E-zine?

So why would anybody in their right mind still use an e-zine to reach their subscribers?

- *There's no spamming.* Evil spammers have made everybody less likely to subscribe than ever.
- *There are no viruses.* E-mail–based viruses are rampant and have further eroded the trust in e-mail delivery. Feeds protect your subscribers.
- *The power is in the recipient's hands.* A feed is like a TV channel—if it becomes annoying, they can just turn it off, for good.
- *Your messages are on par with the recipient's favorite and most important news.* You are important enough to be a part of their customized newspaper.

Feeds and news aggregators are finally starting to be accepted among the general online audience, but it will be a bit longer before they truly hit the mainstream. Once the next version of Windows or AOL supports news aggregation, expect feeds to be ready for prime time. And you can be there, ready to broadcast your content and messages through this fascinating new medium.

MITCH MEYERSON
COACHING AND THE
VIRTUAL BUSINESS

MITCH MEYERSON is a consultant, author, coach, and the founder of the Guerrilla Marketing Coach Certification Program. Over the past 20 years, he has helped clients break through barriers in their personal and professional lives. Mitch is the author of six personal development books and audios including *Six Keys to Creating the Life You Desire, When Is Enough Enough?* and *When Parents Love Too Much*. His books appear in over 21 languages and he has been featured on the *Oprah Winfrey Show*. He has personally trained and certified over 100 coaches through his Guerrilla Marketing Coach Certification Program.

FOR MORE INFORMATION: http://www.mitchmeyerson.com

In This Chapter You Will Learn:

- What the Guerrilla Marketing Coach Program Is

- The Ten Coaching Competencies

- How Coaching Is the Online Marketer's Untapped Opportunity

- How Assessments Are Tools for Success

A WINNING STRATEGY FOR EVERY ONLINE BUSINESS

In *Online Marketing Superstars* you've learned countless strategies and techniques for building a successful online business. In this chapter, we're going to explore one more way, something that most marketers overlook, causing them to leave easy money on the table. I'm referring to coaching. Adding coaching services or programs to your virtual business is an important revenue stream that can extend the value of your core products and services, while providing you with yet another stream of Internet income.

For me, coaching was a natural addition to my online business, blending seamlessly with my more than 20 years of experience as a practicing psychotherapist. It has allowed me to reach out to more people with my products and services, while at the same time doing it in a cost-effective manner. In this chapter, I'm going to teach you about the Ten Coaching Competencies that will help you add this valuable and often untapped area to your new or established Internet business. I'm also going to introduce you to assessments, an effective tool that can be combined with your coaching to maximize benefits to your customers. But, first, I'll share my journey that led me from practicing therapy to running a successful online marketing business.

FROM THERAPIST TO COACH

In 1984, I started my practice as a psychotherapist, counseling individuals and running personal growth groups in my office in downtown Chicago. During that time, I worked with thousands of people to help them identify and break through barriers to success. Most of their challenges focused on relationship difficulties and struggles at work.

As I noticed a variety of recurring patterns among a wide variety of clients, I developed and tested my own theories as to why people do what they do.

In 1990, I cowrote my first book entitled *When Parents Love Too Much*. This book was a success and was featured on the *Oprah Winfrey Show*.

In the years following, I developed a strong interest in the notion of "chronic dissatisfaction" and why some people are never really happy. My second book, *When Is Enough Enough? What You Can Do If You Are Never Satisfied* (1996), explored these ideas in depth and shaped many of the theories underlying the development of my Guerrilla Marketing Coach Certification Program.

BREAKING FREE

In 1999, I simplified these ideas into a workbook entitled *Six Keys to Creating the Life You Desire*. This easy-to-use manual, which can be used for self-coaching, includes over 100 exercises that the reader can complete on their own. All of my books can be found at http://www.breakingfree .com.

Looking back at my evolution as a writer and therapist, I see a gradual but intentional shift in my approach from exploring "why" people do what they do to "how" they could create more productive, fulfilling lives. This natural evolution led me into the field we now refer to as coaching.

In the mid-1990s, I noticed a new business model emerging in the therapy and business arenas called coaching. It was created by a brilliant innovator and businessman named Thomas J. Leonard.

THE VIRTUAL BUSINESS—GUERRILLA MARKETING COACH PROGRAM

One of the most intriguing aspects of the coaching movement was that many coaches worked virtually, interacting with clients using the telephone and through the Internet. Being able to coach this way opened up the amazing possibility of reaching people from all over the world!

By the late 1990s, the coaching field boomed and competition increased. It was difficult for newer coaches to compete with the 10,000 coaches already in the marketplace. Intuitively, if these businesses were to survive, I knew there would be a great need for marketing skills, not only for the coaches, but also for millions of other small businesses.

After a month or so of pondering this problem I came up with what I call my big idea.

For years, I had been familiar with a bestselling series of *Guerrilla Marketing* books by Jay Conrad Levinson. They addressed the issue of marketing a small business without spending a lot of money. Having read many of these books and finding them useful for my own business, I knew they were perfect for the small business owner.

And that's why I developed a coaching program based on *Guerrilla Marketing*—it brings in to play all aspects of marketing. A coach provides the qualities of listening and accountability, and the important aspect of forwarding the client's actions. It was from combining these two important concepts that the Guerrilla Marketing Coach Program was born.

In a matter of months, I created a 12-week Guerrilla Marketing Coach Certification Program, which since 1999 has trained and certified over 130 coaches at GmarketingCoasch.com.

COACHING: THE ONLINE MARKETER'S UNTAPPED REVENUE STREAM

You might be asking yourself, what does coaching have to do with online marketing? Well, everything. Offering coaching services and programs to your clients is the pot of gold at the end of your online marketing rainbow. But, first, let's talk about coaching and what it is.

Coaching versus Consulting

The distinction between coaching and consulting is confusing to many people. Simply put, consulting is a process by which the consultant is the expert. Their role is to lead the client to the best solution that the consultant has determined through prior analysis.

Coaching is a process where the coach asks questions to uncover the answers that the client has within them. The client is considered an expert on their own life, with the coach serving as an objective listener asking questions and providing valuable insight.

In my Guerrilla Marketing Coach Certification Program, we train our coaches to wear the hats of both the coach and the consultant. The key is to be conscious and intentional about which approach you are using and why.

Coaching versus Seminars

Seminars, which can be highly motivational and stimulating, fall short when it comes to promoting permanent life changes. It is very difficult to lay the foundation for long-term change through a seminar that lasts only a day or two. The challenge always seems to be how to maintain and sustain the momentum after the seminar ends.

Coaching, however, is an ongoing process. Unlike a seminar that transports you to a peak experience but doesn't provide follow-through, working with a coach is like taking a journey with an experienced guide who can show you the way. With a coach, you can establish habits that will propel you forward. A professional life coach will encourage you to enjoy not only the scenery along the way, but to enjoy the journey to the top.

COACHING AND TECHNOLOGY

We are living in amazing times when it comes to global communications. In my Guerrilla Marketing Coach Certification Program, I regularly have students calling in from Europe, Japan, Australia, and other countries. With long-distance rates so affordable, the world can easily become our marketplace.

The key to building an international business is in developing a strong Internet presence founded upon a strategic direct marketing Web site and a regular e-mail follow-up program.

WHAT DOES THIS MEAN TO YOU?

Coaching can be a cost-effective, highly profitable addition to your online business. You already have a product or service that can easily be bundled with coaching services to create another lucrative revenue stream for your business.

Engaging clients, after the initial sale, through valued-added services like individual or group coaching, or through coaching programs, is not only an easy way to expand your earnings capability, but also a great way to expand your offerings.

HOW CAN I DELIVER MY COACHING TO MY CLIENTS AND CUSTOMERS?

I market and deliver my Guerrilla Marketing Coach Certification Program exclusively through technology. I use the latest in audio conferencing to host our weekly group calls. This technology allows me to record calls with the push of a button, and also provides me with audio files that can be saved and archived for future playback. My course materials, which are delivered through audio and downloadable content files, are available exclusively through my Web site. I'm currently working on several new products that will be delivered through the Web and combined with audio and video capabilities to create a full-sensory experience for my clients.

IMPLEMENTING COACHING INTO YOUR ONLINE BUSINESS

How might you implement coaching into your online marketing business? How can you extend the value of your core product and service offerings? Here are a few suggestions:

- *Offer individual or group coaching to support your products and services.* For example, you might sell a piece of software that helps people design marketing letters. As an add-on program, you might offer individual coaching or a series of seminars around writing effective headlines, the components of an effective sales letter, or captivating copywriting techniques. These programs can be easily delivered through audio, Web, or video technology.

- *Create a coaching program.* I took the concept of Guerrilla Marketing and developed a 12-week program to not only teach participants how to use these tools in their own businesses, but also how to teach them to others. I added the component of a certification so that participants could brand themselves as an expert. The program, marketed exclusively via the Internet, is delivered through audio technologies as well as the Web.
- *Create coaching products.* Why not record your coaching seminars to sell as an audiocassette program, CD, or video series? You can easily package these items by themselves, or bundle them with a workbook.
- *Develop an e-program or e-book.* Again, building on your coaching and consulting expertise around your core products and services, you can repackage the material to develop an e-program, a series of lessons delivered at predefined intervals via e-mail, or even an e-book, a product available for download, both delivered easily and effortlessly through the Internet.

MORE ABOUT COACHING: BECOMING A GOOD COACH AND THE TEN COACHING COMPETENCIES

What do you need to know to get started with coaching? This short introduction will give you an idea about the types of skills you'll need to develop to add coaching to your offerings.

In my business, Guerrilla Marketing is all about combining effective coaching skills with specific marketing knowledge that will grow your business. Because coaching skills are such an important part of the process, I developed another self-assessment around the Ten Coaching Competencies.

These competencies are important if you want to become a coach, an effective marketer, or simply if you want to coach yourself to success.

Test your coaching competency. Read each statement and score each competency on a scale of 1 to 10 (1 = poor, 10 = excellent).

Test Yourself on the Ten Coaching Competencies

1. *Active listening.* Focus your full attention on another person in order to understand both what is said and what is not said. Notice feelings, beliefs, and motivations.
2. *Accountability and structures.* An intention or system for holding a person to his or her commitments. Structures remind clients of their goals or actions they can take right away (e.g., calendars, e-mail reminders, alarm clocks, rubber band around the wrist, etc.).
3. *Affirmation.* Validation or praise of a person's actions, thinking, or way of being, which serves to affirm and energize.
4. *Key questions.* Questions that deepen understanding of self or that promote discovery of possibilities. The best questions are open ended.
5. *Content versus process.* Rather than just discussing the events or content of the day, identify repeating patterns of interaction (e.g., recurring procrastination, defensiveness, self-sabotage).
6. *Managing resistance.* Noticing and addressing stuck points, procrastination, and avoidance, and addressing them in a productive way.
7. *Challenging.* Making big requests or delivering truthful messages in order to promote a shift in another's thinking or actions.
8. *Strategizing.* Supporting an individual in identifying their vision, mission, purpose, values, and goals, and in creating a solid strategy to reach a desired result. It involves looking at where an individual is, where they want to be, how trends are affecting the overall marketing strategy, and what must shift in order to reach goals in an effective way.
9. *Reframing.* Supporting an individual to overcome limiting beliefs, negative thinking, or inner contradictions by altering the language used to describe one's experience.
10. *Forwarding the action.* Supporting an individual to identify the steps needed to realize a desired goal, and to identify and eliminate barriers that could restrict forward movement.

For a detailed description on each of these competencies, go to CoachingSkillsMasterCourse.com.

ASSESSMENTS: TOOLS FOR SUCCESS

I have always enjoyed developing personal growth tools and, similarly, I encourage my clients to create models, theories, and products of their own. In fact, I think one of the strengths of coaching is the ability to set up systems of accountability with your clients.

I am an advocate of the self-assessment because when we measure our effectiveness in something, it gives us a starting point for improving and raising our proficiency in that area.

One example of an assessment is the "16 Guerrilla Marketing Competencies Assessment" created for the Guerrilla Marketing Coach Certification Program. When I created this inventory, I asked myself, "What are the most important concepts of Guerrilla Marketing and how can I create a self-assessment to assist business owners score and track their skills in each area?"

The following assessment tool is excerpted from the Guerrilla Marketing Toolkit (http://www.gmtoolkit.com). Assessments can be an effective addition to any coaching program. Try this assessment for yourself.

TEST YOURSELF ON THE 16 GUERRILLA MARKETING COMPETENCIES

Read each statement and score each competency on a scale of 1 to 10 (1 = poor, 10 = excellent). Answer each question *not only* from your own perspective, *but as a client or customer* would answer for you.

1. I see every contact with my customers and prospects as marketing. My words, attitudes, and actions are intentional and based on my marketing goals.
2. I look at my marketing activities from the customer's point of view. I consistently make time to ask my customers and prospects what it is they really want.
3. I am aggressive in my marketing efforts.
4. My marketing attack includes an assortment of strategies. I make use of many of the 100 marketing weapons available to me.
5. If I surveyed my customers today, they would agree that I follow up in a consistent and timely manner.

6. I consistently use a marketing calendar to track and measure the effectiveness of my marketing weapons.

7. My friends, prospects, and customers would say I am enthusiastic and consistently positive in all my interactions with them.

8. I have a clearly defined marketing niche.

9. I have a clear and specific marketing plan to guide my weekly actions.

10. I use online marketing as one of my major marketing weapons. I utilize e-mail, a Web site, and the vast power of the Internet to reach new prospects and communicate with customers.

11. I build strong one-on-one relationships with my prospects and customers knowing that people buy from friends rather than strangers.

12. My business is oriented toward giving. I provide free consultations, tips, gifts, and information. I make generosity a part of my overall marketing plan.

13. I look for ways to amaze my customers by providing exceptional service.

14. I consistently use my imagination to develop marketing strategies that are unconventional and that will capture the attention of my target market.

15. I actively work on developing strategic alliances with other businesses.

16. I take consistent action on my marketing plan.

The template in Figure 21.1 allows you to track your progress over a number of weeks. The areas where you consistently score low represent obstacles or roadblocks to your success. Until you address them, they will continue to hold back your progress.

I require my clients and coaches to track their scores once a week for a three-month period. I have noticed that when they utilize this powerful assessment tool and raise their scores, they consistently attract new clients and build their businesses.

What types of assessments can you create to support your online business?

FIGURE 21.1 Tracking Template

Competency	Week 1	Week 2	Week 3	Week 4
1. Intentionality				
2. Sensitivity				
3. Aggressiveness				
4. Assortment				
5. Follow-up				
6. Measurement				
7. Enthusiasm				
8. Niche				
9. Marketing Plan				
10. Internet Marketing				
11. Relationships				
12. Giver Stance				
13. Outstanding Service				
14. Imagination				
15. Marketing Partners				
16. Consistent Action				

© 2004 Mitch Meyerson and Jay Conrad Levinson. For a downloadable version, visit http://gmarketingcoach.com.

LOOKING FORWARD

Clearly, adding coaching to your menu of offerings is a powerful and profitable way to extend the value of your current products and services. Low-cost customer delivery solutions, like audio conferencing as well as Web and video options, makes coaching an efficient and effective addition to any online business.

Over the past year, I have been finding more ways to blend my psychology and personal growth background with marketing strategies delivered through technology. My fascination with the Internet has inspired me to create more digital products and teleclasses to reach more people quickly and inexpensively.

My original Guerrilla Marketing Coach Certification Program will continue to expand and grow as will a new Internet marketing program, based on this book, to be launched in the near future. To keep abreast of new developments, visit www.OnlineMarketingSuperstars.com

Lastly, in the coming year, I will be writing more songs and releasing a CD of my original music, which can be found at http://www.mitchsongs .com.

We are living in a time like no other. Without leaving the comfort of our home or office, we can reach millions of people, globally, with the mere click of a key. We have dozens of tools right at our fingertips to take any business from idea to online marketing success. From Web copywriting to e-mail campaigns, from shopping cart technology to audio, Web, and video delivery strategies, our imaginations are the only limitation to the success that can be ours.

JOE VITALE
JOINT VENTURES:
THE SECRET TO PROFIT
AND PRODUCTIVITY
ONLINE

DR. JOE VITALE is the world's first Hypnotic Marketer and an Internet Marketing pioneer. He is the president of Hypnotic Marketing Inc. and author of way too many books to list here, including *The Attractor Factor,* the bestselling e-book *Hypnotic Writing,* and the bestselling Nightingale Conant audio program, "The Power of Outrageous Marketing."

FOR MORE INFORMATION: http://www.mrfire.com

In **T**his **C**hapter **Y**ou **W**ill **L**earn:

- A Behind-the-Scenes Look at Joint Ventures

- How to Run a Joint Venture Campaign

JOINT VENTURE GOLD: THE SECRET TO PROFIT AND PRODUCTIVITY ONLINE

Scene One

Ten years ago. Mark Joyner is starting an Internet company. He likes my books and audio recordings, writes me an e-mail, and asks if he can release one of my works as an e-book.

"As a what?" I write back.

"An e-book," he replies. "They're computer files containing books. You read them on your monitor."

Being the futurist that I am, I told him I never thought an e-book would ever sell. I love books, but the real ones. The printed, hefty ones that you can see, touch, and hold. E-books are invisible. Who would want one? Not me. I passed on his offer.

Every two months, Mark would send me another e-mail. He always asked the same thing. Sometimes he got a little more persuasive by mentioning the success of one of his own e-books. I still didn't understand the concept. I told him no.

Finally, after two years of e-mail exchanges, Mark writes me again. This time I'm feeling sorry for the guy. I dust off an old manuscript of mine, pay someone to input it into a computer file, and I e-mail it to Mark.

"Here," I say. "See if you can sell this."

He puts up a Web site HypnoticWriting.com. He writes a sales letter for it. The letter is so strong I read it and want to buy my own book.

Overnight he sells 600 copies of it at $29.95 a copy. I quickly sense that this is all profit. There was no printing, inventory, fulfillment, warehousing, or much of anything else as a normal book expense. This is like the Holy Grail of publishing.

"How did you do that?" I ask Mark.

"Do what?"

"Sell so many e-books in just one day?"

"It's all done with joint ventures," he tells me.

"And what is that?"

"That's my army," he says, reminding me of his stint in the service. "Joint ventures are arrangements I have with people out there selling the e-book for me. I don't sell it. They do."

"What's in it for them?"

"Money."

I begin to s-l-o-w-l-y understand the concept of joint ventures.

Scene Two

Five years ago. I receive an e-mail from someone unknown, by the name of Larry Dotson. He said he compiled a book packed with hypnotic words, phrases, statements, mental starters, closers, and more. He wanted to know if I would look at it and maybe write a foreword to it. He was polite. I was curious. I agreed.

He sent the book. One look and I bolted straight up in my chair. This stuff was fantastic. I immediately wrote Larry back and asked if I could contribute to the book in some way. I wanted to be a part of history.

He instantly e-mailed back and wrote, "You can put your name on it and not write a word. Add material if you want. Write a foreword if you want. Don't do anything if you don't want. Whatever you do, I'd be proud to have you be my coauthor."

That became our first collaborated e book. You can see a description of it at HypnoticWritingSwipeFile com. We went on to write seven more e-books together. He helped create my brand recognition as the "hypnotic writer." And it helped Larry Dotson become well known. And we did it all through e-mail, never meeting, or even once talking on the phone.

Why was he willing to joint venture authorship with me?

Before we worked together, Larry was completely unknown. He wanted to hitch a ride on my comet. He also knew I had a mailing list and some online celebrity status. He knew joining forces with me would help him.

And why did I agree to do anything with him at all?

It was only fair. It was his book. We went on to write several of them. Alone, it would have taken me years to write seven books. With us sharing the chores, we did it in a year or more.

I'm starting to like this joint venture gig.

Scene Three

Three years ago. Jim Edwards is a reporter in Virginia. He writes, asks to interview me, and we have a pleasant conversation. The article runs in a local publication. It was nice. I thank him and we go our separate ways.

Months later and he writes me again. This time he asks if he could coauthor a book with me. He says he'll do most of the work. I think about it and give him an old manuscript I had from years ago, on how to write a book in six days. It was the course outline for a class I used to teach in Houston long, long ago, when I was young and had hair.

Jim takes my writing, adds to it, turns it into an e-book, and calls it *How to Write Your Own Outrageously Successful E-book—In Only 7 Days*. He puts up a site at 7Dayebook.com. Like Joyner, he begins selling e-books almost instantly.

That e-book has been a number one bestseller at Clickbank, a popular site for selling digital products, for over three years. Jim and I make thousands of dollars each and every month from that one little digital product. Neither of us thought the pickings would be so good.

Why did I let him take my original idea and turn it into an e-book?

My idea, the old manuscript, was gathering dust in a box in the attic. Jim Edwards breathed life into it. He also turned it into a product. He also found the first affiliates who began selling the e-book for us through their joint venture arrangements with us. Jim is now famous online in his own right. Our joint venture kicked him into the spotlight.

I'm beginning to see that joint ventures are win-wins.

Scene Four

Two years ago. Jo Han Mok and I are in Dallas, attending the first ever Armand Morin Big Seminar. We note that the majority of the people in the room are newbies. They don't have a clue on how to make money online.

"We ought to write a book just for them," I mention to Jo Han.

He quickly agrees. We decide to begin it as soon as we return to our homes, which for him was in Boston at the time, and for me was near Austin.

But wait a minute.

A thought occurs to me.

"Why do we want to write the book?" I ask Jo Han in an e-mail. "Let's pull a 'Chicken Soup' and get others to write the book for us."

I'm referring to the success of Mark Victor Hansen and Jack Canfield's long series of *Chicken Soup* books. They didn't write any of the books. They compiled them. And people keep buying them.

Jo Han agreed to my idea. We then wrote simple e-mails and sent them to every successful Internet person we could find. Within a few days we were receiving contributions from 32 hot shots of the online world. They were writing the book for us. We sat back and let their articles appear in our e-mail box.

Those contributions became *The E-Code*. It's a huge book, brimming with clever ideas from such legendary marketers as Joe Sugarman and Mark Joyner, to brilliant authors, such as Mark Levy and even Jo Han and myself.

When the book is published by J. Wiley later this year, we will ask the 32 authors in the book to help us market it. Because they are in the book, they all have an investment in its success.

This is a joint venture of productivity and of profit. We created a book in less than seven days. We'll sell it with the help of 32 people, all partners desiring the same goal: the book's success.

And this is a glorious example of a joint venture at work.

At this point, I'm addicted to joint ventures.

Scene Five

Last year. Pat O'Bryan is working on a Web site, his first, over at InstantChange.com, and is frustrated. He's working night and day. He's learning as fast as he can. But he can't seem to catch up. He walks into a meeting and jokingly says, "One day I'm going to write a book called *The Myth of Passive Income*."

Everyone laughs.

I don't.

I see an opportunity.

"Write it," I say.

The next thing I know, he's asking me to be the coauthor. Then I'm advising him to follow the joint venture strategy that Jo Han and I used to create *The E-Code.*

Within hours (*hours,* mind you) we're sending out a simple e-mail to people who make a living online. We ask them to tell us about a day in their "passive income life." One day later (one day!) and the submissions are coming in. Seven days later, just one week after we started the process, and the book is done. We put up a site and sell it at MythOfPassiveIncome .com. We go back to all the contributors and ask them to be an affiliate and sell it for us. They do.

Why?

Because this is a joint venture. It was written that way. It is sold that way. Long live joint ventures.

I could go on and on. These are all examples of joint ventures, or JVs. Some were done to create a product. Some were done to sell a product. In every case, the arrangement was a win-win.

And that's why I love joint ventures. In the early days of the Internet, Mark Joyner taught me that most joint ventures are 50/50 arrangements. If I write a book and you sell it, I'll give you 50 percent of the money. That's *very* fair. It's also very unusual in the offline world. On the streets, in brick-and-mortar retail stores, commissions for salespeople are often low. Online, they are often high.

Joe Kumar, for example, made history by selling over $100,000 of an e-book he didn't write, in only 30 days. He created the book by writing to people (including me) and asking us to answer a question. He compiled our answers into a book. He then went back to us and asked us to sell it.

But this wasn't any old joint venture. Joe upped the ante. He said he would pay a 70 percent commission for every book sold. That was unheard of. The news of this new JV deal spread virally across the Net. This caused us contributors to be on fire. We sold like crazy. And Joe Kumar, then only 17 years old (a teenager!) and still in high school in Singapore, got rich.

Or take John Reese. This popular Internet guru made $1,080,496.37 in 24 hours online. He made Internet history. How? He set up joint ventures with people. He said he would pay them 10 percent of every sale they made. Jim Edwards made so many sales, I'm told he received a check for over $75,000.

By now you know as much as me about the possibilities of joint ventures.

Or do you?

HOW TO RUN
A JOINT VENTURE CAMPAIGN

Say Mitch Meyerson, the brilliant author of this very book you are reading, wants to make this book a number one bestseller on Amazon. Here's how he might do it as a joint venture:

Step 1. Make a list of all the people who might spread the word about his Amazon campaign. The list should include the contributing authors in this book, like me. But it doesn't have to be limited to who you know. It's a big mistake to think you can't write to the rich and famous. I've contacted everyone from Donald Trump to Evel Knievel. My rule of thumb is this, if they're alive, they're reachable.

A great tip for expanding your reach is to ask everyone you know, "Who do you know who knows (fill in the blank)?" Then say the name of the person you want to meet. Guaranteed, someone in your circle knows someone in their circle who knows the person you want to reach.

Step 2. Write each person a simple, respectful e-mail. Tell them you plan to make your book a bestseller on a particular day and would they help.

Why would they help?

First, the authors in this book will want to see their chapter promoted. They'll help.

Second, those not in this book may want to do a good deed. People are good natured (believe it or not) and will help, if at all possible.

Finally, get them involved in the book's publicity with the next step.

Step 3. To up the odds of people saying they will help promote your book campaign, ask them to contribute something that you can use as a bonus.

In other words, if Mitch wrote to me, I'd offer him one of my e-books as a bonus. Then he could say, "If you buy a copy of my book on Amazon today, you will also get an e-book by Joe Vitale, for free."

You're creating what's called an "ethical bribe" for the buyer. And you're creating a promotional opportunity for the person who gave you the bonus.

Step Four. The hard part is over. Now write a letter that everyone who agreed to help you in your bestseller goal can send out.

Does this JV strategy for creating a bestseller really work?

Ask Terrie Levine, Kevin Hogan, Peggy McColl, Randy Gilbert, Mark Joyner, Dr. Robert Anthony, Joe Galloway, Robert Allen, Larry Winget, and a long list of authors—some known, most unknown. All used this basic joint venture method to make their book either number one best-sellers or at least in the top ten.

I've had three books hit the Amazon bestseller list. *Spiritual Marketing,* now called *The Attractor Factor,* hit the number one spot at Amazon twice. And two of my other books, *Adventures Within,* and *The Greatest Money-Making Secret in History,* have also hit the top ten list at Amazon.

How?

With joint ventures.

I could write a book on joint ventures. When I do, I'll probably get someone else to help me with it, making the project itself a joint venture. And when the book is complete, I'll get others to help me sell it, all through joint ventures. If there's ever been a good karma way to doing business, it's through joint ventures. It's a win-win for all.

Said another way: Share and grow rich.

MICHAEL PORT AND MITCH MEYERSON
HOW TO CREATE PRODUCTS FOR THE WEB

MICHAEL PORT is the leader of the "Think Big Revolution" and an internationally known marketing and business development expert for the entrepreneur. He's the author of the bestselling *Book Yourself Solid: The 7 Keys to Getting More Clients Than You Can Handle*. Michael is a highly sought after professional speaker.

FOR MORE INFORMATION: http://www.michaelport.com

MITCH MEYERSON is the president of Guerrilla Marketing Coach and creator of 16 products, including 4 published books. He is a visionary in the coaching and psychology industries. Over the past 20 years he has been helping clients break through barriers in their per-

In **T**his **C**hapter **Y**ou **W**ill **L**earn:

- What Defines an Online Product

- Why It's Important to Have Your Own Product on the Web

- Six Easy Steps to Creating Your Own Product

sonal and professional life. He is the cofounder with Michael Port of *The Product Factory: 90 Days to an Information Product or Program* (see http://www.90dayproduct.com).

FOR MORE INFORMATION: http://www.mitchmeyerson.com

HOW TO CREATE PRODUCTS FOR THE WEB

There has never been a more exciting and profitable time to create your own online product. Recent breakthroughs in the costs of software, broadband, online hosting, and teleconferencing combined with the explosion of Internet sales, make it easier than ever before for any entrepreneur to create their own products.

Even better, with the advent of automation, it's never been easier to automate the entire sales and distribution of your product, providing you with a passive stream of income while you sleep. It's an incredible opportunity for entrepreneurs and small business owners to create an arsenal of online products on virtually a shoestring budget.

In this chapter we'll tell you exactly what an online product is, why it's important to have one, and how to create the ideal circumstances for navigating to remarkable products, and then we'll guide you through the steps to creating your own. As coaches, our goal is for you to not just understand the process, but to take action. Throughout this chapter, we'll give you some questions and exercises that will help to get you on the road to action.

What Is an Online Product?

There are many different types of products you can create. In this chapter we'll be focusing primarily on information products, but you can apply these principles to other types of products as well.

An information product conveys knowledge. Why is that so exciting? It's exciting because everyone has knowledge that they can share; knowledge that would benefit and enhance the lives of others, and that others would be willing to pay for, making it possible for you, too, to become an info guru.

An information product can be delivered in many different formats, such as an e-book, e-course, special report, manual, tutorial, home study course, teleclass, intensive program, etc. Audio and video can even be added to any of these formats, simply and easily from home, something that wasn't possible even just a few years ago.

Why Is It Important to Have Your Own Product on the Internet?

Imagine this, you open your e-mail first thing in the morning and you see 15 new orders; one from Switzerland, one from Australia, one from India, and a dozen from all over the United States. All for the product you just recently made available on the Web. It's 7:00 AM, you're still sipping your first cup of coffee and only half awake, and already it's been a very profitable day. While this scenario may seem more like a dream than reality to you right now, it's entirely possible to achieve and it's much easier to do than you might imagine. Besides starting each day with a big, Cheshire cat grin, and dollar signs floating through your mind's eye, there are numerous other benefits to having a product available on the Web.

Positions you as an expert. Perception is everything on the Internet and the creation of your own product results in positioning you as an expert and is a critical step in generating new business.

Builds your brand identity. Your product represents you and your business in the marketplace, and making it available on the Web is the first step toward getting your product into more hands, heads, and homes.

Reaches a global marketplace. Having a product available on the Web means that you've expanded your geographic marketplace from local neighborhoods, where your product sits on a shelf, to the entire world via your Web site.

Creates a 24/7, passive revenue, profit machine. The Web never sleeps, which means that you can literally turn your computer and Web site into a cash register around the clock, and many, if not all, of the processes can be automated.

Levels the playing field. In the past, the entrepreneur or small business owner was unable to compete with the larger companies that could afford to mass market products. The Web makes it possible for even the smallest of businesses to compete.

Instantly increases the effectiveness of your sales cycle. This is especially critical for service professionals. Often a consumer will opt to purchase a product as a trial before deciding to purchase your service. Having a quality product available on the Web allows them to get to know a bit more about you and what you have to offer.

In addition to the great benefits listed above that apply to any on-line product, there are several more that apply specifically to information products and make them an even more attractive choice.

Greater cost-effectiveness. Because traditional production and distribution is unnecessary, your costs are significantly reduced and your margin for profit is significantly increased.

Increase your speed to market. While it might take months or years to get a hardbound book written, edited, published, produced, and distributed to book stores, you can deliver the same content in the format of an e-book and bring it into the world in a matter of days or weeks instead.

Content can be leveraged in several formats. The same content can be presented in several different formats—as an e-book, an e-course, a teleclass, a home-study course, and the list goes on and on.

Opportunity for bold self-expression and learning. The Web allows you to get your message to millions simultaneously while at the same time offering you the opportunity to learn in action as you challenge yourself to create something totally unique.

SIX EASY STEPS TO CREATING YOUR OWN PRODUCT

1. Plan Your Project

The project plan underlies the entire product development process. It outlines key components that you need to be very clear about from the project outset in order to strengthen the quality of your desired outcome. (For a complete project planner visit: http://www.90dayproduct .com/freestuff.htm.)

Define your product. This is the first step toward making your dream a reality. The project definition captures not only what the project is, but your passion around doing it. Passion is a requisite for producing remarkable projects.

What are you passionate about?

What type of product would you get really excited about creating (e.g., an e-book, audio program, home-study course, etc.)?

Now define in detail what the product will be. Include a complete description such as the type of product, an overview of the content, the look and feel you wish to convey through the design and/or packaging, and how you will deliver the product to the consumer.

Identify your resources. It's critical to evaluate the resources you have and the ones you need before beginning. Once you've assessed the resources you have, then you can determine what resources you'll need and begin to plan for how to acquire them.

Begin by considering the resources you were born with, your talents and natural gifts. The use of your talents and natural gifts is a key element of creating remarkable products.

What talents and natural gifts can you bring to the creation of your product?

On the flip side, one thing that keeps people from getting on with their projects is believing they need to know something before they start, instead of learning in action. Couple learning with action to take advantage of the opportunity to enhance your knowledge and your skills.

Consider and list five things, along with the resources you'll need, that you can learn in action, during your product creation.

The next great resource to consider is potential partners. Collaborating with others is the way to produce remarkable results. If you are committed to the creation of something truly great, you've got to bring people in as early as possible as you're developing the product.

What talents and/or resources might you want to look for in a potential partner that would enhance the creation of your product? List five of each.

Who can you contact this week that would be a great partner for you? List five people who would be potential partners and schedule times to contact two of them this week.

Some of the other resources that need to be considered are technology, financial, personal, and time. List five or more of these resources that you have, and five or more that you will need for the creation of your product. Begin to contemplate how, and from whom, you might acquire those resources you need and include any ideas that come to mind for each.

Assess the consumer's need. Thinking about your project's purpose, its deliverables, and what makes it different from everything else available on the market will help you to craft a signature product. One that is uniquely yours.

Why does the consumer need your particular product now?

What does your product need to deliver to meet the consumer's need?

What about your product will be different from similar products on the market?

How can you overdeliver on your promises by adding value to make your product "remark-able?"

Answering these questions will help you to set clear intentions for the product, and to craft a big, bold promise based on your intentions. If you can promise your customers, in advance, that you're going to deliver a specific, tangible product by a certain date, that's going to put you into action and motivate you to not only meet, but exceed, that big, bold, and very public promise.

Write out the biggest, boldest promise you can make to your customers. This will be an essential part of the announcement of your product.

Avoid project breakdown. This is something we hope to avoid, but realistically is bound to happen from time to time with any project. However, with a bit of thought and foresight we can identify the most likely causes of project breakdown in advance and take steps to prevent it.

List the most likely causes of project breakdown, and the steps you will need to take to prevent them.

One of the best ways to prevent project breakdown is by developing habits of commitment making and fulfilling. Progress depends on the successful completion of promises. Making and keeping promises will keep everyone on the project on task, and will go a long way toward preventing project breakdown.

List the promises that you need to make, and those that you need to have from others, to keep the project moving ahead. Keep in mind, that this is an ongoing process. As tasks are completed and promises met, new ones will need to be made.

2. Choose Your Role as a Storyteller

There is a story you'll tell with your product in order to facilitate learning and change. You need to choose the role you'll play when delivering your information.

- *Expert: Here is what I've done and here's my theory on why it works.* If you're an expert in an area or would like to develop yourself as an expert, this is the role to take. Michael Port and Mitch Meyerson's "Product Factory" program and product line is an example (see 90DayProduct.com).
- *Interviewer: Compiling information from experts.* You can compile a product by interviewing others who are experts in the field. This book is an example.
- *Researcher: Go out and gather information to serve the needs and desires of your target market.* Compile the results to create a product that meets these needs/desires. Research can turn you into an expert at a future date.
- *Repurposer: Uses and modifies existing content for a different purpose.* Mitch Meyerson combined his knowledge of coaching with the content in many of Jay Conrad Levinson's *Guerrilla Marketing*

books and created the "Guerrilla Marketing Coach Certification Program."

- *Repackager: Takes content and puts it into a different package.* This could be your own content or that of someone else. However, it is critical to get the author's express written permission if you wish to repackage someone else's content.

Choose and list the role that is best suited to you and your product.

3. Choose the Framework for Your Product or Program

When telling a story, you need a framework from which to tell it. The same thing applies when it comes to product development and presentation. This not only helps you to organize the information when you're creating your product, but it will help the consumer to get the most value from the product. Below are seven different frameworks that you might consider using.

1. *Problem/Solution.* State a problem and then present solutions to the problem. For example, you might develop a product on how to improve your golf score. The problem is your golf score, followed by a number of solutions to improve it.
2. *Numerical.* Create your product as a series of steps or lessons. A well-known example of this is Steven Covey's *The 7 Habits of Highly Effective People.*
3. *Chronological.* Some products need to be presented in a particular order because that is the only way it would make sense. Step A must come before Step B, as in "Your Pregnancy Week by Week" by Glade B. Curtis and Judith Schuler.
4. *Modular.* Michael Port's "Book Yourself Solid" program is a perfect example. The program consists of three modules. Within each module are additional tracks that are presented in a numerical framework. This product has both a main framework and a secondary framework.
5. *Compare/Contrast.* Showcase your creation in terms of presenting several scenarios or options and then comparing them or con-

trasting them. Jim Collins, in his book, *Good to Great,* compares and contrasts successful and not-so-successful companies.

6. *Reference.* Reference is just as it sounds. You may be creating a product that essentially becomes a valuable resource to others. A compilation of information is best showcased in a reference format like that in *Words That Sell* by Richard Bayan.

Choose and list the framework that most appeals to you or to which your product is especially well suited.

4. Choose a Title That Sells

The title of your product or program can make a big difference in whether your product sells. It's the title that initially catches the consumer's attention and determines whether they look any further. Your title must be compelling enough for the prospect to want to know more. Keep your title short, succinct, and focused. The consumer should be able to know exactly what you're offering. Investing time to craft a captivating title can have a significant impact on your bottom line.

Six Types of Titles That Sell

1. *Generate suspense.* "The Secret Life of Stay-at-Home-Moms"
2. *Tell a story.* "Lessons from the Marketing Guru"
3. *Address a pain or a fear.* "The Top Ten Fears Every Leader Has and How to Overcome Them"
4. *Grab the reader's attention.* "CAUGHT! The Six Deadliest Marketing Mistakes"
5. *Create an emotional connection.* "What My Son's Tragedy Taught Me about Living Life to the Fullest"
6. *Solve a problem.* "The Seven Keys to Finding Love after You've Been Left at the Altar"

One of these types of titles may be especially fitting for your product or for the framework you've chosen. Most could potentially work with more than one. List three of the six types of titles that fit your product or that you find especially appealing, along with possible titless that fit each type. Have fun with this. The idea is to get the creative juices flowing. You may or may not decide to actually use any of these titles so don't get stuck trying to decide on the perfect one.

5. Develop Your Content

The table of contents provides the consumer with a framework to understand what content is to be provided, and it provides you with a way to organize the material and ensure that you're covering all the key points. It also allows you to then break down the content development into manageable sections. If you've already created a strong, workable framework for "delivering your story" (see "Choose Your Role as a Story-teller" above), it will be a simple exercise to craft a table of contents.

Whichever role you choose for delivering your story, the consumer will perceive you as an expert and your table of contents should be well organized and professional.

Whether you choose to use only main titles or to include section ti-tles with either a brief synopsis or bullet points about included content, the consumer should be able to quickly and easily scan the table of contents in order to gain a general understanding of the key points and main concepts.

Choose a format (based on your chosen framework) for your table of contents and write a first draft. Remember that the table of contents is simply an outline of the material you'll cover.

Next, using the draft of your table of contents, begin to develop the content further by listing beneath each heading or subheading a brief synopsis or key points that will be covered.

Last, but certainly not least, is to use the table of contents you've just created to fully develop your content. Don't let this step overwhelm you. It's actually a series of steps. Break it down by heading/subheading into manageable pieces.

Create and list a schedule for completion of the first draft of each section.

6. Making Your Product Available to the World

You are so close. Once you've completed steps one through five all you need to do is set up an automated system to market, sell, distribute, and deliver your product, and because you're reading this book you'll have all the marketing strategies and tactics to deliver your product worldwide.

For a comprehensive list of resources for producing and distributing your information product go to http://www.90dayproduct.com/freestuff.htm.

Consider and list which of these production and distribution services you'll need, noting the person to contact and when you plan to do so.

Lay out a schedule for completing the remaining aspects of production and distribution, as well as the revisions of your first draft. Don't forget to include scheduling your advance announcement (your big, bold promise crafted in step one of the "Six Easy Steps" section) to your customers.

Now is the time to get into action and there's no time like the present because you have all the resources you need, right here in this book. Product creation does not have to be difficult. In our very first group in the "90-Day Product Factory," we had 122 people all creating products within 90 days. If you follow the steps we've outlined in this chapter, you can too, and you'll be well on your way to reaping all of the rewards the Web has to offer. Before you know it you'll be hearing the beautiful, melodic, "ka-ching, ka-ching" sound of your Web site turned cash register, as the orders come rolling in.

24

TOM ANTION
USING EXIT STRATEGIES
TO MAKE MORE MONEY

TOM ANTION and Associates Communication Company provides entertaining and informative keynote speeches and educational seminars from advanced public speaking and presentation skills training to high-end Internet marketing training for small business. Tom is the author of the bestselling presentation skills book *Wake 'em Up Business Presentations* and *Click: The Ultimate Guide to Electronic Marketing.*

FOR MORE INFO: http://www.greatinternetmentoring.com

In This Chapter You Will Learn:

- How to Develop Exit Strategies and Pop-Up Boxes

- Sales Exit Strategies

- How to Super Survey Your Market

Well, we're coming to the end of a great book full of strategies that are destined to make you money. Because you soon will be leaving this book, it would be an appropriate time to tell you about an aspect of e-commerce that most businesses totally ignore.

EXIT STRATEGIES

Smart marketers turn people that are leaving their sites into money. The strategies used to do this can turn a business that's losing money into a profitable venture, and a profitable venture into a superstar performer.

There is a very important concept you must come to terms with to be successful with many exit strategies.

Pop-Up Boxes

Every successful online business I know of—whether it's large or small—uses pop-up boxes. Even major online service providers who brag about providing pop-up blockers use pop-up boxes.

You may personally feel that pop-up boxes are irritating. What you have to come to terms with is that however you may feel about pop-up boxes, the cold hard facts are that used judiciously, they make money with little or no backlash.

I'm not talking about the kind of pop-up boxes that hijack your browser and won't let you go about your online activities. I'm talking about those that are clearly related to your content and easy to close if your visitor is not interested.

Pop-Up Blockers

Because I work at very high levels and had some great Internet teachers, I found a way to beat many of the pop-up blockers that block standard pop-up boxes and hurt the income they generate.

I use a pop-up box generator at http://www.amazingpopups.com/power. A programmer wrote me a simple piece of code that changes the standard pop-up boxes created by this generator to a specialized and little known type of pop-up box called "modal." This style finds its way through about 90 percent of standard pop-up blockers.

The first day I changed my standard pop-ups to modal ones, all my pop-up income went back to pre-pop-up blocker levels. You've got to love those programmers.

SALES EXIT STRATEGIES

When your visitor comes to your site you obviously want them to buy. To the new marketer it is not so obvious that a great deal of money can be had from people leaving your site, but only if you know what to do. Savvy Internet marketers make money coming and going; that is, when their visitors are coming and going.

What I really love about exit strategies is that the visitor to your Web site has already decided not to buy and by using these techniques you get them to change their mind.

Let's take a look at a few exit strategies.

Sell-Down Technique

This technique is used to offer a cheaper price when a visitor is leaving a sales page without purchasing. The pop-up box they get is a "pick your price" deal. The simplest way to implement this is to have three cheaper price points to pick from. Just about everyone picks the cheapest price, but occasionally, some incredibly fair people choose one of the higher-priced options.

This technique is best for products like e-books because they are almost entirely profit so you have plenty of room to discount.

For an example of this technique visit http://www.wedding-speeches .org. Exit the page and you'll see a pop-up box that consistently brings in orders.

Finance Option

This technique uses the exact same exit pop-up box as the sell-down technique. The only thing that changes is what is in the pop-up box. Finance options have meant a fortune to me. If a person leaves one of my ads without buying, they see a pop-up box that gives them a chance to finance their purchase. You can use finance options to sell products for which you are willing to take payments. To automate the process, you need a shopping cart with a recurring billing function.

Thank-You Page Selling

After a customer purchases from your Web site, normally a thank-you page is displayed as a nice gesture for your customer. This is a wonderful place to sell! You could put links to your other products, or you could put affiliate links to sites that will send you a commission check if your customer clicks through and buys something.

You can make custom thank-you pages that match what the customer bought. This works really well because you can add links to offer your customer something complementary to what they just bought. This is smart selling!

Coregistration

Savvy Web site owners want to monetize every visitor that comes to their site. One way to do that is to capture e-zine subscribers for other publishers. You get paid for each subscriber.

Confirmation Page Selling

This may not technically be an exit strategy, but it works like a charm.

Do you have some type of sign-up form on your site? Normally after someone subscribes to something on your site, a page confirming the entry is displayed.

This is another great time to sell something.

On my site I have a sign-up form for *Great Speaking*. When someone subscribes, a confirmation page appears. "We've received your subscription. Your welcome letter and bonuses will be e-mailed to you shortly. In the meantime, read this special report on the business of professional speaking." This special report is actually a long copy sales letter for my "Wake 'em Up Video Professional Speaking System."

SUPER SURVEY YOUR MARKET

This technique has two elements:

1. Exit survey
2. Customized autoresponder series

The Exit Survey

Like the other exit strategies, I use an unblockable exit pop-up box. In this case, I put a survey form in the box (see Figure 24.1).

FIGURE 24.1 Exit Survey Form

Wait! Tom will give you an hour-long CD on Professional Speaking for free just for taking a few seconds to give your honest answers to the questions below.

Question 1. Are you interested in using the "Wake 'em Up Video Professional Speaking System" to learn professional level speaking techniques?
Yes ___ No ___

Question 2. What is your main goal with regard to public speaking?
___ It's a hobby.
___ I just want to do better at my presentations at work.
___ I want to promote my business.

(continued)

FIGURE 24.1 Continued

___ I want to get paid to speak locally.
___ I want to get paid to speak in my own country.
___ I want to get paid to speak internationally.
___ I want to do my own public seminars.
___ I want to speak on cruise ships.

Question 3. What brought you to our Web site?
___ Banner
___ Search engine
___ Postcard
___ Magazine ad
___ E-zine article or ad
___ Friend's recommendation
___ Other

Question 4. If you used a search engine, which one did you use?

Question 5. If you used a search engine, what subject or keywords were you using when you found our site?

Question 6. If you did not finish reading the detailed description of our speaking program, what kept you from finishing it?

Question 7. Are you planning on acquiring the "Wake 'em Up Professional Speaking System" along with the consulting that goes with it?
Yes ___ No ___ Maybe ___

Question 8. What is the main thing holding you back?
___ I need more information.
___ I'm concerned about stage fright.
___ Cost.
___ I'm skeptical.

Thank you for your help. To receive your FREE CD or audiocassette and FREE special report, please list your name and address below.

(Then make sure there is enough space for the person to enter their name, address, cassette or CD, e-mail, etc.)

When the person submits the form, the entire results are sent to me and some of the results are used to create a custom e-mail message.

Customized Autoresponder

When the person fills out and submits the form, certain answers trigger prewritten responses to be sent back automatically. I hope you can see the power of this. When my hot prospect fills out the form, they get a totally customized response.

Ok. I'm a sly dog. I hold up the e-mail until about 3:00 AM so the recipient feels like I really looked at their form. It would be pretty obvious the e-mail was automated if it came back two seconds after they submitted the form.

This is a powerful sales tool.

The bottom line on all these exit strategies is to turn your visitors into as much money as you can. It costs you one way or the other to get visitors to your site, so you may as well get that money back and then some by selling them coming and going.

For more information, see OnlineMarketingSuperstars.com.

Automating Your Web Site and Accepting Payments Online
http://www.easywebautomation

Audio for Your Web Site
http://www.instantflashaudio.com

Low-Cost, High-Quality Hosting and Domains
http://www.superstarhostinganddomains.com

Excellent Copywriting Course
http://www.ultimatecopywritingcourse.com

Creating Your Own Products for the Web
http://www.90dayproduct.com

Simple Web Site Design
http://www.onepagewebdesign.com

Automated Headline Creator
http://www.headlinewizard.com

Web Conferencing Systems
http://www.easyliveconference.com

Traffic Creation
http://www.onlinetrafficnow.com

Keyword Search Tool
http://www.goodkeywords.com

Online Freelancers Center
http://www.elance.com

Video for Your Web Site
http://www.instantflashvideo.com

Overcoming Procrastination
http://www.breakingfree.com

Online Marketing Coaches
http://www.gmarketingcoach.com

Internet Mentoring
http://masteringwebmarketing.com

Podcasting
http://www.onlinemarketingsuperstars.com/Podcasting.htm

Blogging and RSS Feeds
http://www.onlinemarketing.com/BlogsandFeed.htm